Paul Virilio

From Modernism to Hypermodernism and Beyond

Edited by
John Armitage

SAGE Publications
London · Thousand Oaks · New Delhi

Paul Virilio is simultaneously published as Volume 16, Numbers 5–6 of *Theory, Culture & Society*

© Theory, Culture & Society 2000

First published 2000

Published in association with *Theory, Culture & Society*, Nottingham Trent University

SAGE Publications Ltd
6 Bonhill Street
London EC2A 4PU

SAGE Publications Inc
2455 Teller Road
Thousand Oaks, California 91320

SAGE Publications India Pvt Ltd
32, M-Block Market
Greater Kailash - I
New Delhi 110 048

British Library Cataloguing in Publication data

A catalogue record for this book is available from the British Library

ISBN 0 7619 5901 7
ISBN 0 7619 5902 5 (pbk)

Library of Congress catalog record available

Typeset by Type Study, Scarborough, UK
Printed in Great Britain by The Alden Press, Oxford

Contents

This book is dedicated to
Barbara and Jeffrey Armitage,
my mother and father

Paul Virilio
An Introduction

John Armitage

> This is a war universe. War all the time. That is its nature. There may be other universes based on all sorts of other principles, but ours seems to be based on war. . . .
>
> (Burroughs, 1991: 95)

> People often tell me: you reason in a political way, like the Ancients. It's true. I don't believe in sociology. It's a mask. Sociology was invented in order to forget politics. For me, all that is social, sociology, doesn't interest me. I prefer politics and war.
>
> (Virilio and Lotringer, 1997: 17)

SELF-PROFESSED 'urbanist', political thinker and 'critic of the art of technology', Paul Virilio is one of the most significant and stimulating French cultural theorists writing today. Increasingly hailed as the inventor of military, spatial, political and 'technocultural' concepts such as the 'oblique function', 'dromology', or the 'science' of speed, the 'aesthetics of disappearance' and 'endo-colonization', Virilio is noted for his proclamation that the logic of ever increasing speed lies at the heart of the organization and transformation of the contemporary world.

Challenging accepted modern and postmodern theories of war, architecture, politics and technoculture, Virilio's phenomenological critique of speed draws on the continental philosophy of Husserl (1964) and Merleau-Ponty (1962), together with the gestalt psychology of forms.[1] Partially converging with the poststructuralist theories of Foucault (1977) and Deleuze and Guattari (1987), Virilio's writings are particularly influenced by war, strategy and spatial planning. Sharing common ground with other contemporary 'hypermodern' cultural theorists like Wark (1994), Kittler

- *Theory, Culture & Society* 1999 (SAGE, London, Thousand Oaks and New Delhi), Vol. 16(5–6): 1–23
  [0263-2764(199910/12)16:5–6;1–23;009956]

(1997), and Kroker and Kroker (1997), Virilio rejects the 'catastrophe' of postmodernism, describing his own main texts such as *Speed & Politics: An Essay on Dromology* (1986), *War and Cinema: The Logistics of Perception* (1989) and, most recently, *Politics of the Very Worst* (Virilio and Petit, 1999), as a modest contribution to the 'archeology of the future'.[2]

But who is Paul Virilio? What is the significance of military space, the organization territory, dromology, disappearance, the 'logistics of perception', 'polar inertia', the 'transplant revolution' and 'technological fundamentalism'? What are the principal architectural, political and aesthetic themes and contributions of Virilio's important dromological and hypermodern writings on the archeology of the future? In this Introduction to *Paul Virilio: From Modernism to Hypermodernism and Beyond*, such questions are briefly addressed in the first two sections through the provision of Virilio's biographical details, theoretical development and contributions to cultural theory. In the following three sections, an outline of Virilio's hypermodernism, the 'war machine', the 'flesh machine', and a short evaluation of the salient propositions and controversies surrounding Virilio's work will be provided prior to the conclusion and, finally, an overview of the contents of this collection.[3]

Military Space and the Organization of Territory

Born in Paris of a French mother and an Italian father in 1932, Virilio was evacuated to the port of Nantes in Brittany in 1939 where he was traumatized by the drama of the *Blitzkrieg* during the Second World War. After the war, he attended L'École des Métiers d'Art in Paris before becoming a craftsman in stained glass and working in churches alongside artists such as Matisse. In 1950, Virilio converted to Christianity in the fraternity of 'worker-priests' – radical clerics who shun religious dress, take an industrial job and live among the workers. Later, after being conscripted into the colonial army during the Algerian war of independence (1954–62), Virilio began campaigning with Abbé Pierre, the post-war patron of the homeless.[4] In the late 1950s Virilio studied phenomenology with Merleau-Ponty at the Sorbonne before turning to existential, political and aesthetic questions involving the architecture of war from the radical political standpoint of an 'anarcho-Christian'. With the architect Claude Parent, he instituted the *Architecture Principe* group and the review of the same name in 1963. However, as Virilio relates to Armitage in the interview in this collection – hereafter, 'the hypermodern interview' – an irreversible split with Parent ensued after Virilio's anarchist- and situationist-inspired political activities during the *événements* of May 1968. In 1969, Virilio was nominated Professor at the École Speciale d' Architecture in Paris, becoming its Director in 1975 and its President in 1990. An experienced organizer of exhibitions on the themes of war, architecture, media and democracy, Virilio has also been a member of the editorial board and a contributor to a variety of influential periodicals, including *Critique*, *Traverses*, *Cahiers du Cinéma* and *Le Monde Diplomatique*. Awarded the coveted 'National Award for

Criticism' in 1987, Virilio's political activities currently involve, among others, active participation in various associations concerned with the housing of the homeless in Paris.

According to Virilio, in a culture overshadowed by war, the military is of critical significance in questions concerning the construction of urban and political space and the technological organization of social existence. As he amply demonstrates in *Speed & Politics* (1986) and in his contribution to this collection, Virilio presents a convincing 'war model' of the evolution of the modern city and the development of cultural and social life using such proposals. The fortified city of the feudal era, for example, was a stationary and largely impregnable war machine connected in Virilio's understanding to an effort to regulate the flow and the speed of the movements of the urban population. Consequently, the fortified city was a political space of habitation, the political form, and the material foundation of feudalism. However, for Virilio, the fortified city of feudalism disappeared because of the arrival of exceptionally mobile and high-speed weapons systems. Such developments not only 'exposed' the city and turned siege warfare into a war of movement but also destroyed the attempts to regulate the population and thus ushered in the free movement of the urban masses. Virilio therefore conceives of the transition from feudalism to capitalism not in economic but in military, spatial, political and technological terms. It is, in short, the military conception of history.

Beginning in 1958 with a critical analysis of military space and the organization of territory, particularly regarding the 'Atlantic Wall' – the 15,000 German bunkers constructed during the Second World War along the coastline of France to prevent an Allied invasion – Virilio developed his research within the *Architecture Principe* group review and through a phenomenologically and gestalt-based theory of the oblique function – a theory that resulted in the erection of a 'bunker church' in Nevers in 1966 and the Thomson-Houston aerospace research centre in Villacoubly in 1969. In the 1970s, Virilio argued that the militarization of urban space was leading to the 'deterritorialization' of the modern city under the sign of speed, or 'chronopolitics'. Outlining the alarming 'dromological' consequences of the technological revolution in transportation and information transmission, Virilio set out to examine the possibilities for 'revolutionary resistance' to 'pure power' and began investigating the relationship between military technologies, the organization of space, culture and society. As a result, throughout the 1980s, Virilio developed the next major phase of his work via aesthetically based conceptions of 'disappearance', 'fractalization', 'pure war', urban space, cinema, logistics, automation, and what I shall call 'pure perception'. Nevertheless, since the early 1990s, Virilio has reflected upon the revolutionary socio-cultural consequences of the deployment of remote-controlled and cybernetic technologies in the city, the Persian Gulf War, and the new information and communications media of hypermodern societies. Focusing on polar inertia, the transplant revolution, technoscience and cybernetic performance art, his post-Einsteinian cultural theory is presently concerned with the invasion of the human body by hypermodern technoscience, or endo-colonization, 'cyberfeminism' and what Virilio calls 'technological fundamentalism'.

The Dromocratic Condition: A Report on Speed

As the articles by Leach on Virilio's architecture and Gane on Virilio's 'bunker theory' in this collection indicate, Virilio's early essays on the oblique function – a proposed new urban order based on 'the end of the vertical as an axis of elevation, the end of the horizontal as permanent plane, in favour of the oblique axis and the inclined plane' – were published in the mid-1960s in *Architecture Principe* (Johnson, 1996; Virilio and Parent, 1996: v). They foreshadowed his military and political critiques of deterri-torialization that surfaced in *Bunker Archeology* (1994a) and *L'Insécurité du territoire* (1976). Virilio's phenomenology, like Merleau-Ponty's, was not so much influenced by the philosophies of structuralism, poststructuralism and postmodernism but, rather, merged with them at various points. In conse-quence, Merleau-Ponty's emphasis on the corporeal dimensions of human existence in terms of the 'situated' 'body-subject' and 'expressive' 'inter-subjectivity' encouraged Virilio to declare 'the total reinvention of architec-tural vocabulary', and the 'third spatial possibility of architecture' (Virilio and Parent, 1996: v).

Virilio's scepticism concerning the political economy of wealth is sustained by his 'dromocratic' conception of politics, revolution and histori-cal progress in 'dromocratic society'. Nonetheless, his writings on chron-opolitics have also been decisively swayed by Sun Tzu's (1993) theory of war and Virilio's long-running debate with himself about the 'positive' (Fascist) and 'negative' (anti-Fascist) political and technological aspects of Marinetti's artistic theory of Futurism (see e.g. Tisdall and Bozzolla, 1977; Virilio and Lotringer, 1997: 45). For Sun Tzu and Marinetti, political economy cannot be subsumed under the political economy of wealth, with an understanding of the management of the economy of the state being its general aim. On the contrary, the histories of socio-political institutions like the military, and cultural movements such as Futurism, demonstrate that war and the need for speed rather than commerce and the urge for wealth were the foundation stones of the city, culture and society. In the present period, then, Virilio insists that politics must be presumed to have a relationship to speed that is equal in importance to its relationship to wealth. The hypermodern city airport is a typical research topic in Virilio's political economy of speed. Here, the terrestrial city is described by him as a mere concentration of 'passengers in transit'. The airport is characterized as signifying the archeology of some future society; a society 'concentrated in the vector of transportation'. Henceforth, '[t]he new capital is no longer a spatial capital like New York ... but a city at the intersection of practic-abilities of time, in other words of speed' (Virilio and Lotringer, 1997: 67).

It is important to state that Virilio is not arguing that the political economy of wealth has been superseded by the political economy of speed, rather, he suggests that 'in addition to the political economy of wealth, there has to be a political economy of speed':

> The physiocrats who provided the basic studies of political economy worked in the tradition of Hume, they were men of perceptions, men of precepts. And when I discuss an economy of speed I'm doing the same sort of work, with the difference that my research examines the comparable power of speed and its influence on morals, on politics, strategies and so on.
>
> My epoch is the epoch of the *Blitzkrieg*! I'm a physiocrat of speed and not of wealth. So I'm working in the context of very old traditions and absolutely open situations. At present we still don't really know what a political economy of speed really means. It's research which still awaits subsequent realization. (Virilio, 1998a: 10–11)

Even so, in *La Dromoscopies ou la lumière de la vitesse* (1978), *Speed & Politics* (1986) and *Popular Defense & Ecological Struggles* (1990), Virilio approaches these and related issues while also developing the breadth of his dromological inquiry to include considerations on pure power – the enforcement of surrender without engagement – and revolutionary resistance, an imaginative case against the militarization of urban space. In later works, as Kellner discusses in his article in this collection, Virilio argues that it is vital to focus on the merciless logic of *Pure War* (Virilio and Lotringer, 1997: 167–85) – the undeclared war of militarized technoscience on the civilian population. The 'rationale' of pure war might be encapsulated as the logic of technoscience in the era of 'cyber-', or, 'Info-' war, an era in which 'terrorists' and other (often unspecified) 'enemies' are invoked by the state in order to justify increased spending on 'the third age of military weaponry'. Moreover, as Cubitt suggests in his piece in this collection, for Virilio, the concept of pure war also incorporates the 'weaponry' of new information and communications technologies, interactivity and the Internet. Why? Because, ultimately, it is the weapons of the military industrial complex that are responsible for 'integral accidents' like the 1987 world stock market crash brought about by the failure of automated programme trading.[5] Thus, for Virilio (Virilio and Lotringer, 1997: 184): '[s]cience itself has become pure war, and it no longer needs enemies. It has invented its own goal.'

In texts such as *The Aesthetics of Disappearance* (1991a) and *The Lost Dimension* (1991b), Virilio, now supporting Mandelbrot (1977) and the geometry of fractals, aims to demonstrate that cultural theory must take account of interruptions in the rhythm of human consciousness and 'morphological irruptions' in the notion of the physical dimension. Utilizing the concept of 'picnolepsy' (frequent interruption) and scientific ideas drawn from Einstein's relativity theory, he argues that hypermodern vision and the hypermodern city are both the products of military power and time-based cinematic technologies of disappearance. Furthermore, although there are political and cinematic aspects to our visual consciousness of the cityscape, what is indispensable to them is their ability to designate the technological disappearance of the grand aesthetic and spatial narratives and the advent of micro-narratives. In Virilio's terms, Mandelbrot's geometry of fractals reveals the appearance of the cinematic, or 'overexposed' city – as when the morphological irruption 'between space and its form-image and between time and its technical de-realization' splinters into a countless number of visual interpretations, 'open conflict with the regime of telecommunication' and 'the crisis of whole dimensions' (1991b: 9–28, 59–68). Significant here is that Virilio's concerns about the aesthetics of disappearance and the crisis of the physical dimension are not exercised by the textual construction of totalizing or developmental intellectual 'explanations' and 'systems', but with the strategic positioning of productive interruptions, suggestions, jumps and the creative dynamics of what he, following Churchill, calls the 'tendency', or the 'change of level' (1989: 80; Virilio and Lotringer, 1997: 44). As McQuire and Crogan argue in their individual contributions to this collection, the rule in Virilio's fully fledged dromocratic society is the disappearance of aesthetics and whole dimensions into a militarized and cinematographic field of retinal persistence, interruption and 'technological space-time'. In other words, the screen becomes the new 'city square' and 'the crossroads of all mass media', the 'phantom landscape' of all those driven blind by the speed of light (Virilio, 1991b: 25–7).

Virilio's chief ambition, therefore, is to raise the critical question of perpetually increasing speed, or dromology. For him, the relentless logic of speed plays a crucial part in the militarization of urban space, the organization of territory and the transformation of social, political and cultural life. Dromology is an essential component of urban space, the politics of transportation and information transmission, and the aesthetics of technologically generated perception. Pursuing the accelerating and organizational logic of the political economy of speed and drawing on the ancient military texts of Sun Tzu, the artistic work of Marinetti, and the scientific writings of Mandelbrot and Einstein, Virilio accordingly rejects the notion that the political economy of wealth is the sole driving force of cultural and social life. Instead, it is the tyranny of eternally intensifying acceleration that makes history progress 'at the speed of its weapons systems' (Virilio, 1986: 68).

From Modernism to Hypermodernism and Beyond

Virilio's exegesis of speed in terms of military space, the organization of territory, dromology and the aesthetics of disappearance is an important contribution to the fields of critical cultural and social theory because it diverges from the increasingly sterile current debate over the differentiation of modernism and postmodernism. It is, for instance, quite wrong of critical cultural and social theorists such as Harvey (1989: 351), Waite (1996: 116), Gibbins and Reimer (1999: 143) and various others like the positivist physicists Sokal and Bricmont (1998: 159–66) to characterize Virilio's cultural theory as either postmodern or poststructuralist cultural theory. In fact, such characterizations are so far wide of the mark it is difficult to know where to begin. I will explain.

First, although the concept of postmodernism, like Virilio himself, originally came to prominence in architectural criticism in the 1950s and 1960s, Virilio's cultural theory is neither an overt reaction against the International Style nor a reaction against the concept and culture of modernism in general. The concept of postmodernism, Virilio proposes in the hypermodern interview, has been a catastrophe in architecture and has nothing to do with his phenomenological critique of speed. In reality, like Deleuze's, Virilio's cultural theory draws extensively on the modernist tradition in the arts and sciences.[6] In it, Virilio constantly references modernist writers such as Kafka and Aldous Huxley, and modernist artists like Marinetti and Duchamp. His most consistent philosophical reference points are Husserl and Merleau-Ponty, phenomenologists and modernists. Furthermore, Virilio's later writings regularly cite Einstein's works on relativity theory and quantum mechanics. Here, then, are clear instances of Virilio's broad commitment to the philosophy of scientific modernism established in the early part of the 20th century.

Second, as Virilio points out in the hypermodern interview, he sees no connection between his cultural theory and that of deconstructionists like Derrida. Additionally, there are only a small number of associated links between Virilio's work and poststructuralism. For instance, Virilio has never shown any interest in de Saussure's structural linguistics, preferring instead to remain to this day within the orbit of phenomenology and existentialism. As an anti-Marxist (and anti-Sartrean), committed anarchist and cultural theorist who has 'absolutely no confidence in psychoanalysis', he has little in common with many of the pioneers of structuralism such as the semiologist Barthes, the Marxist philosopher Althusser, the psycho-analyst Lacan and the anthropologist Lévi-Strauss (Virilio and Lotringer, 1997: 39). As a number of contributors to this collection suggest, Virilio's theoretical connections with Foucault's (1977) *Discipline and Punish* and Deleuze and Guattari's (1987) *A Thousand Plateaus* also need to be treated with care. This is because, unlike most postmodern or poststructuralist cultural theorists, Virilio is a *humanist* and a practising Christian. He is, as he insists unequivocally in the hypermodern interview, completely opposed to the viewpoint of anti-humanism and to the philosophy of Foucault's and Deleuze's messiah, Nietzsche. Interestingly, Guattari always denied that he was a Nietzschean, not that anyone seems to have taken any notice (e.g. 1996: 23). There are, as a result, only indeterminate and convergent relationships between Virilio's cultural theory and Foucault and Deleuze's poststructuralist cultural theories. This is also something that Virilio has pointed out on a number of occasions (e.g. Virilio and Lotringer, 1997: 44–5). For Virilio, the crucial pointers on all his work on dromology and related topics have been the Second World War, military strategy and spatial planning.

Third, in contrast to many postmodern cultural theorists, Virilio does not provide a blanket condemnation of modernity. Rather, as he argues in the hypermodern interview, he views his cultural theory as a 'critical analysis of modernity, but through a perception of technology which is largely... catastroph*ic*, not catastroph*ist*'. Arguing that 'we are not out of modernity yet, by far', it is, then, 'the drama of total war' that lies at the core of Virilio's cultural theory. Choosing to concentrate his thought on the fluctuating rhythms and varying speeds of modernity, Virilio's texts thus concern themselves with its key characteristics such as science, rationality, surveillance, urbanism, democracy and, above all, alienation. In addition, and despite his reputation as a technological Cassandra, Virilio often insists that his conception of modernity, as distinct from the philosophers of postmodernism, is essentially optimistic. As he recently suggested to Zurbrugg:

> Many people only seem to notice the pessimistic side of my writing. They don't realize that it's the global dimensions of the twentieth century that interest me – both the absolute speed and power of the twentieth century's telecommunications, nuclear energy and so on, and at the same time the absolute catastrophe of this same energy! We're living with both of these things! (Virilio, 1998a: 2)

Furthermore, Virilio is not wholly antipathetic to reason as such, even if he is critical of some aspects of the 'Enlightenment project'. But, like Deleuze, he certainly is inimical to Hegelian and Marxist theories of knowledge and ideology, including, on occasion, those proposed by 'messianic' Marxists and critical theorists like Benjamin (see e.g. Virilio, 1991b: 72). To some extent, therefore, as Kellner proposes in this collection, Virilio can be considered as a kind of 'left Heideggerian'. In brief, Virilio's critical relationship to modernity is far more complex and removed from the caricatured description of it given by many modern and postmodern cultural theorists.[7]

Fourth, as Virilio argues in the hypermodern interview and elsewhere, his writings have very little to do with those of the advocates of postmodernism like Lyotard (1984) and, arguably, Baudrillard (1983, 1994). Unlike Lyotard's work, for example, Virilio's work remains true to the principle of hope with regard to making sense of history. Actually, one could make a good case for suggesting that nearly the entirety of Virilio's cultural theory is a sustained attempt to make sense of his own history and, through it, ours too. Still less does Virilio accept the demise of *all* the 'metanarratives', insisting in the hypermodern interview, for instance, 'that the narrative of justice is beyond deconstruction'. Likewise, Virilio's general hostility to Marxism, semiotics and Nietzschean 'nihilism' largely explains his antagonism toward Baudrillard's concept of simulation. Again, unlike many postmodern cultural theorists, Virilio does not share Baudrillard's admiration for McLuhan's (1994) 'drooling' (Virilio, 1995: 10) over new media technologies. Similarly, Virilio's writings are less concerned with Baudrillard's 'hyperreality' and 'irony' and more concerned with social reality, the celebration of ordinary people and the poor in particular.[8]

For these reasons, it is very difficult to characterize Virilio's cultural theory as either postmodern or poststructuralist cultural theory. It is also why – in my view – it is preferable to interpret it as the work of a cultural theorist whose thinking addresses what might be termed the question of hypermodernism, or, perhaps alternatively, 'the cultural logic of late militarism'. Consequently, in Virilio's hypermodern world, it is time 'to face the facts: today, speed is war, the last war' (1986: 139).

From the War Machine to the Flesh Machine

Since the publication of *War and Cinema: The Logistics of Perception* (1989) and *L'Horizon negatif* (1985) in France in the mid-1980s, Virilio has periodically applied the concept of 'substitution' when touching on the different classes of reality that have unravelled since the origin of time. It must be said that this concept bears a remarkable likeness to Baudrillard's (1983, 1994) concepts of 'simulation' and 'simulacra'. For all that, in *War and Cinema* in particular, Virilio does not so much explain his idea of substitution as introduce and demonstrate its growing cultural significance. Writing on the cinema in the 1930s, for example, he notes that 'it was already clear that film was superimposing itself as a geostrategy which for a century or more had inexorably been leading to the direct substitution, and thus sooner or later the disintegration, of things and places' (1989: 47). Virilio's primary concern, however, is with the link between cinematic and geostrategic substitution, the disintegration of things and places, and what he calls the logistics of perception. The logistics of perception is perhaps less complicated than one might imagine and simply denotes the supplying of cinematic images and information on film to the front-line. The idea of the logistics of perception arises because, in the context of hypermodern wars like the Persian Gulf War of 1991 or NATO's war in 1999 against Milosovic's Serbia, not only do settled topographical features disappear in the midst of battle but so too does the architecture of war. For the military high command entombs itself in subterranean bunkers with the chief aim of evading what one of Coppola's helicopters in the film *Apocalypse Now* announced as 'Death from Above'.[9] Consequently, and in a similar manner to Baudrillard's (1983: 2–3) conceptualization of simulation, hyperreality, and the 'precession of simulacra', Virilio (1989: 66) conceptualizes a logistics of perception where 'the world disappears in war, and war as a phenomenon disappears from the eyes of the world'.

Thus, at the forefront of Virilio's interests in texts such as *L'Écran du désert: chroniques de guerre* (1991c) is the relationship between war, substitution, human and synthetic perception. Such interests are fuelled by the fact that, for Virilio, military perception in warfare is comparable to civilian perception and, specifically, to the art of film-making; in brief, both groups are increasingly concerned with directing images. According to Virilio, therefore, the notion of substitution eventually results in a 'war of images', a sort of 'video game', cyber-, or, more commonly, Infowar. Yet Virilio's war of images is not a traditional war, where the images produced are images of actual battles. Instead, for him, the disparity between the images of battles and the actual battles is currently being 'derealized'. As Virilio puts it: 'People used to die for a coat of arms, an image on a pennant or flag; now they [die] to improve the sharpness of a film. War has finally become the third dimension of cinema' (1989: 85). Of course, like Baudrillard's (1995) infamous claim that the Gulf War did not take place, Virilio's assertion that war and cinema are virtually indistinguishable is open to dispute. Conrad, for example, reviewing *War and Cinema*, claimed that 'Virilio is himself the victim of the 'interpretation mania' which he maniacally discovers in the impediments of war' (1989: 939). Virilio, though, remains unimpressed by such criticisms. One reason for this is that his stance on the appearance of Infowar is also consistent with his view that the only way to match cultural and social developments in the war machine is to adopt a radical and critical theoretical position with regard to the various parallels that exist between war, military weaponry, eyesight, photography and cinema. In 'A Travelling Shot Over Eighty Years', the final chapter of *War and Cinema*, Virilio vividly describes such parallels as the 'conjunction between the power of the modern *war* machine, the aeroplane, and the new technical performance of the *observation* machine' (1989: 71, original emphases). Virilio's work on the relentless automation of the war machine and related cinematic topics published in the late 1980s, together with his deepening preoccupation with remote-controlled technologies, accordingly betokens his vehement critiques of *The Vision Machine* (1994b) and *Polar Inertia* (1999a) that were to appear over the next few years.[10]

In Virilio's hypermodern epoch, then, when people 'no longer believe their eyes, when their *faith in perception* became slave to the faith in the technical *sightline*', contemporary cultural and social substitution has reduced the 'visual field' to the 'line of a sighting device' (1994b: 13, original emphases). Seen from this perspective, *The Vision Machine* (1994b) is a survey of what I call pure perception. For, although substitution has been revealing different categories of cultural and social reality over the entirety of human history, in the contemporary era, ominous technological substitutions and potentialities such as Virtual Reality, the Internet and cyberspace have been developed by the military industrial complex. In Virilio's terms, and returning to earlier themes, 'the main aim' of pure perception is *'to register the waning of reality'*. Indeed, for him, 'an aesthetic of disappearance' has 'arisen from the unprecedented limits imposed on subjective vision by the instrumental splitting of modes of perception and representation' (1994b: 49, original emphases). Hence, as in the case of NATO's Cruise missiles 'disappearing' over the horizon and filming their own and civilian destruction in the cities of the Balkans, Virilio conceives of vision machines as the accelerated products of *'sightless vision'*; a vision that 'is itself merely the reproduction of an intense blindness that will become the latest and last form of industrialization: *the industrialization of the non-gaze*' (1994b: 73, original emphases). Even so, the far-reaching cultural and social relationships between vision, remote-controlled technologies, pure perception, post-industrial production and human stasis are illustrated in their most complex form by Virilio in *Polar Inertia* (1999a).

In this text, Virilio considers various kinds of pure perception, speed and inertia. For instance, in his contribution to this collection, 'Indirect Light', Virilio examines the difference between the new synthetic video screens adopted by the Paris Metro system and traditional or 'real' perceptual objects such as mirrors, from a theoretical standpoint that broadly conforms to what Foucault (1977) labelled 'surveillance societies' and Deleuze (1995) later called 'control societies'. In contrast, in 'The Last Vehicle', Virilio notes the discrepancy between technologically generated inertia and biologically induced human movement in the context of a discussion about the introduction of 'wave machines' in Japanese swimming pools. 'Kinematic Optics' relates the effacement of a variety of 'local times' around the world and their gradual replacement by a single 'global time', while 'Environmental Control' contemplates the disparity between 'classical optical communication' and 'electro-optical commutation'. In the era of substitution and pure perception, though, Virilio argues that it is not the creation of relative speeds, acceleration and deceleration that becomes important but the creation of 'Polar Inertia'.

Polar inertia? Here, Virilio proposes that in the early modern era of mobility, in his terms the era of emancipation, inertia did not exist. The concept of polar inertia thus excludes what would have been alternate aspects of the speed equation – simple acceleration or deceleration – in the industrial age. But, today, as Virilio suggests in the hypermodern interview, in the post-industrial age of the absolute speed of light, 'it is no longer necessary' for anyone to 'make any journey' since 'one has already arrived'. As he tells Lotringer in *Pure War*:

> We're heading towards a situation in which every city will be in the same place – in time. There will be a kind of coexistence, and probably not a very peaceful one, between these cities which have kept their distance in space, but which will be telescoped in time. When we can go to the antipodes in a second or a minute, what will remain of the city? What will remain of us? The difference of sedentariness in geographical space will continue but real life will be led in a polar inertia. (Virilio and Lotringer, 1997: 64)

In such circumstances, then, the geographical difference between 'here' and 'there' is obliterated by the speed of light. Additionally, in its terminal mode, as exemplified by reclusive billionaires such as the late Howard Hughes, polar inertia becomes a kind of Foucauldian incarceration. Holed up in a single room in the Desert Inn hotel in Las Vegas for 15 years, endlessly watching Sturges' *Ice Station Zebra*, Hughes, Virilio's 'technological monk', was not only polar inertia incarnate but, more importantly, the first inhabitant of an increasingly '*mass situation*, the quest for the progress of speed without the knowledge of the engine's exterminating character' (Virilio and Lotringer, 1997: 77, original emphasis). So, at the broadest level, Virilio's writings on vision machines and polar inertia seek to show that artistic practices and physical geographical spaces no longer have significant human content. As a result, it is not too surprising to find that, in the contemporary era and in works such as *The Art of the Motor* (1995), Virilio has turned his attention to the transplant revolution, technoscience, cybernetic performance art, endo-colonization and technological fundamentalism.

On the eve of the 21st century, therefore, Virilio's cultural theory is predominantly concerned with how various forms of technological substitution have begun to permeate the totality of dromocratic society. For him, one of the most important cultural developments in this field is what he calls the transplant revolution – the almost total collapse of the distinction between technology and the human body. Intimately linked to the technological enhancement and substitution of body-parts through the miniaturization of technological objects, dynamic inserts and cardiac simulators, the third revolution is a revolution conducted by technoscience against the human body through the promotion of what the Critical Art Ensemble (CAE) (1998: 118–37) calls 'second wave eugenics' to the wealthy. As Zurbrugg reveals in his contribution to this collection, such disturbing developments are also the foundations of Virilio's (1995: 109–12, 1998a: 3) scathing criticisms of the 'psycho' and cybernetic, or 'terminal' convictions of Stelarc, the 'Antonin Artaud of technology' and Australian performance artist (see e.g. Stelarc, 1997). However, it should be stressed that Virilio's criticisms of the transplant, or 'third revolution', in concert with his critique of artists such as Stelarc, are also closely linked to the development of his notion of endo-colonization – what takes place when a political power like the state turns against its own people or, as in the case of technoscience, the human body. As Virilio argues in the hypermodern interview, 'there is no colonization' of territory 'without control of the body. One has, for example, 'only to watch those nerdy "internaut" types to see to what extent their behaviour is already being shaped by technology'.

Virilio's criticisms of the transplant revolution, in conjunction with those of 'neo-eugenics', Stelarc and the technocultural endo-colonization of the human body thus demonstrate how, in the contemporary era, the dromocratic regime is conceivably a 'pancapitalist' system that involves 'the coming of age of the flesh machine', the development of 'cyborgs', 'designer babies' and a 'new eugenic consciousness' (CAE, 1998). For these reasons, in *Open Sky* (1997a: 116–17) and other recent works such as *La Bombe informatique* (1998b) and *Politics of the Very Worst* (Virilio and Petit, 1999), Virilio has elaborated a critique of cyberfeminism that Plant (1997), following Haraway's (1985) 'manifesto for cyborgs' and the declarations of Australian artists such as VNS Matrix, speaks of as a kind of revolution on the part of cybernetic technology and feminists against the rule of patriarchy. Cyberfeminism thus endeavours to delete what might be termed the *différance* between technology and women, or, as Plant puts it, '"if machines, even the machines of theory, can arouse themselves, why not women?"' (1997: 59).

Plant's question relates to issues of technology, cyber cultural theory, cybersexuality and the politics of cyberspace. But, as Conley makes clear in her contribution to this collection, Virilio has little time for notions such as cyberfeminism and 'cybersex'; notions that in the hypermodern interview he criticizes, likening cybersex, for instance, to the technological replacement of the emotions. For Virilio, it is imperative to reject cybernetic sexuality, refocus theoretical attention on the human subject, and resist the domination of both men and women by technology. He sums up his current political position well in the closing pages of *La Bombe informatique*, announcing, '*Homo est clausura mirabilium dei*' – Man is the end point of the marvels of the universe (1998b: 152, original emphasis). In the world according to Virilio, then, cyberfeminism is merely one more form of 'technological fundamentalism' – the religion of all those who believe in the absolute power of technology (Virilio and Kittler, 1999, forthcoming). In brief, in the realm of what he labels '*technoculte totalitaire*', the lure of cyberspace is terminal because, through it, human subjects allow themselves to be dominated by cybernetic and technological objects (1998b: 48). Consequently, cyberfeminists and numerous other groups, lacking any awareness of 'cyberesistance', are characterized by Virilio as 'collaborators' with the 'Occupation' forces of multimedia 'generals' such as Microsoft's CEO, Bill Gates (1999b: 1–3). Having departed from the religious sensibility required in order to understand the ubiquity, instantaneity and immediacy of new information and communications technologies, cyberfeminists, like the Heaven's Gate sect that performed mass self-destruction recently in the USA in order to migrate to the stars, have now capitulated to the raptures of cyberspace (Virilio, 1998b: 51). In Virilio's terms, cyberfeminists are moving inexorably towards a technologically fundamentalist political position with regard to new information and communications technologies such as the Internet; a position he recently denounced in the following apocalyptic style:

> No longer the monotheism of the Written Word, of the Koran, of the Bible, of the New Testament, but a monotheism of information in the widest sense of the term. And this information monotheism has come into being not simply in a totally independent manner but also free from controversy. It is the outcome of an intelligence without reflection or past. And with information monotheism comes what I think of as the greatest danger of all, the slide into a future without humanity. (Virilio and Kittler, 1999, forthcoming)

A Brief Sortie into the War Zone

As the previous sections, and the final article in this collection by Der Derian, clearly suggest, Virilio's numerous activities and 'conceptual cosmology' have courted controversy since the 1960s. For example, when

Virilio and Parent wrote their articles in the *Architecture Principe* review,
they claimed that the world should abandon horizontal planes and organize
itself on inclined planes instead. Nonetheless, as Parent recalls: 'We might
have been forgiven if we had just called the things "slopes". As it was we
encountered absolute opposition. The magazine was our counter-attack'
(Johnson, 1996: 54). Similarly, Virilio's later conceptions of the 'suicidal
state' (1998c: 29–45), the 'state of emergency' (1986: 133–51), technology
and speed have also been subject to considerable critique. In the 1980s, for
instance, Deleuze and Guattari (1987: 351–423, 559) attempted what
Crogan (1999, forthcoming) calls a problematic effort to 'subsume' Virilio's
investigations into their own poststructuralist approach to the state, technology and speed. Even so, as Crogan argues in his article, Deleuze and
Guattari's 'static, ahistorical model' of the state and technology cannot
easily be combined with Virilio's ideas without undoing 'its own coherency
in the process'. In turn, Virilio's *The Aesthetics of Disappearance* (1991a) has
outraged the neo-Marxian geographer Harvey (1989: 293, 299 and 351). For
Harvey, Virilio's 'response' to what the former calls 'time–space compression' 'has been to try and ride the tiger of time–space compression
through construction of a language and an imagery that can mirror and
hopefully command it'. Harvey places the 'frenetic writings' of Virilio (and
Baudrillard) in this category because 'they seem hell-bent on fusing with
time–space compression and replicating it in their own flamboyant rhetoric'.
Harvey, of course, has 'seen this response before, most specifically in
Nietzsche's extraordinary evocations in *The Will To Power*'. Yet, in *The
Aesthetics of Disappearance* (1991a), Virilio's unfolding and wholly intentional reactions to the emergence of the dromocratic condition are actually
concerned with 'the importance of interruption, of accident, of things that
are stopped as *productive*' (Virilio and Lotringer, 1997: 44, original emphasis). As he told Lotringer: 'It's entirely different from what Gilles Deleuze
does in *Mille Plateaux*. He progresses by snatches, whereas I handle breaks
and absences. The fact of stopping and saying "let's go somewhere else" is
very important for me' (Virilio and Lotringer, 1997: 45). What Virilio's
'frenetic writings' actually substantiate throughout the 1980s are the material and, crucially, the *immaterial* consequences of dromological changes
in aesthetics, military power, space, cinema, politics and technology. In an
era increasingly eclipsed by the technologically produced disappearance of
socio-cultural life, war, matter and human perception, this is a very significant achievement. In the 1990s, though, the limitations of Virilio's cultural
theory are likely to rest not – as Harvey suggests – with his similarities but
with his *differences* from Nietzsche. As Waite, quoting the American performance artist Laurie Anderson, and others have argued:

> Virilio still desperately holds on to a modicum of modernist *critique* of
> postmodern military tactics, strategies, and technologies, whereas Nietzsche
> basically would have been impatient with mere critique, moving quickly to
> *appropriate* them for his own *use*, at least conceptually and rhetorically, as

metaphors and techniques of persuasion to preserve power for elites over corpses – 'now that the living outnumber the dead'. (Waite, 1996: 381–2, original emphases)[11]

Conclusion

Although there are many controversial features and vexing questions connected to Virilio's cultural theory, there is also little doubt that his hypermodern critique of military tactics, strategies and technologies is presently colliding with the work of a rising number of other cultural theorists like the Krokers. Naturally, the main reason why such collisions are taking place is that Virilio's latest texts, such as *Politics of the Very Worst* (Virilio and Petit, 1999), address head on some of the most alarming and significant contemporary cultural and social developments of our time; developments often designed to preserve the power of the increasingly virtual global elites over the creation of actual local corpses. As I write this conclusion in June 1999, for example, the living are rapidly increasing the numbers of the dead in Kosovo, Angola, southern Mexico, East Timor and almost anywhere else on the planet one cares to look. As Burroughs maintained, this is a war universe. War all the time. A child of Hitler's *Blitzkrieg*, Virilio has theorized the cultural logic of late militarism and the organization of territory, the central theme and the most important aspect of his work. Revealing the probable dromological and political conditions of the 21st century, Virilio interprets modernity in terms of a military conception of history and the endo-colonization of the human body by technoscience. As the title of this collection indicates, the concept of hypermodernism needs to be uppermost in any understanding of Virilio's particular contribution to cultural theory.

Virilio is, therefore, one of the most important and thought-provoking cultural theorists on the contemporary intellectual battlefield. He is, as Brugger argues, an 'archeologist' who 'examines the technological inventions of our time in order to find the *signs* that indicate where the acceleration of speed will be seen in the future' and, in addition, 'tries to point out the possible *negative effects*' of the dialectic of speed and disappearance (1997: 17, original emphasis). However, unlike Lyotard's or Baudrillard's postmodernism, Virilio's hypermodernism does not articulate itself as a divergence from modernism and modernity but as a critical analysis *of* modernism and modernity through a catastrophic perception of technology. Indeed, Virilio put his general position forward recently and succinctly in the context of a discussion about technology:

When someone says to me I don't understand your position, my response is, I'll explain it to you: I am a critic of the art of technology. Fair enough? That's all. If they still don't understand, then I say: just look at what an art critic is to traditional art, and then substitute technology for traditional art, and you have my position. It's that simple. (Virilio and Lotringer, 1997: 172)

Virilio's theoretical position, current trajectory and cultural sensi-
bilities concerning technology thus remain almost *beyond* the realm of even
the critical social sciences. He simply does not depend on intellectual
'explanations', 'constructing clear systems', or writing 'machines that work
well' (Virilio and Lotringer, 1997: 44). Rather, he relies on 'suggestion' and
'the obvious quality of the implicit'. On the one hand, then, it is possible to
describe a critic of the art of technology like Virilio as a cultural and a
political theorist who movingly considers the tendencies of the present
period. On the other, it makes little sense to describe someone who utterly
rejects the many 'masks' that sociology wears 'in order to forget politics' as a
typical social theorist.

As a result, and as several contributions to this collection suggest, it is
still open to debate as to how much there is to be gained from the growing
army of social theorists currently attempting to establish the 'truth' or
otherwise of Virilio's cultural and political theory. Such projects might be
questioned from the outset because, to a considerable extent, Virilio's
critical responses to the military, speed politics, cinema, art and technology
are, basically, ethical, artistic and emotional responses to the arrival of
technological culture. In his words:

> I'm so involved in the world of painting and the world of art that I don't speak
> about it much in my books because I live it! I'm a painter who writes, you
> know! Surely you feel that my books are very visual – they're very, very,
> visual books! They're not words, they're visions! (1998a: 9)

Moreover, Virilio is well aware that his work is 'often dismissed in
terms of scandalous charges!' As he recently pointed out, in France '(t)here's
no tolerance' for 'irony, for wordplay, for argument that takes things to the
limit and to excess' (1998a: 12). Consequently, to raise the question of the
advantages and disadvantages of Virilio's cultural theory is also to raise the
critical question of whether, outside France, his work should be dismissed
in terms of scandalous charges, received in terms suffused with praise, or a
mixture of both? In other words, it is to raise the question of how much
tolerance there is in the English-speaking world for irony, for wordplay, for
argument that takes things to the limit and to excess? For these and other
reasons, Virilio's hypermodern cultural theory looks set to continue eliciting
theoretical argument, cultural and social debate well into the next millennium.

The Contents

To my knowledge, Wark's 'On Technological Time' was the first critical
evaluation of Virilio's work in English. Investigating 'Virilio's Overexposed
City', Wark advocated reading Virilio 'as something of an *accidental* mouth-
piece for certain observations' (1988: 87, original emphasis). Today, in view
of the expanding influence of Virilio's writings on a growing number of other
cultural theorists in the English-speaking world, the time has surely come

for a *re*-evaluation of many of his ideas. For one thing, as I have tried to show in the previous sections, the developing critical literature on Virilio presently encompasses much more than his critical reflections on the over-exposed city. For another, many readings of Virilio's work are intentional and unintentional agents for a variety of inaccurate, hostile and often superficial pronouncements. In contrast, the contributions to this collection engage in an assortment of fact-finding, broadly sympathetic and detailed explorations of Virilio's cultural theory from the perspectives of the critical social sciences and the humanities.

As a consequence, while some contributors scrutinize Virilio's biographical and intellectual development, others present supportive assessments of the central themes and conceptual significance of his work. In his hypermodern interview with Armitage, Virilio discusses aspects of his life and explains the main impetus behind his theoretical efforts to strengthen our comprehension of modern and hypermodern culture. Virilio's 'Indirect Light', meanwhile, criticizes contemporary developments in video surveillance and miniaturization. Challenging the relentless illumination of the urban environment, Virilio outlines the likely consequences of cultural life lived under conditions of real time.

Virilio's own particular offering, though, sits alongside studies that present somewhat critical readings of his theoretical claims regarding architecture, war and other issues of current concern such as technology and new media. Leach demonstrates how Virilio and Parent's theory of the oblique can elucidate the spaces of architecture and typology. Examining the contributions of Virilio's writings on dromology, 'post-architecture', cultural space and the body, Leach points to various questions surrounding Virilio's 'aestheticization' of the political. In turn, Gane analyses Virilio's work on bunker archeology and compares his visions of the desert and ecological struggle with those of Baudrillard. Kellner reflects on Virilio's 'flawed' contribution to a militarized and politicized cultural theory of war and technology, an undertaking developed through Virilio's later writings on pure perception and disappearance. Similarly, Cubitt provides a critical overview of Virilio's 'liberal individualism' in the context of a discussion about his understanding of picnolepsia, 'big optics', war, politics, art and technology.

Further contributors, however, provide a more sympathetic response to Virilio's cultural theory in terms of speed, the tendency, and the integral accident. McQuire examines Virilio's analyses of mechanical and media 'vehicles', specifically with reference to their capability to change space and time within the frame of human interaction. Supporting Virilio's theory of speed, Crogan incorporates the writings of Hottois and Derrida, suggesting that Virilio's concept of dromology is useful in explaining the accident, the tendency and the 'untimely'.

In his piece, Zurbrugg appraises Virilio's writings and judgments on the Australian performance artist, Stelarc, arguing that Virilio's artistic concerns are, to some degree, resolved in the technocultural practices of artists and composers such as Viola and Holtzmann. Showing how Virilio's and Stelarc's work fuses at a number of places, Zurbrugg suggests that both Virilio and Stelarc are best understood as artists in the manner of Duchamp. Although Virilio's writings have had an impact on a number of female artists such as Louise K. Wilson (Virilio, 1997b: 41–8) and, arguably, the prevalent elaboration of technocultural practices, his work has not so far seriously affected the development of feminist or cyberfeminist theory. In her contribution, Conley considers whether it might be conceivable to clear a space for feminism in Virilio's oeuvre or, more precisely, whether it may be possible to accompany Virilio into the time and space of cyberfeminism.

In a lively article discussing Virilio's conceptual cosmology, Der Derian highlights the importance of Virilio's prolific conceptual production in a post-Einsteinian world of instant information, chronopolitics and virtual disappearance. Finally, the collection is drawn to a close by Armitage's select bibliography of Virilio's main published works, articles, interviews and studies of Virilio in French and English.[12]

Thus, the 12 contributions to this collection denote the significant areas in which Virilio's cultural theory and important concepts have drawn on the work of others, while also demonstrating how his concepts can be applied in the present period by theorists in the cultural and social fields. Virilio is a decidedly contentious cultural theorist whose 'calculation', as Baudrillard puts it, 'is to push the military to a kind of extreme absolute of power, which can only ultimately cause its own downfall, place it before the judgment of God and absorb it into the society it destroys' (1987: 109). Such extreme calculations about the role of the military in the realm of chronopolitics, not to mention the apocalyptic and religious tones in which Virilio delivers such forecasts, arouse immoderate and censorious reactions from critical and positivist theorists alike. As noted, Virilio is well aware that, in France and elsewhere, his work is often dismissed as excessive. Hence, it is crucial to emphasise that *Paul Virilio: From Modernism to Hypermodernism and Beyond*, like the broader project of *Theory, Culture & Society*, attempts to provide a genuinely *critical* exploration of Virilio's cultural theory within the framework of the social sciences and the humanities.

Notes

1. Gestalt psychology originated in Germany in the early part of this century. Its founders were Wertheimer, Kohler and Koffka. For gestalt psychologists, mental phenomena are extended 'events', or gestalts. According to Gestalt theory, cognitive processes cannot be understood in terms of their individual components. Rather, when some new piece of information is acquired, an individual's entire perceptual field has been altered. However, as Virilio makes clear in the interview in this collection, his own particular influence is Guillaume (1937).

2. First, although Virilio does not use the concept of hypermodernism to describe his work, as he clearly indicates in the interview in this collection, he certainly agrees with this interpretation of it. Broadly, and following the pioneering work of Arthur and Marilouise Kroker (see e.g. Kroker, 1992; Kroker and Kroker, 1997), I

will define hypermodernism as a tentative term and embryonic tendency in the contemporary critical social sciences and the humanities that seeks to move away from the polarized assumptions of modernism and postmodernism and toward a deeper theoretical understanding of the 'excessive' intensities and displacements inherent within cultural and social thought about the modern world and how it is represented. In the critical social sciences and the humanities the term might be put to use in the near future to describe the amalgam of styles employed by architects such as Virilio, Nouvel (1996), political theorists like the Krokers, 'sociologists' such as Bataille (Botting and Wilson, 1997), 'amodern' philosophers and political activists like Deleuze and Guattari (1987), and artists and cultural theorists such as Stelarc (1997), Critical Art Ensemble (1998) and Golding (1997). It is perhaps worth stressing that, as editor, I have not sought to establish any consensus on the concept of hypermodernism among the collection's contributors.

Second, since I have already compiled and contributed a detailed biography of Virilio's main works to this collection, in this Introduction I shall only refer to Virilio's most important texts and make use of the English translations of such works. For more detailed references, the reader is referred to 'Paul Virilio: A Select Bibliography' in this volume.

3. In this Introduction my aim is merely to introduce Virilio's cultural theory to those unfamiliar with it. The limitations of Virilio's work are only briefly considered. This is owing to the fact that the 12 other pieces in this collection provide a wealth of detail and a whole variety of critical evaluations and assessments of the impact of Virilio's cultural theory. Additionally, I have borrowed the concept of the 'flesh machine' from the innovative work of the Critical Art Ensemble (1998).

4. Abbé Pierre began campaigning on behalf of the French homeless in the winter of 1954 and quickly became an icon. So much so that one of the numerous 'mythologies' contained in Barthes' (1993: 47–9) famous work of the same name is entitled 'The Iconography of the Abbé Pierre'. However, in May 1996, Abbé Pierre fell rapidly from his esteemed position after supporting the former communist philosopher Roger Garaudy's self-published and 'revisionist' explanation of the Holocaust, *The Founding Myths of Israeli Politics*. Abbé Pierre has since retired to an Italian monastery.

5. For an excellent, detailed, and considered 'Virilian' assessment of the world stock market crash of 1987, see Wark's 'Site # 4, Wall Street, New York City, Planet of Noise', in his *Virtual Geography* (1994: 165–228).

6. A broad allegiance to the concept and culture of modernism is a crucial but so far little remarked upon link between Deleuze's work and that of Virilio. As Marks observes of Deleuze's aesthetics: 'It is striking that the objects of Deleuze's interest are frequently taken from the canon of high modernism. He favours writers such as Kafka, film-makers such as Godard and Antonioni, and painters such as Francis Bacon' (1998: 27). Much the same could be said of Virilio.

7. Virilio is, of course, not the only apocalyptic or catastrophe theorist and adherent of modernity to emerge from post-war French continental philosophy. Deleuze, for example, has also written on the apocalypse in relation to the writings of D.H. Lawrence. Moreover, in the article cited, he also references Virilio's work (Deleuze, 1998: 36–52). Williams has written on the theme of 'catastrophism' in Deleuze's writings (1997: 233–46). Meanwhile, and in the same volume, Ansell Pearson argues – correctly in my view – that Deleuze's philosophy 'needs to be situated

within the general problematic of modernity' (1997: 180–1). For a review of the latter volume, see McLure (1998).

8. However, it is worth pointing out that although Virilio frequently criticizes Baudrillard's work quite sharply in interviews, such criticisms are rarely returned by Baudrillard, who is more often than not complimentary about Virilio's cultural theory (see e.g. Baudrillard, 1987: 109).

9. Apart from the obvious contemporary relevance of the conflict in former Yugoslavia, I mention it in this context because Virilio is currently in the process of writing a book on what he recently called the 'final conflict of the twentieth century'. The book will be published in France towards the end of 1999 (personal communication, 30 May 1999).

10. Many of Virilio's most important texts from the 1980s can be found in his *Un paysage d'événements* (1996).

11. Even though I disagree with Waite's description of Virilio as a Nietzschean thinker, I certainly do agree with his critique of Virilio in this instance. In fact, I have made a very similar criticism in another article (see Armitage, 1997: 206).

12. This collection emerged from a chance meeting between Mike Featherstone and myself at the 'Time and Value' conference, held at the University of Lancaster in the UK in April 1997. I am very much indebted to Mike for his patient support over the past two years. However, the work on this project was made easier than it might have been by financial and administrative research assistance from the Division of Government & Politics at the University of Northumbria at Newcastle, the *TCS* Centre in Nottingham and Sage Publications. Credit is therefore respectfully due to Ken Harrop, John Fenwick, Neal Curtis, Chris Rojek, and Robert Rojek. I would also like to thank all the contributors to this collection who not only responded to the challenge of the enterprise so magnificently but furnished me with – by now – hundreds of (mostly!) friendly e-mails, letters, reader's reports and other exchanges. Finally, I am grateful once more to Joanne Roberts who endured far too many lengthy monologues about this venture over countless breakfasts, lunches and dinners. It is enough to say that Joanne can now reluctantly add the life and works of Paul Virilio to her many other specialisms.

References

Ansell Pearson, Keith (1997) 'Viroid Life: On Machines, Technics, and Evolution', pp. 180–210 in K. Ansell Pearson (ed.) *Deleuze and Philosophy: The Difference Engineer*. London: Routledge.

Armitage, John (1997) 'Accelerated Aesthetics: Paul Virilio's *The Vision Machine*', *Angelaki* 2(3): *Intellectuals and Global Culture*: 199–209.

Barthes, Roland (1993) 'The Iconography of the Abbé Pierre', pp. 47–9 in R. Barthes *Mythologies*, trans. Annie Lavers. London: Vintage.

Baudrillard, Jean (1983) *Simulations*, trans. Paul Foss, Paul Patton and Philip Beitchman. New York: Semiotext(e).

Baudrillard, Jean (1987) 'Forget Baudrillard: An Interview With Sylvère Lotringer', pp. 65–137 in J. Baudrillard *Forget Foucault*, trans. Philip Beitchman, Lee Hildreth and Mark Polizzotti. New York: Semiotext(e).

Baudrillard, Jean (1994) *Simulacra and Simulation*, trans. Sheila Faria Glaser. Ann Arbor: University of Michigan Press.

Baudrillard, Jean (1995) *The Gulf War Did Not Take Place*, trans. Paul Patton. Bloomington and Indianapolis: Indiana University Press.

Botting, Fred and Scott Wilson (eds) (1997) *The Bataille Reader*. Oxford: Blackwell.

Brugger, Niels (1997) 'Connecting Themes in the Work of Paul Virilio', unpublished seminar paper, presented at 'Paul Virilio, Technoscience and Society'. Convened by Mark Elam at the University of Copenhagen.

Burroughs, William S. (1991) 'The War Universe' (Interviews with Raymond Foye), *Grand Street* 37: 92–108.

Conrad, Peter (1989) 'Screen Spectaculars', *Times Literary Supplement* 4509: 939.

Critical Art Ensemble (1998) *Flesh Machine: Cyborgs, Designer Babies, and New Eugenic Consciousness*. New York: Semiotext(e).

Crogan, Patrick (1999, forthcoming) 'Theory of State: Deleuze, Guattari, and Virilio on the State, Technology, and Speed', *Angelaki* 4(2). Special Issue. *Machinic Modulations: New Cultural Theory & Technopolitics.*

Deleuze, Gilles (1995) 'Postscript on Control Societies', pp. 177–82 in G. Deleuze *Negotiations: 1972–1990*, trans. Martin Joughin. New York: Columbia University Press.

Deleuze, Gilles (1998) 'Nietzsche and Saint Paul, Lawrence and John of Patmos', pp. 36–52 in G. Deleuze *Essays Critical and Clinical*, trans. Daniel W. Smith and Michael A. Greco. London: Verso.

Deleuze, Gilles and Félix Guattari (1987) *A Thousand Plateaus: Capitalism and Schizophrenia*, trans. Brian Massumi. Minneapolis: University of Minnesota Press.

Foucault, Michel (1977) *Discipline and Punish: The Birth of the Prison*, trans. Alan Sheridan. Harmondsworth: Penguin.

Gibbins, John R. and Bo Reimer (1999) *The Politics of Postmodernity: An Introduction to Contemporary Politics and Culture*. London: Sage.

Golding, Sue (1997) *The Eight Technologies of Otherness*. London: Routledge.

Guattari, Félix (1996) 'Desire is Power, Power is Desire: Answers to the Schizo-Culture Conference', pp. 15–23 in F. Guattari *Soft Subversions*, trans. David L. Sweet. New York: Semiotext(e).

Guillaume, Paul (1937) *La Psychologie de la forme*. Paris: Flammarion.

Haraway, Donna (1985) 'A Manifesto for Cyborgs: Science, Technology, and Socialist Feminism in the 1980s', *Socialist Review* 80(2): 65–108.

Harvey, David (1989) *The Condition of Postmodernity: An Enquiry into the Origins of Cultural Change*. Oxford: Blackwell.

Husserl, Edmund (1964) *The Idea of Phenomenology*, trans. W. Alston and G. Nakhnian. The Hague: Martinus Nijhoff.

Johnson, Pauline (ed.) (1996) *The Function of the Oblique: The Architecture of Claude Parent and Paul Virilio*, trans. Pauline Johnson. London: Architectural Association.

Kittler, Friedrich A. (1997) *Essays: Literature, Media, Information Systems*, edited and introduced by John Johnston. Amsterdam: G & B Arts.

Kroker, Arthur (1992) *The Possessed Individual: Technology and Postmodernity*. Basingstoke: Macmillan.

Kroker, Arthur and Marilouise Kroker (eds) (1997) *Digital Delirium*. Montreal: New World Perspectives.

Lyotard, Jean-François (1984) *The Postmodern Condition: A Report on Knowledge*, trans. Geoff Bennington and Brian Massumi. Minneapolis and Manchester: Minnesota University Press and Manchester University Press.

McClure, Bruce (1998) 'Machinic Philosophy', *Theory, Culture & Society* 15(2): 175–85.

McLuhan, Marshall (1994) *Understanding Media: The Extensions of Man*. Cambridge, MA: MIT Press.

Mandelbrot, Beniot (1977) *The Fractal Geometry of Nature*. New York: Freeman.

Marks, John (1998) *Gilles Deleuze: Vitalism and Multiplicity*. London: Pluto Press.

Merleau-Ponty, Maurice (1962) *The Phenomenology of Perception*, trans. C. Smith. London: Routledge.

Nouvel, Jean (1996) 'Once the Morning Mist has Cleared', pp. 160–9 in P. Virilio and C. Parent (eds) *Architecture Principe 1966 et 1996*, trans. George Collins. Besançon: L'Imprimeur.

Plant, Sadie (1997) *Zeros + Ones: Digital Women + The New Technoculture*. London: Fourth Estate.

Sokal, Alan and Bricmont, Jean (1998) 'Paul Virilio', pp. 159–66 in A. Sokal and J. Bricmont *Intellectual Impostures: Postmodern Philosophers' Abuse of Science*. London: Profile Books.

Stelarc (1997) 'From Psycho to Cyber Strategies: Prosthetics, Robotics, and Remote Existence', *Cultural Values* 1(2): 241–9.

Tisdall, Caroline and Bozzolla, Angelo (1977) *Futurism*. London: Thames and Hudson.

Tzu, Sun (1993) *The Art of War*, trans. Yuan Shibing. Hertfordshire: Wordsworth Editions.

Virilio, Paul (1976) *L'Insécurité du territoire*. Paris: Stock.

Virilio, Paul (1978) *La Dromoscopies ou la lumière de la vitesse*. Paris: Minuit.

Virilio, Paul (1985) *L'Horizon negatif*. Paris: Galilée.

Virilio, Paul (1986) *Speed & Politics: An Essay on Dromology*, trans. Mark Polizzotti. New York: Semiotext(e).

Virilio, Paul (1989) *War and Cinema: The Logistics of Perception*, trans. Patrick Camiller. London and New York: Verso.

Virilio, Paul (1990) *Popular Defense & Ecological Struggles*, trans. Mark Polizzotti. New York: Semiotext(e).

Virilio, Paul (1991a) *The Aesthetics of Disappearance*, trans. Philip Beitchman. New York: Semiotext(e).

Virilio, Paul (1991b) *The Lost Dimension*, trans. Daniel Moshenberg. New York: Semiotext(e).

Virilio, Paul (1991c) *L'Écran du désert: chroniques de guerre*. Paris: Galilée.

Virilio, Paul (1994a) *Bunker Archeology*, trans. George Collins. Princeton, NJ: Princeton Architectural Press.

Virilio, Paul (1994b) *The Vision Machine*, trans. Julie Rose. Bloomington and London: Indiana University Press and British Film Institute.

Virilio, Paul (1995) *The Art of the Motor*, trans. Julie Rose. Minneapolis: University of Minnesota Press.

Virilio, Paul (1996) *Un paysage d'événements*. Paris: Galilée.

Virilio, Paul (1997a) *Open Sky*, trans. Julie Rose. London: Verso.

Virilio, Paul (1997b) 'Cyberwar, God, and Television: An Interview with Paul Virilio', (interview with Louise K. Wilson), pp. 41–8 in A. Kroker and M. Kroker (eds) *Digital Delirium*, trans. Louise K. Wilson, Magali Fowler and Rania Stesan. Montreal: New World Perspectives.

Virilio, Paul (1998a) 'Not Words but Visions!', (unpublished interview with Nicholas Zurbrugg), trans. Nicholas Zurbrugg. Paris.

Virilio, Paul (1998b) *La Bombe informatique*. Paris: Galilée.

Virilio, Paul (1998c) 'The Suicidal State', pp. 29–45 in J. Der Derian (ed.) *The Virilio Reader*, trans. Michael Degener, Lauren Osepchuk and James Der Derian. Oxford: Blackwell.

Virilio, Paul (1999a) *Polar Inertia*, trans. Patrick Camiller. London: Sage.

Virilio, Paul (1999b) 'Virilio – Cyberesistance Fighter: An Interview with Paul Virilio' (interview with David Dufresne), trans. Jacques Houis. *Aprés Coup*. Archived at: *http://www.apres-coup.org/archives/articles/virilio.html*

Virilio, Paul and Friedrich A. Kittler (1999, forthcoming) 'The Information Bomb: Paul Virilio and Friedrich Kittler in Conversation', *Angelaki* 4(2). Special Issue. *Machinic Modulations: New Cultural Theory & Technopolitics*, trans. Patrice Riemens. (Edited and Introduced by John Armitage).

Virilio, Paul and Sylvère Lotringer (1997) *Pure War*, rev. edn, trans. Mark Polizzotti, Postscript translated by Brian O'Keeffe. New York: Semiotext(e).

Virilio, Paul and Claude Parent (1996) *Architecture Principe, 1996 et 1966*, trans. George Collins. Besançon: L'Imprimeur.

Virilio, Paul and Philippe Petit (1999) *Politics of the Very Worst*, trans. Michael Cavaliere, ed. Sylvère Lotringer. New York: Semiotext(e).

Waite, Geoff (1996) *Nietzsche's Corps/e: Aesthetics, Politics, Prophecy, or, the Spectacular Technoculture of Everyday Life*. Durham, NC and London: Duke University Press.

Wark, McKenzie (1988) 'On Technological Time: Virilio's Overexposed City', *Arena* 83: 82–100.

Wark, McKenzie (1994) *Virtual Geography: Living With Global Media Events*. Bloomington and Indianapolis: Indiana University Press.

Williams, John (1997) 'Deleuze on J.M.W. Turner: Catastrophism in Philosophy?', pp. 233–46 in K. Ansell Pearson (ed.) *Deleuze and Philosophy: The Difference Engineer*. London: Routledge.

John Armitage teaches at the Division of Government & Politics, University of Northumbria, Newcastle upon Tyne, UK. Currently working on *Virilio Live: Selected Interviews*, he recently edited *Machinic Modulations: New Cultural Theory & Technopolitics*, a special issue of *Angelaki*, the journal of the theoretical humanities.

From Modernism to
Hypermodernism and Beyond
An Interview with Paul Virilio

John Armitage

Postmodernism and Hypermodernism

JA: Professor Virilio, I would like to begin by charting your place within the contemporary intellectual landscape.[1] For instance, your work is closely associated with the cultural movement known as postmodernism. Certainly, your most recently translated study *Open Sky* (1997 [1995]) is being received as such in the English-speaking world.[2] However, you have always been sceptical of the idea of postmodernism. Could you explain the basis of your critique of this concept?

PV: Postmodernism is a notion that makes sense in architecture, through the work of [Robert] Venturi (Venturi et al., 1977) and so on. Since I am teaching architecture, to me, postmodernism is a 'suitcase' word, a syncretism. In architecture it is a clear-cut phenomenon: styles are mixed up, history is ignored, one goes for a 'melting pot' of approaches. But as far as thought is concerned, thought as developed in the years 1970–80, I simply cannot understand why people are talking about postmodernism. Poststructuralism? Yes, OK. Postmodernism? It doesn't make any sense to me. Hence, I do not feel linked at all with postmodernity. Moreover, as a teacher in a college of architecture, I believe postmodernism was a catastrophe in the history of modern architecture. Therefore there is no linkage between me and postmodernism. I know that many people tend to associate postmodernism with relativism, especially with cognitive relativism. Well, this is a new polemic that is cropping up, especially here in France, and which does not concern, let alone interest me in the slightest measure. Another

■ *Theory, Culture & Society* 1999 (SAGE, London, Thousand Oaks and New Delhi),
   Vol. 16(5–6): 25–55
   [0263-2764(199910/12)16:5–6;25–55;009957]

thing is that I am a very marginal thinker, I do not relate to any established school of thought. Of course, I am a phenomenologist. When young, I was a pupil of [Maurice] Merleau-Ponty, I loved [Edmund] Husserl. You could call me a 'Gestaltist', I was enthusiastic about the psychology of form, Paul Guillaume, and the Berlin school: these are my intellectual origins.[3] I have been associated with the end phase of structuralism, with [Michel] Foucault, of course, and [Gilles] Deleuze. But I am essentially a marginal figure. The main influence in my work has been the Second World War, that is, strategy, spatial planning, and this body of thinking about total war of which I was victim in my youth.

JA: It seems to me that your work, which is primarily concerned with technological, urban and socio-cultural change, is the work of someone whose thinking addresses the problem of what might be called 'super' or 'hypermodernism'?[4] I say this because your theoretical interventions appear to be aimed not only at intensifying but also at displacing traditional forms of thought about the modern world and the way it is represented. How do you respond to this interpretation?

PV: I totally agree. As a so-called 'war baby', I have been deeply marked by the accident, the catastrophe, and thus by sudden changes, and upheavals. I am a child of the *Blitzkrieg*, the 'lightning war', I am a child of history's acceleration, as Daniel Halévy put it in 1947.[5] Hence, it is clear that my work is a critical analysis of modernity, but through a perception of technology which is largely, I might say, catastrophic. I say catastro*phic*, not catastro*phist*. This is because I have witnessed the drama of total war myself, I have lived through it, the millions of deaths, the cities razed to the ground, all that. As far as 'hyper' or 'super' modernism is concerned, I think we are not out of modernity yet, by far. I think that modernity will only come to a halt within the ambit of what I call the 'integral accident' (Virilio, 1989b [1986], 1997). I believe that technical modernity, modernity taken as the outcome of technical inventions over the past two centuries, can only be stopped by an integral ecological accident, which, in a certain way, I am forecasting. Each and every invention of a technical object has also been the innovation of a particular accident. From the sum total of the technosciences does arise, and will arise a 'generalized accident' (1997). And this will be modernism's end.

JA: Do you consider yourself a modernist author? Your writing style, for example, seems to many people to replace traditional narrative and structure with the 'stream of consciousness' technique...

PV: Yes, I do. Well, let me put it this way: to be concerned with speed, like I am, means to be involved in music. For 20 years now I have been working on 'dromology', that is, on the importance of speed in history, and thus of acceleration (Virilio, 1986 [1977]). Now, if there is a realm where speed is really an important element, it is music, rhythm, tempo. And thus my writing is a dynamic, cinematic process. Moreover, and I state this as modestly as possible, it is my belief that philosophy is a mere subdivision of literature. To me, Shakespeare is really a great philosopher, perhaps above Kant and a few others.

Relativity

JA: *Open Sky* (1997 [1995]) brings to the fore one of the most under-appreciated themes of your writings, namely, your interest in Albert Einstein's theory of relativity. This scientific concept is also occasionally viewed as a facet of modernism. How does the theory of relativity relate to your current projects?

PV: Well, frankly, this is quite simple. There is no way one could study the phenomenon of acceleration in all these domains, whether that is in the realm of transportation, or in the realm of information, that is, in the transfer of information, without stepping full scale into the issue of relativity. It is unavoidable. Ours are cinematic societies. They are not only societies of movement, but of the acceleration of that very movement. And hence, of the shortening of distances in terms of time, but, I would also add, of the relation to reality. It is thus simply impossible to ignore the theory of relativity. We're all going through the gates of relativity. It is well known that the theory of relativity is very poorly popularized, it is not at all well-understood by the general public. One cannot skip the theory of relativity for the mere reason that it is difficult to understand. Why so? Because we live it. We live it through mobile phones, through 'live' programmes on TV, through the telecommunications media, through Virtual Reality (VR), through cyber-space, through video-conferencing, through supersonic air travel and so on. Thus, as we live it, we interpret it, in the musical sense of the word. Like one says, 'to interpret a musical score', we, all of us, interpret the theory of relativity through our own lived lives. We do that through our calendar, through our time planning, our relationships, our involvement in love affairs even. We do that through the telephone, for instance, we do that through education, and through 'tele-learning'. We have become deterritorialized. Our embedding in our native soil, that element of *hic et nunc* (here and now), 'in situ', that embedding belongs, now, in a certain way, to the past. It has been overtaken by the acceleration of history, – by the acceleration of reality itself – by 'real time', and by the 'live', all of which are in a stage beyond the *hic et nunc*, 'in situ' condition. Caught as we are between this territory-based embedding, which is of a geographic, geophysical nature, or even of a geostrategic nature in the case of the military, and total deterritor-ialization, what remains in order to interpret our world? Nothing but relativity! Not the physicists' relativity, but our relativity, the relativity of our own lived lives, for which we are responsible, and of which we are the victims, at the same time. Relativity is no longer the exclusive domain of (natural) scientists, it has become the property of all those who live in the modern world.

Phenomenology and Marxism

JA: Before we move on to discuss your relationship to deconstruction (Derrida, 1973 [1967], 1976 [1967]) and post-structuralism, I would like to ask one or two questions about your own intellectual formation. For example, one of the leading philosophies in France and elsewhere in the immediate aftermath of the Second World War was structuralism...

PV: Yes, indeed, absolutely so. And certainly not existentialism...

JA: Even so, your own philosophical background developed through an engagement with Merleau-Ponty's *Phenomenology of Perception* (1962 [1945]). What would you say you learnt most from Merleau-Ponty's work and how has it influenced your own?

PV: First of all, I was a pupil of Merleau-Ponty, of Jean Wahl and of Vladimir Jankelevitch, to name three French philosophers who were teaching at the Sorbonne at that time. The one to which I felt most attracted was quite naturally Maurice Merleau-Ponty, and his *Phenomenology of Perception*. Why? Because I am so totally involved with perception myself, through my childhood, through painting. Yes, I painted, I even worked with famous painters such as [Henri] Matisse and [Georges] Braque when I was young. I am a man of perception, a man of the gaze, I am a man of the visual school of thought. Therefore, Merleau-Ponty's *Phenomenology of Perception* appeared to me to form a crossroads with the psychology of form, with Gestalt and the whole Berlin School. And thus it is at this crossroads of the psychology of form, Gestalt theory and the *Phenomenology of Perception* that I position myself. And to that one of course has to add the reading of Einstein, of the big scientific names of the time, [Paul] Dirac, [Werner] Heisenberg and yes, of course, [Henri] Bergson.[6] So you have a crossroads there, and it's where I stand, at the intersection.

JA: Merleau-Ponty was, for a large part of his life, associated with the philosophy of humanist Marxism. One thing that has always surprised me about your writings, particularly within the intellectual context of postwar France, is the absence of any reference to Marx. What is your relationship, if any, to Marxism?

PV: I am no Marxist, nor have I ever been one. But my father was a communist. We'll come back to that later. You see, my mother was a Breton, and my father Italian. Like every young boy (laughs) I had to choose between my mother and my father. So, although I have a lot of respect for my father, I totally reject his political views. I absolutely cannot be a communist. I might well feel at home as a 'communard', as in the Paris

Commune, or as an anarcho-syndicalist, these would suit me. But Marxism, no! Take it as a reaction against my father.

JA: Are you saying that your reasons for rejecting the Marxism of your intellectual contemporaries like Merleau-Ponty were autobiographical rather than theoretical?

PV: Yes, you're right, my intellectual contemporaries were communist to a man. I was not. But my reasons were theoretical also. This is because, when I was young, I converted to Christianity. I converted when I was 18, as an adult. The war had just ended then, and I had seen terrible things, and that was also one of the reasons for my conversion to Christianity. But then, you must know that I converted in the company of 'worker-priests'. Worker-priests are, in France, those priests who take an industrial job and go to live with the factory workers. They do not display their pastoral cross. I chose to convert with a worker-priest because I wanted something real, not some religious show with a guy in a costume. It is since that time that I have worked with Abbé Pierre.[7]

JA: Would it be correct, then, to suggest that you have no *theoretical* objections against socialism, against the left as a body of thought?

PV: No, of course not, I have nothing against socialism. I belong to the left, that is quite clear...

JA: Nevertheless, in the immediate aftermath of the Second World War, many of your friends were not merely on the left but also committed Marxists...

PV: True...

JA: Can you recall why you felt it necessary to develop your own political perspective at that time?...

PV: I feel that many of my contemporaries have totally blacked out the war from their minds. Many of them never experienced totalitarianism. I lived through that experience. With a communist father, who was Italian to boot, we had to make our escape from totalitarianism, from Nazism and so on. It was no joke to be both communist and Italian during the Second World War (in occupied France). This meant that I never could get involved in something that appeared to me, right from the beginning, to be a totalitarian phenomenon. Yet I have always remained interested in the leftist dimension within Marxism.

'Anarcho-Christianity'

JA: You spoke earlier of your conversion to Christianity. What role does it play in your work? Do you see yourself, for example, as part of a French Catholic moral tradition that might include other Christian and existentialist critics of technology like Gabriel Marcel or Jacques Ellul?[8]

PV: Yes, I do see linkages, especially with Jacques Ellul, rather than with Gabriel Marcel, who is from an earlier generation. But I cannot really place myself within what you call a Catholic tradition. The reason is that I have always been utterly unable to write about my faith. I do not have the gift for that. I have always considered that my life as a follower of Christ was something happening through my everyday life, not through my theoretical writings. It is not that I refuse to do it, I would gladly write a book about it, but I simply do not have the gift for it. You see, I do not have much of a theological culture. My conversion was an affair of the heart, a love affair you may say, more than an intellectual one. Speaking of religion, I feel much more at ease with an ordinary, poor person. When I am writing, I am somewhere else.

JA: In the late 1950s and throughout most of the 1960s the philosophy of structuralism began to challenge Christian existentialism, phenomenology and humanist Marxism. Structuralism was, of course, profoundly *anti*-humanist. Could your own theoretical approach be described as anti-humanist?

PV: Oh, not at all. I am an anarcho-Christian. It sounds quite paradoxical, but to me the definition of man is subsumed, and I quote it often, in a saying by someone I have come to like very much, Hildegarde of Bingen. St Hildegarde wrote, composed music, played harp, and was many other things at once. The saying is: *'Homo Est Clausura Mirabilium Dei'*: 'Man is the closing point of the marvels of the universe' (i.e. God). Thus, for me, Man is not the centre of the universe, he is the end of the universe, the end of the world. This has nothing to do with ideas like 'transcendental ego' or 'egocentrism'. For me, there is nothing beyond man. Forget about technology, eugenism, robotics, prostheses. Forget also about [Friedrich Nietzsche's] *'Uebermensch'* [Overman]. I do not believe these ideas are at all humanist. I think they're far worse. This is a very important point for me, because I am absolutely against this newfangled form of totalitarianism which I call technoscience and its cult. I see there a yet unheard-of eugenics programme, eugenics written very large, far beyond [Sir Francis] Galton's.[9] The idea behind this new brand of eugenicism being to perfect man, to make a better man. Well, there is no such thing as the possibility of 'improving' man, of tinkering man into something better. No way. Never.

JA: You would say that such a programme would not be a desirable aim?

PV: No indeed, I believe it is not. Yet it is exactly the programme of technoscience. Take, for instance, 'Dolly' [the recently cloned sheep], take neo-eugenicism, clones, take all new technologies. We see now a eugenic desire running amok.

From Military Space to Cyberspace

JA: The initial significance of your theoretical work flows from your architectural and photographic enquiries, documented in *Bunker Archeology* [sic] (1994a [1975]), into the 'Atlantic Wall' – those 1500 German bunkers constructed during the Second World War along the French coastline to prevent an Allied invasion ...

PV: There were in fact 15,000 of them, one zero more! And they stretched along the West European coast all the way up to Denmark. But about me: I spent my youth in the town of Nantes. Nantes lies at the mouth of the Loire, just before the Atlantic Ocean. Its true oceanic harbour is St Nazaire, where there was a German submarine base, and in fact an Allied landing took place there at some stage. Thus I spent the war time as a boy, with the sea just one hour away, yet without ever being able to go and see it: the seashore was a forbidden zone. So when liberation finally came, I rushed to the sea, to the beaches, like everybody else did. And there I encountered structures which were littering the beaches: the bunkers of the Atlantic Wall. And thus at the same time as I saw the sea for the first time, I also discovered these mysterious, enigmatic architectural structures. To me, they were like the statues on Easter Island. And so, for ten years, I went on a quest after these structures. I sketched and photographed these bunkers in order to come to grips with the totalitarian dimension of the war. My first snapshots were taken in 1957, the last ones in 1965.

JA: What was the connection between this discovery and your thinking on military space?

PV: First, it was an emotional discovery, which you might compare with Victor Segalen's first encounter with Chinese sculpture. You can also call it an archaeological experience, and a shocking one. Another element, aside from this encounter with military space, and which led me to write *Bunker Archeology*, was that I wanted to get involved in the study of urban phenomena, in the city and its technique. I switched over to urbanism, to architecture and thus to the study of the technique's impact on the space of the city, and the way it alters the urban landscape. And at this point, you of course meet Gestalt theory, the psychology of forms. Military space is an organized form of perception. When I was a conscript – I served in the artillery – I was a gunner. Part of my military service was in Germany, in the French occupation zone. I was stationed in Freiburg, at the HQ of the First French Army. I ended up as a cartographic officer in the staff of Field Marshall Juin. In this function I made a good number of military surveys in the Black Forest region, to be used in manoeuvres taking place in the occupied zone. So everything is linked up. There is an aesthetic kind of involvement with bunkers, and an urbanistic one in the field of regional planning. Over thousands of kilometres, the coast was organized in such a way as to be controlled by sight. It is that logic that made me understand to what extent the war had been a total one. War had not only conditioned the people through manslaughter, Auschwitz and wholesale executions, it had also reorganized the territory, just like the Great Chinese Wall had done. One could say that military architecture was the first incarnation of Land Art. In fact, minimalist and Land artists like Robert Morris came to me later to reflect on my book, and said they had found it most interesting.[10]

JA: In *The Function of the Oblique* (Johnston, 1996) you, along with the architect Claude Parent, outline your efforts in the 'Architecture Principe' group of the early 1960s to initiate an urban regime based on the theory of the 'oblique function', which, while founded on uneven planes and bodily disorientation, nevertheless resulted in the construction of several major works. Looking back, what do you think were the major achievements and disappointments of Architecture Principe and the theory of the oblique function?

PV: Architecture Principe was the name of a group. That period lasted five years in all (1963–8). You must know that this was at a time when many artists, philosophers and the like would come together to do things. For instance, we did quite a few things together with 'Archigram'. You also had Paulo Soleri in the United States, and there was also the 'Metabolic' group in Japan.[11] And so, Claude Parent and myself decided to start a research group together, and the main thing I contributed to was a church. That was the St Bernadette church in Nevers, and that church is a so-called 'Bunker church'. Why? Because I wanted to 'Christianize' the bunker. Of course, at the time, the prevailing myth was that of the crypt – the atomic shelter. One was then living under the permanent threat of the atomic bomb, and hence the atomic shelter. And so, you get a cross-point between the theme of St Bernadette of Lourdes, and that of the bunker. In Lourdes, the Virgin Mary appeared to St Bernadette in a grotto. Now, both the grotto and the bunker are crypts, hidden places, as in the English word, cryptic. And thus there was an opportunity to make a cross-over happen between that monolithic branch of architecture and a religious building. There is another reason: I had frequently been to Germany, to look at bunkers, and there I had seen a lot of so-called '*Luftschutzraum*', air-shelters and, in Dusseldorf, I suddenly saw *Luftschutzraums* which had been converted into Protestant or Catholic churches. And a correspondence dawned on me as between these places of shelter from danger, and places of worship, which are also places of salvation. We had another big project, a factory, and we also designed a number of private homes with inclined planes. Now if you want me to explain the concept of the oblique function as succinctly as possible it is this: simply to have people inhabit places with inclined, not horizontal, planes...

JA: And the disappointments?

PV: We published things. But, basically, this was a typical 'youth group'. And it broke up with the 'events' of May 1968. I was myself very much involved in those events, whereas Claude Parent was against the whole thing. So our ways parted, I went to the left, and he went to the right.[12]

JA: Much of your work in the late 1960s and early 1970s is overtly concerned with the idea of 'critical space'. Could you elaborate on this concept?

PV: Critical space is indeed a very important concept. You must see it as the direct outcome of me joining the École Spéciale d'Architecture, in 1968, at the formal request of the students there. And then, I immediately realized that the *prima materia* of the architect is not matter, bricks, stones and concrete, but space. And that it is necessary to construct space first before you can build up matter, with materials. Now, about the *critical* aspect of space: this means that space finds itself in a critical situation, just like one would speak of critical times, or of a critical situation. Space is under threat. Not only matter is threatened, space too is being destroyed. But it is being rebuilt at the same time. This is what I started to feel in the 1960s, and it was by then that I got the foreboding of cyberspace! I got the foreboding of virtual space, through Benoit Mandelbrot and the new geometry of fractals.[13] I came to see that the unity of space, which served as a basis for Le Corbusier, for the Archigram group, for all of us in sense, is in the process of being broken up. And the curious thing is that I published *The Lost Dimension* (1991b [1984]) in the same year as William Gibson published *Neuromancer* (1984). So here you have someone who writes on virtual space, on cyberspace, and someone who works on critical space. And both approaches will come to mesh into each other. To me, the reason why space is critical is because it is on the verge of becoming virtual space. Let me give you another example: whole dimensions no longer exist. For the modern architect, there exist the three dimensions, and time on top of them. This is what you might call 'ancient space'. It's modern space too, but it is conventional. From Mandelbrot onwards, dimensions are no longer whole, they are broken up. Space is fractured too. Nothing remains whole, as space, from approximately the 1970s onwards. And, to me, this is a great joy, since I am an anti-totalitarian. Newtonian absolute space disappears with the break up brought about by fractals, and by Einsteinian relativity in the first place, of course. The entire unity of space, which was the basis of architecture, modern architecture included, is deconstructed, fractionalized. This is what I call an 'accident'. It is a far better situation than that of totalitarian space. Geometry has now encountered its accident in fractalization.

JA: In *The Lost Dimension* and elsewhere, you present critical analyses of the nature of electronic space and the spread of new information and communications technologies. Why is it necessary to criticize, say, the Internet and cyberspace?

PV: I do not criticize the Internet and cyberspace as such. What I criticize is the propaganda unleashed by Bill Gates and everything that goes with it. What I loathe are the monopolies of Microsoft, of Time Warner, etc. I cannot stand those! I am an Apple fan, I am for Apple's convivial approach. I am not fretting against technology per se, but against the logic behind it. But first and foremost I'd like to position myself as an art critic of technology. Everybody is familiar with the conventional art critic, the musicologist. But art criticism of technology is a taboo. 'Yes and Amen' is the only allowed position. Well, not for me, thanks!

Nietzsche, Derrida, Power

JA: Although you were working on critical space in the late 1960s and early 1970s, it was also in that period when both structuralism and Marxism came under attack. Deconstructionists and post-structuralist philosophers like Jacques Derrida, for example, looked to Nietzsche rather than Marx for inspiration. Would it be correct to say that Nietzsche's philosophy is close to your own?

PV: It is true that I always have felt close to Deleuze and Derrida, who were very intimate friends, and Derrida still is, but I must confess that I have never been convinced by their 'Nietzscheanism'. I love 'Nietzschean music'. But, to me, Nietzsche is a man of the grand opera! His linkage with Wagner is not at all fortuitous. And I really admire the operatic part of Nietzsche. But his underlying philosophy? I'm sorry, I cannot stand it! It's physically repulsive! All that crap about the *'Uebermensch'*, and 'the Will to Power'! I do, though, profoundly admire the dramatic, the literary dimension, in Nietzsche. But I cannot assign any philosophical value to that brand of thinking. Here we encounter Shakespeare again. It is clear that I prefer Shakespeare to Nietzsche, by far. When I link Nietzsche's writings to the opera, it is because, to me, philosophy is spread out over the arts. Take Marcel Duchamp: for me, he is a philosopher who happens to paint. Shakespeare is a philosopher who writes plays. Kant is a philosopher who writes philosophical treatises. But philosophy transcends all this. When reading Nietzsche, I admire the literary music, the 'heroization' of concepts. As half Italian, I admire! I clap my hands! I love theatre! To me, Nietzsche is like Verdi. I applaud. But at the same time, I cannot, simply cannot, accept his philosophy. You see, I remain an art critic.

JA: Do you see any points of contact between your work and that of Derrida? Derrida (1984, 1996 [1995]) has, for instance, not only written on Nietzsche but also on speed and technoscience...

PV: No. The fact is that I do appreciate Derrida very much, but I do not encounter him. There are parallels in our work, but we do not share common ground. I cannot formulate it better. We are friends, but there are no points of contact in our writings.

JA: Earlier, you rejected the Nietzschean conception of power. How would you define power?

PV: This is a rather difficult type of question to respond to. The question of power is a long and vexed one. The ancient Chinese had an extraordinary phrase for it. When a representative of the Emperor would meet some local or regional power holder, his first words would be: 'Tremble and Obey!' To me, this is the best definition of power. Fear! That is, to instil fear, to frighten. The first thing power is about is fear, and from that compliance follows. Fear is of course also about emotions, about astonishment. And speed frightens. There is an awful lot more to say, naturally.

The Political Economy of Speed

JA: Power and speed are central to perhaps what is your best known book, *Speed & Politics: An Essay on Dromology* (1986 [1977]). Could you explain the nature and significance of dromology?

PV: Dromology originates from the Greek word, *dromos*. Hence, dromology is the science of the ride, the journey, the drive, the way. To me, this means that speed and riches are totally linked concepts. And that the history of the world is not only about the political economy of riches, that is, wealth, money, capital, but also about the political economy of speed. If time is money, as they say, then speed is power. You see it with the velocity of the predators, of the cavalry, of railways, of ships and maritime power. But it is also possible to see it with the velocity of dispatching information. So all my work has been about attempting to trace the dromocratic dimension of societies from ancient Greek society right up to our present-day societies. This work is of course about unrelenting acceleration, but it is mostly about the fact that all societies are pyramidal in nature: the higher speeds belong to the upper reaches of society, the slower to the bottom. The wealth pyramid is the replica of the velocity pyramid. Examples are easy to find: it was true in ancient societies, through maritime power and cavalry, and through their ways of dispatching messages, and it holds true in our modern societies, through the transport revolution, and through the current revolution in data transport and information processing. Thus my work is all about stating that it is of paramount importance to analyse acceleration as a major political phenomenon, a phenomenon without which no understanding of history, and especially history-that-is-in-the-making since the 18th century is possible.

JA: In *Speed & Politics* you also suggest that successive waves of acceleration imply both the 'disappearance' of physical geographical space and a
new politics of real time. What, for you, is the most important aspect of the
relationship between the physical dimension and the political space of real
time?

PV: Well, the old politics of acceleration were mainly about transport. That
is, the possibilities inherent in moving goods from one place to another, or,
perhaps equally importantly, moving *troops* from one point to another. This
means that acceleration bore next to no relationship to information. You had
pigeons, and other methods of despatching, but through the ages there was
hardly any acceleration of information transmission. But today, that is, since
the beginning of the 20th century, acceleration is mainly about the increasing speed of information transmission. Sure, transportation has been constantly speeded up too, but, today, the major development is the increasing
speed of information transmission, and the quest for the attainment of real
time. Information transmission is thus no longer concerned with the bringing about of a relative gain in velocity, as was the case with railway transport
compared to horse power, or jet aircraft compared to trains, but about the
absolute velocity of electromagnetic waves.

Pure War and the Politics of Everyday Life

JA: Your concerns about what might be called 'the dromocratic condition'
led, in the late 1970s, to the publication of your *Popular Defense &
Ecological Struggles* (1990 [1978]). This seems to me to be one of the few
books of yours which, while discussing the theoretical concept of 'Pure
War', also makes a *practical* political case for 'Revolutionary Resistance'
against the tyranny of speed politics and, in particular, the military-
industrial complex. Could you elaborate upon these concepts? Are they
still relevant today?

PV: Here, one must state that the book might also have been titled *Pure
War* (Virilio and Lotringer, 1997 [1983]) since that is the heading of the
Introduction.[14] That was the time when we were living with the unadulter-
ated balance of terror. What I mean is that one cannot understand the
concept of pure war outside of the atomic bomb, the weapon of the
apocalypse. At that time, and this has been somewhat forgotten, we were
living with the potentiality of a pure war, which, nevertheless, failed to
materialize. What is pure war? It is a war of a single utterance: Fear! Fear!
Fear! Nuclear deterrence can be conceived of as pure war for the simple
reason that nuclear war never took place. However, such deterrence did
spawn a technoscientific explosion, inclusive of the Internet, and other
satellite technologies. And so one saw that the history of warfare, of siege
war, of the war of movement, of total war, of world war, all somehow merged
into pure war. That is, into a blockade, into nuclear deterrence. What had
been reached was the dimension of the integral accident, the moment of the

total destruction of the world. And there it stopped. Thus, at that stage, the whole concept of resistance to war became a new phenomenon. It was no longer about resisting an invader, German or other, but about resisting the military-scientific and industrial complex. Take my generation: during the Second World War you had resistance, combat against the Germans who invaded France. During the 1960s and 1970s there was resistance, among others by me, not against an invader, but against the military-industrial complex, that is against the invention of ever crazier sorts of weapons, like the neutron bomb, and 'Doomsday machines', something that we saw, for instance, in Stanley Kubrick's film, *Dr Strangelove*. Thus resistance to pure war is of another nature than resistance to an oppressor, to an invader. It is resistance against science: that is extraordinary, unheard of!

JA: At this point, I would like to ask a question on behalf of my students. For when I give a lecture on your work there is one question that comes up over and over again at the end of the session. It usually runs something like this: 'While I find Paul Virilio's analyses of pure war, and revolutionary resistance against the military-industrial complex extremely thought-provoking, I'm not quite sure what he is suggesting I actually *do* about these issues at the political level, at the level of the everyday?' What, in your view, should one tell them?

PV: Well, tell them the following. I was a militant against the atomic bomb. I joined leftist movements during the events of May 1968. But I must say that I became very disappointed about political struggles, since they appear to me to lag very much behind developments both within the post-industrial revolution and technoscience. Thus I am, and many people with me, out of phase with real existing political movements. I feel henceforth marginalized, and the only action I can partake in takes place within the urban realm, with homeless people, with travellers, with people whose lives are being destroyed by the revolution brought about by the end of salaried work, by automation, by delocalization. You may call it street-corner work in a sense. For instance, together with Abbé Pierre, I was member of the High Committee for the Housing of Destitute People that was instituted by President [François] Mitterand and [Jacques] Chirac. I was on that Committee for three years. That work has stopped now, but, for the last 15 years, I have been a member of private associations which work together with homeless people. These are Christian associations for the most part, and there lie my political activities these days. I am a disappointed man of the left. By the way, this is no fun because at the same time there is the rise of extremist political parties like [Jean-Marie] Le Pen's Front National, and so on.

Modernity and 'Globalitarianism'

JA: If we can broadly define modernity as an attempt to understand the present period by contrasting it with the recent past, what key features, *other* than speed, would you point to in the contemporary era as being of most political significance?

PV: Globalitarianism! This is what transcends totalitarianism. Let's take an example, and excuse the neologism, but I cannot find another word. Totalitarianism covered my life, through the Second World War and through the period of nuclear deterrence, so you may say through Nazism first and then Stalinism. Totalitarianism was thus a central issue at that time. But now, through the single market, through globalization, through the convergence of time towards a single time, a world time, a time which comes to dominate local time, and the stuff of history, what emerges – through cyberspace, through the big telecommunications conglomerates, is a new totalitarianism, a totalitarianism of totalitarianism, and that is what I call globalitarianism. It is the totalitarianism of all totalities. Globalization, in this sense, is a truly important event. But, when people say to me, 'We'll become world citizens!', I reply, 'Forget it'. I was a world citizen long before globalization. After the war, I met Gary Davis, I went to meetings which took place in the Père Lachaise neighbourhood of Paris. I was 16–17–18 at that time. I was half Italian, I felt a world citizen. But when people say that Bill Gates, cyberspace and VR are the stuff of world citizenship, I say, no way! Globalitarianism is social cybernetics. And that's something infinitely dangerous, more dangerous even, perhaps, than the Nazi or communist brands of totalitarianism. It is difficult to explain globalitarianism but it is simple enough in itself. Totalitarianisms were singular and localized. Occupied Europe, for example, was one, the Soviet empire another, or China. That's clear. The rest of the world was not under totalitarianism. Now, with the advent of globalization, it is everywhere that one can be under control and surveillance. The world market is globalitarian. It is on purpose that I use the doublet total/totalitarian, and global/globalitarian. I consider this phenomenon a grave menace. It is manifest that Time Warner and the large conglomerates like Westinghouse, MCIWorldCom and all the other gigantic companies are not the exact equivalent of Hitler or Stalin. Yet, bad things are possible . . .

JA: Undoubtedly, I believe that one of the leading microelectronics conglomerates has even adopted 'One World, One Operating System' as its corporate logo . . .

PV: Yes. I can't stand it. Let me remind you of a sentence by Saint Just, one of the main protagonists of the French Revolution who got guillotined in the end, and who said once: 'There's this new idea in Europe: happiness.' Well, his other phrase, which I like very much is: 'If the people can be oppressed, even if they are not actually oppressed, then they are oppressed already.' It is a very interesting statement, because it says that the possibility is already the reality. Even if you are unaware of it, it has already happened. Hence the menace in the present period.

Lyotard

JA: Shortly after the publication of *Popular Defense & Ecological Struggles*, Jean-François Lyotard published his seminal book *The Postmodern Condition* (1984 [1979]). Does this book's renowned scepticism about the possibility of historical understanding, along with its rejection of the 'grand narratives' of progress, have any significance for you?

PV: Well, yes. We see here the fractalization of history, and Lyotard expressed – at an early stage – the end of the grand ideological narratives. But then, there was a question put by a Jewish friend of mine, Gerard Rabinowich – it was just after the book's publication, and we had gathered among friends in St Germain des Prés. My friend asked: 'Well, Lyotard, what do *you* have to say about that grand narrative called justice? Is that too a grand narrative belonging to the past?' A fine point indeed! Needless to say, Lyotard was at a loss for an answer. And indeed, to me, even if I accept the demise of the grand historical and ideological narratives in favour of the small narratives, the narrative of justice is beyond deconstruction. If that was the case, I would not be a Christian. You cannot deconstruct the absolute necessity of justice. Hence that issue remains intact. Justice cannot be divided up, be fractalized, on pain of descent into barbarism. We have reached a limit there.

Speed and Inertia

JA: While some cultural theorists are sympathetic to your critique of speed, few of them appear to appreciate the stress you place on the relationship between absolute speed and its 'Other' – *inertia*? Indeed, you have written a book about speed and the environmental crisis entitled *Polar Inertia* (1999 [1990]). Why is speed inextricably bound up with inertia?

PV: That is quite simple. When what is being put to work are relative speeds, no inertia obtains, but acceleration or deceleration. We are then in the realm of mobility and emancipation. But when absolute speed, that is the speed of light, is put to work, then one hits a wall, a barrier, which is the barrier of light. Let me remind you that there exist three recognized barriers: the sound barrier, which was passed in 1947 by Chuck Jaeger, the barrier of heat, which was crossed in the 1960s with rockets, at what is called 'escape velocity' and, finally, the speed of light, which is the effectuation of the 'live' in almost all realms of human activity. That is, the possibility to transfer over distance sight, sound, smell and tactile feeling. Only gustation, taste, seems to be left out of it. From that moment onwards, it is no longer necessary to make any journey: one has already arrived. The consequence of staying in the same place is a sort of Foucauldian imprisonment, but this new type of imprisonment is the ultimate form because it means that the world has been reduced to nothing. The world is reduced, both in terms of surface and extension, to nothing, and this results in a kind of incarceration, in a stasis, which means that it is no longer necessary to go towards the world, to journey, to stand up, to depart, to go to things. Everything is already there. This is, again, an effect of relativity. Why? Because the earth is so small. In the cosmos, absolute speed amounts to little, but at that scale, it is earth which amounts to nothing. This is the meaning of inertia. There is a definite relationship between inertia and absolute speed which is based on the stasis which results from absolute speed. Absolute stasis leads – potentially – to absolute stasis. The world, then, remains 'at home' [in English], already there, given. I repeat: this is a possibility, a potentiality, but here we are back to what I said before: when the people are in a situation of possible inertia, they are already inert.

The Integral Accident

JA: You said before that 'modernity will only come to a halt within the ambit of the integral accident' . . .

PV: Indeed, the accident has always fascinated me. In fact, I am currently preparing my end-of-the-century book, the one for the year 2000, which will be on the integral accident, although I am writing another book before that. The integral accident is the one that integrates all others.

JA: Could you elaborate on the concept of the integral, or, generalized accident, a little further?

PV: Let me put it this way: every time a technology is invented, take shipping for instance, an accident is invented together with it, in this case, the shipwreck, which is exactly contemporaneous with the invention of the ship. The invention of the railway meant, perforce, the invention of the railway disaster. The invention of the aeroplane brought the air crash in its wake. Now, the three accidents I have just mentioned are specific and localized accidents. The *Titanic* sank at a given location. A train de-rails at another location and a plane crashes, again, somewhere else. This is a fundamental point, because people tend to focus on the vehicle, the invention itself, but not on the accident, which is its consequence. As an art critic of technology, I always try to emphasize both the invention and the accident. But the occurrence of the accident is being denied. This is the result of the hype which always goes together with technical objects, as with Bill Gates and cyberspace, for instance. The hype in favour of technology dismisses its negative aspects. It is a positive thing to have electricity, it is a wonderful device, but at the same time it is based on nuclear energy. Thus what these three types of accidents have in common is that they are localized, and this is because they are about relative velocities, the trans-port velocities of ships, trains and planes. But from the moment that the absolute velocity of electromagnetic waves is put to use, the potential of the accident is no longer local, but general. It is no longer a particular accident, hence the possibility arises of a generalized accident. Let me stress the point by giving you two examples: the collapse of the stock exchange and radioactivity as result of a nuclear conflict. These examples mean that when an event takes place somewhere today, the possibility arises that it might destroy everything. A virus in an electronic network, an atomic leakage in Chernobyl – and that was not much, compared to a massive nuclear strike. Today's collapse of the stock exchange is a nice icon for the integral accident, in the sense that a very small occurrence changes everything, as the speed of quotations and programmed trading spreads and enhances any trend instantaneously. What happened a few weeks ago in [South East] Asia is an integral accident, well, almost an integral accident.

The Aesthetics of Disappearance

JA: In works such as *The Aesthetics of Disappearance* (1991a [1980]) you argue that modern culture is not simply characterized by speed but also by what you call the 'aesthetics of disappearance'. What is the relationship between speed and the aesthetics of disappearance?

PV: These are the cinematic effects, which are characteristic of the contemporary arts, and stem from film, television, video, etc. Let me explain: in ancient societies you had an aesthetic of *appearance*, which means that there was an enduring material support to the image: wood or canvas in the case of paintings; marble, in the case of sculptures, etc. Save for music, most aesthetics-related phenomena were phenomena of appearance, of emergence. Painting enabled the emergence of a figure on the canvas, which was subsequently 'fixed' with a varnish, for example, Leonardo's *Mona Lisa*. The image had appeared, as it were, through the medium of the canvas. The same could be said of Michelangelo, shaping *Moses* out of a block of marble, and that block of marble, suddenly *becoming* Moses. Persistence had a material basis. But with the invention of photography, of the photogramme, that is of instant photography, and of cinematography, from that moment onwards, one enters into an aesthetic of disappearance. At that stage, persistence is no longer material but cognitive, it is in the eye of the beholder. Things owe their existence to the fact that they disappear, like they do on a screen for instance. They are there, they appear, and are in motion, *because* they vanish afterwards. Quite different, therefore, from frescoes, paintings, etc. It is a sequential phenomenon. In the first phase, there was a cinematic effect of painting: if you take snapshots of an artist at work, you see that the painting develops in stages. But this is a very slow cinematic phenomenon as opposed to the film where we are talking about 24 frames per second – even up to 60 frames per second with special effects. So, this is the aesthetics of disappearance, it means that most of the art has vanished. Hence, by the way, the current crisis in contemporary art. Hence, too, 'the art of the motor'. When I write about *The Art of the Motor* (1995 [1993]), I mean that there has been a motorization of art. And, by 'motor', I mean the French cinematographic word *'moteur'*, for 'action'! This motorization of art is a very important phenomenon, and you cannot come to grips with the current crisis in the contemporary arts – I am thinking of *documenta* in Kassel, among others – without it (Joly, 1996). All branches of the arts are involved in this motorization, that is, in acceleration.

JA: So, you are arguing that the crisis in the contemporary arts is the direct outcome of motorization?...

PV: Yes, it is the result of the motorization of images. Let's take ships, for instance, and compare the grace of a sail-boat with a motor vessel: you're not talking about the same kind of marine vessel any longer. The same holds true for figurative images: whether they are from paintings, or from photo stills, or the cinema, or video: it's not the same. You must see that. Meanwhile, photography and cinema have influenced painting. They have also influenced the theatre, and other realms too. Motorization has exerted its influence over art in general. Every time there is a gain, there is a loss too. By losing the slow pace of the revelation of things, we have lost one sense of time in favour of another. Let me give you another example: the moment we acquired the mechanical lift, we lost the staircase. It became the service or emergency staircase, and was no longer the magnificent grand staircase of old. But we gained in speed – as is always the case. When transatlantic air services were invented, we incurred the loss of the ocean liners. This holds true in all possible realms.

Foucault and Baudrillard

JA: Much of your recent work is concerned with cyberspace and imaging technologies of various kinds such as VR. However, it appears to be less influenced by Jean Baudrillard's writings on the nature and impact of *Simulations* (1983) and 'hyperreality,' and more by Foucault's work on surveillance in *Discipline and Punish: The Birth of the Prison* (1977 [1975]). Why is this?

PV: *Discipline and Punish* is the source, obviously. Let me remind you that when Foucault published *Discipline and Punish*, one of his collaborators – he had quite a few of them at the time – was Jacques Donzelot. And Jacques Donzelot happened to sit on the examination board of one of my students who was doing research on prisons. We were working on prisons together, on the panopticon and so on, as part of the college curriculum at the time, and that was before *Discipline and Punish* came out. The proof of that is that the illustrations provided in Foucault's book can be directly traced to my student's thesis! His name, incidentally, is Carthoux, and his thesis – for the Ecole Spéciale d'Architecture – was entitled 'The Place of Detention'. So, whether there is mutual influence or not, there are, again, clear parallels. Another link is of course my work about war and its particular field of perception.

   Now, as far as Baudrillard is concerned, there is for sure something about his work that I have never liked at all, and that is his concept of simulation. I do not believe in simulation. To me, what takes place is substitution. Seminars have already been convened on this theme. The reason why is that I believe that different categories of reality have unfolded since the beginning of time, from the Neolithic Age to the present day. This means that reality is never given, but is the outcome of a culture. And thus we have a category of 'class I reality', and then there is a simulation of that reality, through a new technology, such as photography, or some other thing, or VR, for instance, and then you have a fresh substitution, a second reality. Hence simulation is a mere intermediary phase, without import. What is important is substitution; how a class I reality is substituted by a 'class II reality', and so on, up to the 'nth' reality.

JA: For you, then, one class of reality is continually substituted by other realities?

PV: Well, reality is produced by a society's culture, it is not given. A reality that has been produced by one society will be taken over, and changed by another, younger society, producing a fresh reality. This happens first by mimicry, then by substitution, and the original reality will, by that time, be totally forgotten. Take, for instance, the reality of the ancient Egyptians, of the Chinese of thousands of years ago: we cannot make any sense out of it, we are clueless about what it looked like, about what it sounded like.

JA: You talked before of the 'disappearance aesthetic'. At the same time, Baudrillard suggests that the advent of simulation and hyperreality have led to the 'disappearance of the social'. Isn't there some kind of connection between your work and his?

PV: Absolutely none whatsoever. As I have said and repeated often: there is a nihilistic dimension in Baudrillard's writings which I cannot accept. It is quite clear to me that Baudrillard has totally lost faith in the social. To me, this is sheer nihilism. I have not at all lost faith in the social. First of all, I believe that the social eludes the so-called social sciences, and always has – that's why I am not a sociologist! So I am disappointed, and very much so, about politics, but I am not disappointed by the social. You need only to go into the streets, and meet the poor: they're extraordinary, superior people. The social drama leaves the stunts of the political class far behind. The power and resilience of individual people in the streets puts the intelligence of today's political leaders to shame. And as far as the social scientists are concerned, the less said the better!

Technological Culture
JA: Would you say that your work on the aesthetics of disappearance is characterized by a disenchantment with the modern world? Do you advocate a return to some kind of religious sensibility, one that might place limits, for instance, on the social effects of cinematic disappearance?

PV: I believe that, without some religious culture, it doesn't matter which, one will never be able to understand technological culture and cinematics. I believe that a society, a society which has moved to such an extent into virtuality, will not be able to advance further, without an appreciation of moral virtues, that is, of mystical thought. I mean by that all that has been contributed by philosophers and theologians, of all religions, not only Christianity. The new technologies bring into effect the three traditional characteristics of the Divine: ubiquity, instantaneity and immediacy. Without some cultural familiarity with these themes, mediated by Christianity, Protestantism, Buddhism, Judaism, Islam, etc., they remain incomprehensible. One cannot come to grips with the phenomenon of cyberspace without some inkling of, or some respect for, metaphysical intelligence! That does not mean that you have to be converted. I believe that the new technologies demand from those who are interested in them that they have a substantial measure of religious culture – not merely some religious opinion. I may emphasize that all this has nothing to do whatsoever with 'New Age', and the like...

JA: Don't you think that some people invest technology with a mystical dimension already?

PV: Yes, of course. 'Transhumans', New Age types, cyberpunks and the like. There are plenty of them in the United States, you need only to read Mark Dery's book.[15] I think this is a scary development, leading up to the Heaven's Gate sect, whose members committed suicide in order to depart for the stars. But this is not the sort of thing I am talking about. My point is simply that without a knowledge of the history and philosophy of religions, one cannot come to grips with what I have termed 'technological fundamentalism'. Which is the possibility of a *Deus ex Machina*. Just like there is a Jewish fundamentalism, or an Islamic or Christian one, you have also now got a technological fundamentalism. It is the religion of those who believe in the absolute power of technology, a ubiquitous, instantaneous and immediate technology. I think a balance is needed to remain free vis-a-vis technology, a balance which consists of a knowledge of religion, even if this entails the risks of fundamentalism and intolerance. Without this knowledge one is without balance, and one cannot face the threats of technological fundamentalism, of cyberspace and of the extreme lunacy of social cybernetics.

The War Model

JA: To many people, your work in *Bunker Archeology* and later is associated with what has come to be known as 'the war model'. Could you explain this model?

PV: Well, as a child of the Second World War, a 'war baby', you may say that the war was my university. I learned to know the world through the fear brought about by war. So for me the archetypal war was the Second World War, which lasted from 1939 to 1945. This war produced both Auschwitz and Hiroshima – in fact I keep a stone from Hiroshima on my desk. The war model is a method of total control over a territory and of a population. The aim is to have total control of the population, to bring a whole region or a continent into subjection, through radio, telephone, and a combination of both of these was already very much there during the Second World War. Hence my work is about defining total war as a conflict model, in all realms, not only in the realm of the military, but also in the realm of the social, and in what I would call 'colonization'. Colonization is already a model of total war. To quote [Jules] Michelet, the 19th-century French historian: 'Without a powerful navy, there are no colonies.' It is the power of technology which makes colonization possible; maritime power is one. Later, other forms of colonial power followed. Thus it is clear that my writings on the war model are linked to the history of the colonial empires, that is, to the times of colonial imperialism and ideological totalitarianism.

JA: Does the notion of the war model flow only from the Second World War? Or, is it linked in some way to your resistance to the Algerian war? Or both?

PV: What is for sure is that, as far as my approach to war is concerned, I have passed through three stages in my life: I suffered from the Second World War as a child; I was called into military service during the Algerian War and served six months in Algeria – in the Aurès, the mountainous region south of Constantine. And I opposed nuclear war, that is, the total war *par excellence*. So the three wars that have moulded me, we could say, are the Second World War, the Algerian war and the epoch of nuclear deterrence. These wars, of course, carry the seeds of their followers, especially the Malvinas War and the Persian Gulf War.

The War of Images

JA: In the early 1980s you produced one of your most well-known books, *War and Cinema: The Logistics of Perception* (1989a; [1984]). In this book you discuss the use by the military of cinematic technologies of perception. Why is the analysis of the relationship between war and the cinema so important for you?

PV: Because images have turned into ammunition. Logistics deals in the first place with the supply to the front-line of ammunition, energy and so on. The front-line is constantly being replenished with ammunition, energy and foodstuffs. Now, from the end of the First World War onwards, but especially with the Second World War, the front-line is also being fed with images and information. That means that a 'logistics of perception' will be put in place, just as there is a logistics of fuel supplies, of explosives and shells. For instance, one can observe that the First World War was fought on the basis of maps. Maps were being drawn, lines were sketched on them and height-lines established, whereupon the artillery was told where to fire. But at the close of the war, maps were being displaced by aerial photography, shot by planes and then assembled on tables like mosaics – I did that kind of job myself, when I was a HQ staffer. How did that come about? Well, because the destructive power of artillery is such that the ordinary topographical landmarks simply disappear – here, again, the aesthetics of disappearance at work! Only film or photography keep the memory of the landscape as it was, and as it is constantly being reshaped. The film substitutes for the ordnance survey and, at the same time, architecture goes underground. It buries itself in the soil, in bunkers, in order to escape control from the skies. If you look at the Second World War, there was no bombing without photographs of the planned bomb site being taken back, being scrutinized with specialized equipment. Images thus become a product of extraordinary strategic importance. And if we switch to contemporary military conflicts, what you get are video missiles, unmanned miniature planes or 'drones', observation satellites and more wondrous things. War has morphed into images, into the eyes . . .

JA: According to you, war is now a war of images?

PV: Absolutely. It is impossible to imagine war without images. And, if possible, 'live' images.

Cyberwar in the Persian Gulf

JA: Your reflections on the so-called 'cyberwar' in the Persian Gulf were published as *L'Écran du desert* (1991c). What, for you, are the qualitative differences between conventional warfare and cyberwar?

PV: First, about the book's title. It is very important because there were three phases in the Gulf War. Two are well-documented, and the third has been named by myself: 'Desert Shield', 'Desert Storm' and then, '*Desert Screen*' – the latter is my invention. You may say the title is 'War TV'. The Gulf War was truly a war of images. This is because it was fought out, on the one hand, with drones, that is, with flying cameras on unmanned planes. On the other hand, one also saw Cruise missiles, which were making surveys all the time about where they were flying, with televised bombs which were streaming into Saddam's bunkers, with video missiles. A jet fighter pilot turns on his screen, fires a missile equipped with a camera, and the missile lights up what is on the horizon, while the pilot sees *beyond* the horizon. And, as soon as he sees an adversary, he directs the missile towards him. We have, therefore, now entered a type of war which is about directing images, hence the invention of C^3I – a type of war management which means command, control, communication and intelligence – a kind of (film) director's way of running a war, with images and information coming up from everywhere at once. One observes that in the very first armed conflict after the Cold War, the image is right in the middle of the mechanism. The war is being directed straight from the USA, through communication satellites which are guiding the Patriot missiles. There is a kind of video-game war going on. This perfectly illustrates what I wrote seven years before in *War and Cinema*. In fact, quite a few friends told me that they couldn't make anything out of my book in 1984 but now, after the Gulf War, they tell me that they have got the message – seven years too late. So when there is talk today about the 'new war', the 'info war', the war of information, well, now we are in quite an uncharted territory.[16] It is quite clear that the USA is currently entering a period of great upheaval in military affairs. This means that the command of 'globalitarian', or total information, by the last remaining Big Power, leads to a repositioning of its powers. What we now see happening in its relations with Iraq goes a long way to show the limitations of this war of information, as far as the 'how-far-to-go', 'what-to-do', issues are concerned. It is very difficult to make pronouncements about these developments, save to say that 'cyberwar' manoeuvres have already taken place in Germany, and have been witnessed by my friend James Der Derian.[17] Here we enter a realm of electronic gamesmanship of which very little can be said. It's still quite tricky, and confidential. I am presently working on that, of course, but there is simply not very much open information about this war of information. What is certain is that the locale of war is no longer the 'geosphere', military geography, the realm of geostrategy, but the 'infosphere', cyberspace. We have entered a new world.

The War Machine: Deleuze and Guattari

JA: Before we leave the subject of war, could I ask you about your relationship to Deleuze and Guattari's philosophy and politics of desire? Their 'Treatise on Nomadology: The War Machine', in *A Thousand Plateaus: Capitalism and Schizophrenia* (1987 [1980]) is obviously influenced by your writings about pure war, military space, speed and power. But what, if anything, have you learnt from their writings and how has it influenced your thinking?

PV: I do not think there is influence here but, rather, convergence. If you care to look in *A Thousand Plateaus*, I believe there are 27 references to my work. That's not nothing. Now, I am not stating this in order to claim as my own the qualities of Deleuze and Guattari, whom I have loved very much, but to emphasize that, here again, there were parallels at work. However, I felt rather closer to Deleuze than to Guattari because I am totally devoid of any psychoanalytic background or culture. Guattari and I were, though, on extremely friendly terms, and we did things together. You see, Deleuze was, like me, a man of 'the event', someone who not only worked with the concept of the event but who also rose to the occasion when an event occurred and who reacted with feeling, as befits a phenomenologist. Hence, to me, the interest of *A Thousand Plateaus* lies chiefly in its liberating effect from a certain kind of academic discourse, one which belonged to the end phase of structuralism. I am not talking about Foucault here. I am referring to

[Claude] Lévi-Strauss, to [Louis] Althusser and so on. Here, again, liberation took on a kind of musical hue. For me, *A Thousand Plateaus* is also a form of, shall we say, *'ritornello'* (a recurring couplet or refrain in a folk song), as they called it themselves. So what I like about Deleuze and Guattari is their poetic language, a language which enables them to convey meanings which cannot be conveyed otherwise...

JA: Do you mean that Deleuze and Guattari have a poetic understanding of the world, as opposed to a prosaic or an analytical one?

PV: Yes, but even better, a 'nomadological' understanding of the world – they have that word of their own after all – stemming from the fact that the world is constantly on the move. Today's world no longer has any kind of stability; it is shifting, straddling, gliding away all the time. Hence their ideas about superimposition, strata, layers and cross-currents. Ours is a world that is shifting, like the polar ice-cap, or 'Continental Drift'.[18] Nomadology is thus an idea which is in total accordance with what I feel with regard to speed and deterritorialization. So, it is hardly surprising that we clearly agree on the theme of deterritorialization.

The Gaze of the Machine

JA: Your interest in the acceleration and automation of perception was further developed in *The Vision Machine* (1994b [1988]). What was your central aim in that book? ...

PV: There was, for me, this crucial development, of which nobody, once again, seemed aware of. Everybody was talking about Orwellian remote control and surveillance, with cameras all over the place, scanning the city. I agree, it is scary, the Orwell scenario, police cameras everywhere. But there is something worse, which gives its title to *The Vision Machine*: a device to see with. For it means that an inanimate object now can see *for itself*. A remote camera, for example, is for the use of a policeman or a security guard. There is someone behind it who does the viewing. Nothing special about that and nothing to worry about. But behind the vision machine there is nobody. There is only a micro-receiver, and a computer. A door can 'recognize' me, as it were. This set up without a human spectator means that there is now vision without a gaze. And let me remind you that the research on the vision machine – that is its official name, I did not invent it – was for the Cruise missile! Cruise missiles were equipped with detection radar and built-in mapping systems. They had maps charting their course towards Teheran or Leningrad. The device was constantly surveying the ground with radar and checking it against the map to make sure the missile was on course. No need for a vision machine here, the radar does the work. But, at the final approach stage, a vision machine is necessary, in order to film the target and choose the window to enter the building or the door to the bunker. These vision machines are an improvement on what are called 'shape recognition devices'. They are like those industrial machines that punch holes in metal sheets. They come equipped with a microchip that enables them to recognize the shape of the sheet they're supposed to punch holes in. This is termed contour recognition, which is not fully fledged vision yet. A further development has led to the devising of highly sophisticated vision machines for Cruise missiles. This means that Cruise missiles are endowed with a gaze even though it is an automatic one . . .

JA: But all this is not being carried out for the machines themselves. It is being carried out by, or at least on behalf of, human beings, even if none are directly involved? . . .

PV: No, nobody is there. Well, ultimately, yes, of course, but when you've got a camera, you make a film, and then you view it. Here the object is looking *for itself*, the Cruise missile looks for itself. To me, something like this is an unheard of event. Imagine this table we are sitting around starting to look for itself!

The Transplant Revolution

JA: In *The Art of the Motor* (1995 [1993]) another shift seems to take place in your thinking. For, in that work, you focus on the invasion of the human body by technoscience. Could you explain your interest in what you call 'the transplant revolution'?

PV: Oh yes, this is the 'Third Revolution'. In the realm of speed, the first revolution was that of transportation, the invention of the steam engine, the combustion engine, the electrical motor, the jet engine and the rocket. The second revolution is the revolution of transmission, and it is happening right now in electronics, but it began with Marconi, radio and television. The third revolution, which is intimately linked to the minaturization of objects, is the transplantation revolution. By this term I mean that technology is becoming something physically assimilable, it is a kind of nourishment for the human race, through dynamic inserts, implants and so on. Here, I am not talking about implants such as silicon breasts, but dynamic implants like additional memory storage. What we see here is that science and technology aim for miniaturization in order to invade the human body. This is already true of the cardiac stimulator, a device I am especially interested in, since much of my work is about rhythms and speed, and the cardiac stimulator is what *gives* the rhythm to the life of a human patient. I am writing about that in my next book, and about the case of those twin sisters, which were prematurely born, and who had a cardiac stimulator implanted in them practically from birth: their life-rhythm, thus, is that of a machine, a stimulator. Here is an icon of the transplant revolution, of the human body being eaten up, being possessed by technology. Technology no longer spreads over the body of the territory, as with railways, motorways, bridges and large factories, but now enters the innards of the human body . . .

JA: And, in your view, this is a negative development?

PV: It is absolutely scary. It means that the machine enters into the human. It is no longer a prosthesis, it is a new eugenicism in fact...

JA: Nonetheless, this is a difficult position to maintain with someone whose life may depend upon the insertion of a cardiac stimulator?

PV: Well, here again you see how the indisputable is always put forward in order to foster extremely dubious measures. It all starts by saying how great those things are for people who need them, and then comes the day when it is being forced upon people who don't need or want them. There lies the problem.

JA: Is this the basis of your criticisms, in *The Art of the Motor*, (1995 [1993]) of the Australian performance artist Stelarc?

PV: Yes. This is because Stelarc has opted for 'eugenic suicide'. Instead of committing plain suicide, he does so by grafting himself into various gizmos, so that in the end, there will be no Stelarc left, pffuuut!, gone! Only a pure automaton will remain. That being said, his work is absolutely fascinating.

JA: How does the transplant revolution relate to your concept of 'endo-colonization'?

PV: First, endo-colonization happens when a political power turns against its own people. I have lived through this during the Second World War. Totalitarian societies colonize their own people. You cannot understand Nazi Germany without accounting for the fact that it had been deprived of colonies and embarked on a programme of colonization at home. So Germany's colonization was a programme of colonizing the East (*ostkolonization*), inclusive of Poland, Russia and France for that matter. But, by necessity, Germany's colonization was also a logic of endo-colonization, that is, to force upon its own population the fate that the British – or the French – had forced upon the Aboriginals in Australia or the blacks in South Africa, or, in other words, brute force. And, in the case of the transplant revolution, what takes place is an endo-colonization of the human body by technology. The human body is eaten up, invaded and controlled by technology...

JA: Are you suggesting that the idea of the transplant revolution is identical to the concept of endo-colonization?

PV: Yes, it is, but on the person, on the human body. There is no colonization without control of the body. We are here back to Foucault, evidently. Every time a country is being colonized, bodies are colonized. The body of the Negro, of the slave, of the deportee, of the inmate of the labour camp, is a *colonized body*. Thus technology colonizes the world, through globalitarianism, as we have seen earlier, but it also colonizes bodies, their attitudes and behaviours. You need only to watch all those nerdy 'internaut' types to see to what extent their behaviour is already being shaped by technology. So we have this technology of absorption, or as the Futurists used to say: man will be fed by technology, and technology will colonize human behaviour, just as television and the computer are doing, but this last form of colonization is a much more intimate, and a much more irresistible form. This is scary! It is neo-eugenicism, endo-technological eugenicism!

Cyberfeminism

JA: In *Open Sky* (1997 [1995]) you make reference to 'cyberfeminism', a movement which some see as one of the most important theoretical and political developments in the past decade with regard to our understanding of the human body, technology and subjectivity. Could you describe your response to these developments?

PV: Well, I have become very interested in the notion of 'cybersexuality'. Even if it is still at the gimmick stage, it is a well-known fact that research is very advanced in the field of 'tele', 'remote' or cybersexuality, especially in Japan. And thus, I am quite baffled to see feminists – far from opposing, like I do, the conditioning of the female body, or the male body for that matter – projecting themselves as followers of cybersexuality. I cannot understand it. I cannot understand why opposing machismo does not also imply opposing cybersexuality. Do the cyberfeminists really believe that cybersexuality is going to liberate them? Come on. ... Give me a break!

JA: Are you arguing that feminists have much more to lose than they have to gain by embracing cybernetic technologies?

PV: I believe that the question of technology is predicated upon the question of sexuality, be it male or female. If cyberfeminists do not want to understand the replacement of emotions by electrical impulses – because that is what we are talking about – the replacement of emotional involvement by electrical impulses, it is clear that they will never be liberated. Instead, they will become the servants of a new type of sexual control. Remote or tele-sexuality is by definition machine-controlled sexuality.

JA: The American cyberfeminist, Donna Haraway (1985) has stated that she 'would rather be a cyborg than a goddess'. What is your reaction to such claims?

PV: (laughs – out loud) I want to be neither a God nor a cyborg! I want to be man. It suffices to be a man – or a woman. As I said before, 'Man is the endpoint of the wonders of the universe'!

Georgio Agamben

JA: One final question. Are there any other cultural theorists writing today whose work you admire?

PV: Hm, this is a difficult question to answer, but, yes, there is one book which I've just reviewed, and liked very, very much. It is Giorgio Agamben's *Homo Sacer: le pouvoir souverain et la vie nue* (1997). In ancient Roman law *Homo Sacer* means a human being whose life is considered worthless, meaning someone whom one could kill without committing homicide, and who is also unfit for sacrificial purposes. Such a man stands condemned to summary execution. Killing him is no worse than squashing an insect. I must say I have a boundless admiration for Agamben. I was asked by several papers to give my choice of the best books of the year and I mentioned *Homo Sacer*. It is a remarkable book, and one with which I could not agree more.

Translated by Patrice Riemens

Notes

1. This interview was conducted on 27 November 1997 at the Ecole Spéciale d'Architecture in Paris. I would like to thank Mike Featherstone for his encouragement, Ken Harrop for personal and institutional support, and Mark Little for practical help in setting up the interview. However, I am also heavily indebted to Magali Fowler for interpretation and to Rob Turner and Patrice Riemens for translating numerous letters, tapes and texts. Lastly, I am especially grateful to Paul Virilio for giving his time and energy so freely to this project.

2. See, for example, Kerrigan (1997: 14–15).

3. Gestalt psychology is a body of thought which springs from the experimental studies conducted by German psychologists like Max Wertheimer and Kurt Koffka around 1910. Briefly, the Gestaltists argued that philosophical, artistic, scientific, perceptual and aesthetic configurations endowed with qualities as a whole could not be characterized simply as the totality of their parts.

4. 'Hypermodernism' is a term I reserve for a forthcoming book on Virilio.

5. Here, Virilio is referring to Daniel Halévy (1872–1962). Halévy was an anti-clerical radical French historian and well-known 'Dreyfusard'.

6. Paul Dirac and Werner Heisenberg were both instrumental in developing Einstein's theory of relativity and quantum mechanics in the early part of this century. For a recent and accessible introduction to this fascinating but complex field see Milburn (1996). Henri Bergson (1859–1941) founded a philosophy based on 'creative evolution' and, like Virilio, was much preoccupied with questions relating to the nature of knowledge, time and religion. See, for instance, Bergson (1910).

7. Abbé Pierre is a figure held in high regard in France for his championing of the poor.

8. See, inter alia, Marcel (1950) and Ellul (1965).

9. Sir Francis Galton coined the term eugenics in 1883. Eugenics is, of course, the 'science' which purports to 'improve' humanity through the application of genetic policies.

10. Robert Morris (1931–) is an American minimalist sculptor and Land artist. However, in recent years he has turned increasingly to figurative painting. For a general overview that includes Morris' work, see, for example, Lucie-Smith (1995: 74–133).

11. Archigram is the name of an English utopian architectural group, founded in 1960 by Peter Cook (1974). It disbanded in 1975. Paulo Soleri (1919–) is an Italian architect who, since the 1950s, has worked in the USA on alternative planning schemes at the Cosanti Foundation in Scottsdale, Arizona (see Wall, 1971). The science fiction inspired Metabolic Group in Japan was initiated by Kenzo Tange (see Kurokawa, 1972).

12. For a somewhat different explanation of the break up of Architecture Principe see, I. Scalbert and M. Mostafavi, 'Interview with Claude Parent', in Johnston (1996: 49–58).

13. See, for instance, Mandelbrot (1977).

14. As indicated in the references below, *Pure War* (1997) is the title of a recently revised book-length interview with Virilio conducted by Sylvère Lotringer. The English edition of *Popular Defense & Ecological Struggles* (1990 [1978]) does not contain an Introduction.

15. Virilio is referring to Dery (1996).

16. 'Info War' is the title of the Postscript in the new edition of *Pure War* (Virilio and Lotringer, 1997: 165–86).

17. See, for example, Der Derian (1992).

18. 'Continental Drift' is the title of a chapter in *Open Sky* (1997 [1995]).

References

Agamben, G. (1997) *Homo Sacer: le pouvoir souverain et la vie nue*. Paris: Seuil.

Baudrillard, J. (1983) *Simulations*, trans. P. Foss, P. Patton and P. Beitchman. New York: Semiotext(e).

Bergson, H. (1910 [1889]) *Time and Free Will: An Essay on the Immediate Data of Consciousness*, trans. F.L. Pogson. London: George Allen and Unwin.

Cook, P. (1974) *Archigram*. London: Klotz.

Deleuze, G. and F. Guattari (1987 [1980]) *A Thousand Plateaus: Capitalism and Schizophrenia*, trans. B. Massumi. Minneapolis: University of Minnesota Press.

Der Derian, J. (1992) *Antidiplomacy: Spies, Terror, Speed, and War*. Oxford: Blackwell.

Derrida, J. (1973 [1967]) *Speech and Phenomena, and Other Essays on Husserl's Theory of Signs*, trans. D.B. Allison. Evanston, IL: Northwestern University Press.

Derrida, J. (1976 [1967]) *Of Grammatology*, trans. G. Spivak. Baltimore, MD and London: Johns Hopkins University Press.

Derrida, J. (1984) 'No Apocalypse, Not Now (Full Speed Ahead, Seven Missiles, Seven Missives)', trans. C. Porter and P. Lewis, *Diacritics* 14 (summer): 20–31.

Derrida, J. (1996 [1995]) *Archive Fever: A Freudian Impression*, trans. E. Prenowitz. Chicago, IL: University of Chicago Press.

Dery, M. (1996) *Escape Velocity: Cyberculture at the End of the Century*. New York: Grove Press.

Ellul, J. (1965) *The Technological Society*. London: Jonathan Cape.

Foucault, M. (1977 [1975]) *Discipline and Punish: The Birth of the Prison*, trans. A. Sheridan. London: Penguin.

Gibson, W. (1984) *Neuromancer*. London: Victor Gollancz.

Haraway, D. (1985) 'A Manifesto for Cyborgs: Science, Technology, and Socialist Feminism in the 1980s', *Socialist Review* 80(2): 65–108.

Johnston, P. (ed.) (1996) *The Function of the Oblique: The Architecture of Claude Parent and Paul Virilio: 1963—1969*, trans. P. Johnston. London: Architectural Association.

Joly, F. (ed.) (1996) *documenta. documents 1*. Stuttgart: Cantz Verlag.

Kerrigan, J. (1997) 'When Eyesight is Fully Industrialised', *London Review of Books* 19(20): 14–15.

Kurokawa, K. (1972) *The Concept of Metabolism*. Tokyo: Architectural Foundation.

Lucie-Smith, E. (1995) *Art Today*. London: Phaidon Press.

Lyotard, J.-F. (1984 [1979]) *The Postmodern Condition*, trans. G. Bennington and B. Massumi. Minneapolis: University of Minnesota Press.

Mandelbrot, B. (1977) *The Fractal Geometry of Nature*. New York: Freeman.

Marcel, G. (1950 [1949]) *The Mystery of Being, vol. 1: Reflection and Mystery*, trans. G.S. Fraser. London and Chicago: Harvill Press.

Merleau-Ponty, M. (1962 [1945]) *Phenomenology of Perception*, trans. C. Smith. London: Routledge.

Milburn, G. (1996) *Quantum Technology*. St Leonards: Allen and Unwin.

Venturi, R., D. Scott Brown and S. Izenour (1977) *Learning From Las Vegas*. Cambridge, MA: MIT Press.

Virilio, P. (1986 [1977]) *Speed & Politics: An Essay on Dromology*, trans. M. Polizzotti. New York: Semiotext(e).

Virilio, P. (1989a [1984]) *War and Cinema: The Logistics of Perception*, trans. P. Camiller. London: Verso.

Virilio, P. (1989b [1986]) 'The Museum of Accidents', trans. Y. Leonard. *Public 2: The Lunatic of One Idea*: 81–5.

Virilio, P. (1990 [1978]) *Popular Defense & Ecological Struggles*, trans. M. Polizzotti. New York: Semiotext(e).

Virilio, P. (1991a [1980]) *The Aesthetics of Disappearance*, trans. P. Beitchman. New York: Semiotext(e).

Virilio, P. (1991b [1984]) *The Lost Dimension*, trans. D. Moshenberg. New York: Semiotext(e).

Virilio, P. (1991c) *L'Écran du desert*. Paris: Galilée.

Virilio, P. (1994a [1975]) *Bunker Archeology*, trans. G. Collins. New York: Princeton Architectural Press.

Virilio, P. (1994b [1988]) *The Vision Machine*, trans. J. Rose. Bloomington and Indianapolis: Indiana University Press and British Film Institute, London.

Virilio, P. (1995 [1993]) *The Art of the Motor*, trans. J. Rose. Minnesota: University of Minnesota Press.

Virilio, P. (1997 [1995]) *Open Sky*, trans. J. Rose. London: Verso.

Virilio, P. (1999 [1990]) *Polar Inertia*, trans. P. Camiller. London: Sage Publications.

Virilio, P. and Lotringer, S. (1997 [1983]) *Pure War*, revised edn, trans. M. Polizzotti, Postscript trans. B. O' Keeffe. New York: Semiotext(e).

Wall, D. (1971) *Visionary Cities: The Arcology of P.S.* London: Banham.

Paul Virilio is Director of the École Spéciale d' Architecture in Paris.

John Armitage teaches at the Division of Government & Politics, University of Northumbria at Newcastle, United Kingdom.

Indirect Light
Extracted from *Polar Inertia*

Paul Virilio

Light is the name of the shadow of the living light.

Bernard de Clairvaux

I STILL REMEMBER MY astonishment, ten years ago, when I saw video screens replacing mirrors on Paris Metro platforms.

Soon after 1968, it is true, surveillance cameras had appeared at the entrances to the *grandes écoles* and universities, and this new equipment was also used to keep watch on the boulevards and major junctions of the capital.[1] Today, I am astonished once again when I see the lens of a micro-camera rising above the keypad that gives coded access to a block of flats. Evidently entry phones are no longer enough to do the job of the old concierges.

As an electro-optical substitute, *videoscopy* seems to come into its own with this role of indirectly lighting a domestic environment for which electric light, a direct form analogous to daylight, is no longer sufficient. Rapid miniaturization is indeed making the video camera and its monitor more and more akin to a *warning light* that comes on to let us see who is here or who is there.

Even the old 35 mm cine-camera has had its eyepiece viewfinder replaced to advantage with a screen that actually displays the recorded images.

How can one fail to see here the essential characteristic of video technology: not a more or less up-to-the-minute 'representation' of an event, but *live presentation of a place* or an electro-optical environment – the result, it would seem, of *putting reality on waves* by means of electro-magnetic physics?

■ *Theory, Culture & Society* 1999 (SAGE, London, Thousand Oaks and New Delhi),
Vol. 16(5–6): 57–70
[0263-2764(199910/12)16:5–6;57–70;009958]

It is logical, then, to find here not any performance space, any 'screening room', but only a *control room*.

In furnishing the image of a place, videography does not itself require any 'space' except for its supporting camera and monitor, themselves integrated – or dissolved, as it were – into other equipment having nothing to do with 'artistic' televisual or cinematic representation.

Just as one is not bothered by the dials and lights on a car dashboard or by the lighting in a shop window, so one is not really troubled by the 'broadcasting' or 'diffusion' area of a video camera. That area is solely *what is lit up*, and not the 'theatre' or site of a cinema performance screened at some distant location.

So great is the difference between video observation, cinema and television that the TV set has itself been overtaken through the incorporation of monitors into the most ordinary domestic equipment – for example, the 'electro-optical porter' that makes people visible as the entry phone only made them audible.

The whole debate on the crisis of cinemas, on the miniaturization of public film theatres, will no doubt soon be repeated in relation to private homes and the 'living room', where the TV set is still often located. For the emancipation of the screen will involve not only its sudden expansion into the giant open-air Jumbotron or Olympic stadium screen, but also its *compression* into a scattered array of ordinary objects unconnected with televisual performance or information.

Who still cares about the electrical wires in domestic appliances? Who tomorrow will care about the optical fibres built into commonly used materials or equipment?

Alongside the *broadcasting* of current political or artistic events, video 'illuminates' us about phenomena instantaneously *transmitted* across varying distances and thus becomes itself a new type of tele-topographic 'site' or location. (Is there not already talk of 'neighbourhood television'?) Just as Edison's invention of the electric light-bulb caused daytime places to appear at night, the new electro-optical lamp causes places to become visible amid generally invisible surroundings. As the site of the non-site of instantaneous transmission (at varying distances), it effects a kind of commutation of perceptible appearances similar to that which occurs in para-optic perception and quite unrelated to ordinary mass-media communication.[2]

Thus, alongside the well-known effects of 'telescopy' and 'microscopy', which have revolutionized our perception of the world since the 17th century, it will not be long before the repercussions of 'videoscopy' make themselves felt through the constitution of an instantaneous, interactive 'space–time' that has nothing in common with the topographical space of geographical or even simply geometrical distance.

Whereas theatrical or cinematic *mise en scène* involves the spatio-temporal organization of stage action or film narrative in an area used for public performances, and whereas, to a lesser degree, production for television requires a private stage or broadcasting area (the rooms of a private home), this no longer applies to video transmission. For 'cine-videography' solely consists in the *commutation* of more or less distant and disjointed appearances, and also in the commutation of interactive actors at varying distances. Commutation of the emission and reception of the video signal, at the monitoring terminal, indicates the *mutation-commutation* of distances (topology) into *power* (tele-topology), that is, into light energy as the union of relativist cinema and wave optics.

The present crisis of cinemas is not therefore mainly due to an increase in domestic film-viewing; rather, it expresses a crisis in the idea of representation linked to rapid spread of the 'live' dimension. The live 'real-time' spectacle is a result of the development of videoscopy, not only in people's homes, but here, there and everywhere, in the very body of the various pieces of equipment in which it began to be incorporated nearly twenty years ago. (The most striking example is the weaving of optical fibres into composite materials.) The crisis, then, is a crisis of *delayed* broadcasting as such, so that electro-optical imaging techniques now impose the idea – or, to be more precise, the 'ideography' – of a veritable presentation of places and milieux, a 'presentation' which corresponds, on a human scale, to what telescopic presentation meant for astronomy or microscopic presentation for the innermost properties of materials.

Video is no more the eighth art than cinema was the seventh. The crisis affecting cinema box-office, rival TV channels but also what is called art video stems from the fact that, ever since the beginnings of photography and cinema, as well as of radio and television, the showing of *events* or entertainments has been more important than *the lighting up of the places* where they happen. Notwithstanding Edison, Marey, the Lumière Brothers, Vertov and a few others, the fun of the fair nearly always took priority over illumination (and did so more than ever with the coming of television), but the appearance of an *active optics* has suddenly replaced the feats of passive optics (of glass and other transparent lens material) in the organization of perceptible reality. This startling new *presence of tele-reality* transforms the nature of both the object and the subject of traditional representation, so that *pictures of places have now taken over from the 'picture houses'* where performances used to occur. Only the theatre, thanks to its unity of time and place, still escapes the transmutations of electro-optical lighting whose immediacy excludes 'unity of place' for the sole benefit of 'unity of time', albeit of a *real time* which seriously affects the space of real things.

In fact, alongside the 'radio-activity' of emission and reception, with its 'electro-acoustic high fidelity', there is now what might be called the 'opto-activity' of videoscopic commutation, with all the problems of 'electro-optical high definition' that this implies.

When there is talk in Toulouse and elsewhere of the imminent introduction of neighbourhood television (*télé locale*), people do not realize that they are borrowing a term from videoscopy or, in the case of a cabled city, from a 'videography' that allows the town to *see itself* and to *make itself visible* – that is, to become its own 'production', its own film.

The city of Rennes, for example, has a plan for 'electronic public lighting' to boost the political and economic existence of the urban area – hence the requirement for a municipal tele-noticeboard and the inevitable telesales that will replace the local press with one huge cathode shop-window. But is this not already how things are with the more limited proximity of objects and places in our everyday environment, with the Metro video terminals, the company's closed-circuit television, or the shops that are able to see the faces of window-gazers? And that is nothing compared with 'wall-socket' cameras and 'light-bulb' monitors built into ordinary objects, much as the microphone and loudspeaker were earlier incorporated into alarm-clock, tape recorder or Walkman, or the digital displays of quartz watches were implanted into pen tops, cigarette lighters and all manner of other objects. In the realm of videoscopic display, however, commutation is different. 'Geographically close' television and 'geometrically close' video are *parasitic* upon clear perception of the here and now: they interpenetrate and interchange places *teletopologically*, thanks to sudden 'live' revelation of the 'space-speed' at present supplanting the space–time of our ordinary activities. Merging with para-optical illumination, the upper speed limit of live transmission defines itself as indirect lighting at the speed of the video signal.

It is often claimed in the West that miniaturization, like giant screens, is a Japanese gadget. But this is not true. What is happening in image physics is also happening in astrophysics, where the Hubble space telescope is soon to come into operation with *adaptive optics*, that is, with image correction that depends on the computer's capacity and not just on the properties of the lens.

Screen and picture size therefore have nothing to do with it; the dimensions of the object are no longer what counts. For now the cathode screen displays *spatial distance that changes before our eyes into luminous energy, into illumination power.*

As a new kind of distance – the 'light (zero sign) of the new physics'[3] – suddenly takes the place of the customary distances of time (positive sign) and space (negative sign), every surface of whatever size has an objective existence only in and through the interface of an observation which, instead of just being the visible result of direct solar or electric lighting, is due to indirect lighting by the radio-electrical field of a Hertzian system or an optical fibre cable.

What we see for the *maximal surface* of the globe subjected to constant scrutiny by military, meteorological and other satellites is also true for the *minimal surfaces* of objects and places subjected to the intense lighting of videoscopy. In fact, a mysterious 'tele-bridge' is established between an ever-growing number of surfaces, from the largest to the most minute, in a kind of sound-and-image feedback which triggers for us observers a (video-geographical or video-geometrical) 'tele-presence' or 'tele-reality' essentially expressed by the concept of real time.

What Einstein's 'point of view theory' taught us in 1905 about the relativity of extension and duration – that is, the inseparable face-to-face meeting of observer and observed surfaces, a relativist interface without which extension has no objective dimension – is *visibly* confirmed by instantaneous video feedback in which the electro-optical environment wins out over the classical 'ecological' environment. A kind of 'electronic meteorology' thereby asserts itself without which the meteorology of the earth's atmosphere would soon become incomprehensible. At a time when the major US television channels ABC, CBS and NBC are faring worse and worse, Ted Turner's live news channel, CNN, is planning a 'News Hound' service for a million subscribers with video equipment. 'That's a million opportunities for us,' Earl Casey, the man in charge of this future interactive system, said recently, '*a million witnesses able to provide us with pictures*; all we'll have to do is select.'

In the military sphere, eminently strategic research into *stealth* aircraft points in the same direction. While a complex environment of electromagnetic detection is established at global level, active research is being pursued into ways of escaping 'radio-electrical sight' through special new materials such as the PBZ super-polymer, which is said to be capable of avoiding detection by radar waves. At the same time, however, aeronautical producers are asked to embed in the same material optical fibres capable of sounding, or permanently illuminating, the dense cells and organs driving the combat aircraft.

For the philosopher Schopenhauer, the world was its representation. For the 'video-maker' or electronics expert, we may say, matter is becoming its presentation – direct and external 'presentation' and, at the same time, internal and indirect presentation, the object or instrument becoming not only present to the naked eye but remotely present or '*tele-present*'.

This *physical non-separability* of outside and inside, near and distant, is also exemplified by the road-haulage industry and by the development of 'star' publicity. Thus the American Geostar company, and soon its European counterpart Locstar, are due in the near future to place the first piece of their 'Radio Determination Satellite Service' in orbit. Thanks to this surveillance system, the headquarters of a haulage company will know at any moment the geographical position of each of its vehicles, a geo-stationary navigation satellite enabling it to monitor and control movements. We can see why the magazine *Match* has just had its logo drawn in the Chott Djerid (dear to Bill Viola) of central Tunisia, suddenly turning the desert into a kind of screen, as all the continental and oceanic surfaces have become for the gaze of orbiting satellites.

But this ceaseless *rapprochement* of above and below would not be complete if, after the nadir, we left out the zenith – that is, the minor miracle of high-orbit billposting which is Coca-Cola's plan to leave its indelible mark on our nightly firmament.[4]

Once again we notice the decline of the sites of representation and projection. Theatre, stage or screen become simply *the sky and the ground*, all the surfaces from the smallest to the largest that are exposed, nay, *overexposed*, to the inquisitive gaze of automatic instant-relay cameras — surfaces or, more exactly, 'interfaces' which have objective existence only as a result of videoscopic examination by live-relay recording material. *This 'real-time' tele-reality is supplanting the reality of the real-space presence* of objects and places, now overridden by electro-magnetic paths.

For Einstein, what distinguished a correct theory from a wrong theory was only the length of time for which it remained valid: a few years or decades for the former, a few moments or days for the latter. Is it not perhaps the same with the duration of images, with the difference between the 'real-time' and the 'delayed-time' image?

In the end, the whole problem of 'tele-reality' (or 'tele-presence', if that seems preferable) hinges on this same question of the validity of a short duration; the real value of the *object* or *subject* instantaneously present at a distance entirely depends upon the *passage*, that is, the speed, of its image, the speed of light of contemporary electro-optics. It is the same with 'remote' or 'tele' action, thanks to the capacity for instantaneous interaction in telemetry. The *opto-activity* of the online image is similar to the *radio-activity* of a device that handles objects at a distance (remote-controlled vehicles, transfer machines, various kinds of instrument).[5]

This advent of the real 'passage' to the detriment of the real object and subject — a phenomenon so indicative of the primacy of image over thing resulting from the new supremacy of real time over real space — clearly reveals the wave character of reality. For the sudden *commutation of perceptible appearances* is ultimately only the herald of a general derealization resulting from the new illumination of perceptible reality — a reality not just 'apparent' as before, but 'transparent' or, to be even more precise, *trans-apparent*.

There is a fusion/confusion of transmitted appearances and immediate appearances, with indirect lighting capable of soon supplanting direct lighting — not only, of course, artificial electric lighting but above all natural lighting, with the revolutionary changes in perception that this implies. The advent of passage as instantaneous and ubiquitous is thus the advent of *time light*, the intensive time of electro-optics which is supplanting for ever traditional passive optics.

We can bet, though, that the status of reality will not long resist this sudden illumination of places, happenings and events. For while improvements in the *spatial* definition of optical camera lenses have made it easier to see contrasts and increased the luminosity of the habitual image, recent improvements in the *temporal* definition of filming and electronic transmission procedures have increased the clarity and resolution of videoscopic images. Thus, audiovisual speed primarily helps us to see and to hear, or, in other words, *to move forward in the light of real time*, as automobile speed helped us to move forward in the real space of an area of land.

The greater 'transparency' of high-speed communications (TGV, supersonic aircraft, etc.) is thus compounded by the sudden (electro-optical and acoustic) trans-appearance of the means of information and telecommunication. High fidelity and high image definition serve greatly to modify the nature of the (acoustic or visual) relief, which in the end comes down to the greater or lesser reality of the things perceived, a spatio-temporal relief conditioning our apprehension of the world and of present time. Since the eye interprets any change in luminous intensity as a change in form, the light (direct or indirect, natural or artificial) produces not only the colour of objects and places but also their relief. Hence the importance of research into high definition of the image, definition at once spatial and temporal of a video signal capable of achieving for visual space what high fidelity of the radio signal has already done for the stereophony of sound volumes: *a veritable stereo-optics integrated into the domestic environment.*

Thus, just as star-filming techniques continually improve the image resolution of remote detection satellites, so the constant improvement of TV picture definition increases not the electrical transparency of the local environment (as at the beginning of the century, with the electrification of town and country), but the *electro-optical trans-appearance* of the *global* environment. This means the emergence of a new kind of 'relief' or audio-visual volume applying to the totality of transmitted appearances, a 'stereo-videoscopy' whose significance at macroscopic level is similar to that of the sudden breakthrough of electron microscopy in disclosing the infinitely small. In order to see, one is no longer content to dispel the shadows of surrounding darkness; the commutation of appearances can also remove the obstacle of extension, the opacity of great distance, thanks to ruthlessly penetrative videoscopic equipment that is analogous to the most powerful of floodlights. As the electro-optical *faux jour* of indirect public lighting dawns, as the real is put on air as the figurative, a new artificial light now complements electric lighting in much the same way that electric lighting once filled in for daylight.

At 1.32 p.m. local time, on 26 October 1987, a Titan-34D rocket launched a KH11 satellite from Vandenberg air base in California. *From its polar orbit covering the whole planet*, this satellite is able, at any moment of its ceaseless electronic scanning, to zoom in, spin round and transmit pictures in the form of electronic impulses. The average life of this military light is 36 months.

The invention of cinema can no more be separated from the invention of searchlights than it can from that of snapshot photography. Did not Thomas Edison, inventor of the incandescent lamp in 1879, work on the kinetograph a few years later? As to Louis Lumière, at the Universal Exhibition of 1900 the French Navy lent him its most powerful searchlight to project his films on a large screen, in the famous Gallery of Machines. And in 1948, shortly before his death, the pioneer of the cinema was still working to improve lighthouses for the Navy.

Today, the projection of wide film on to planetarium domes is only possible with a 15 kW xenon lamp initially designed to illuminate NASA's rocket-launching sites.

Finally, in 1969 when the astronauts returned from the Apollo XI lunar mission, the President of the USA ordered all the coastal cities to be lit up, as ordinary lampposts are lit up in the evening along marine boulevards. This was meant as a homage not only to the conquerors of the moon but also to the sudden power of public lighting to reveal man's presence to the farthest reaches of the atmosphere.

If one thinks of the illumination of theatres and palace festivities in the age of Louis XIV or the introduction of electric street lighting at the end of the last century, it is clear that the history of public spectacle has been inseparable from the history of light – from fireworks through the diorama of Daguerre (a decorator at the Paris Opera and the Ambigu Comique) to the *son et lumière* displays of recent times. The birth of the cinema was itself inseparable from the development of artificial light, the famous 'arc lamps' being necessary both for the shooting of films in studios and for their screening in public theatres.

The other revealing aspect of this sudden extension of transparency has more to do with police requirements, for lighting makes the streets safer and so prolongs the time for commercial enrichment. Already in 1667, long before the days of video surveillance, Police Lieutenant La Reynie issued a famous ordinance that led to Paris's world reputation as the *ville lumière*. Then came the electrification of town and country in the early 20th century, an undertaking rather like the present laying of cable to carry video along optical fibres throughout the big conglomerations. But now the shift concerns the very nature of the light, which is no longer just artificial but *indirect*, differing from direct light as much as candlelight once did from the light of the stars.

We should also mention here the *light-intensification* camera (or binoculars) currently used by the Army to see in the middle of the night over considerable distances. Often replacing infrared systems, this 'low-light television' amplifies the surrounding light, however weak, by nearly a hundred thousand times. In a way it is similar to a particle accelerator. Consisting of a tube placed in a powerful and continuous electrical field, the film camera has successive levels of photon acceleration which increase accordingly the luminosity of the final image; the accelerated light particles strike a screen with a phosphorus film at the other end of the tube, causing each particle of the film to glow. Lately this kind of indirect lighting equipment has started to be used by the German and British police, especially for football stadium surveillance.

In fact, where the *real time* of live television broadcasting prevails over the real space of a land actually crossed, the mere distinction between natural and artificial light is no longer enough; one has to add the difference in kind between *direct light*, natural or artificial, and *indirect light*, for electro-optical lighting now replaces electrical lighting as the latter once did the rising of the day.

And this is while we wait for the active optics of computer graphics to achieve its next feat: that is, the coupling of the passive optics of cameras with a computer capable of rectifying the transmitted image as only glass lenses used to do. *Digital optics* will then succeed analogue optics, as the latter once cleverly complemented the ocular optics of the human gaze.

As the image is the most sophisticated form of information, it is logical to expect that advances in computing will also end in the deployment of this indirect light: *digital light* this time, capable of piercing reality's shadows and of most realistically conveying an unknown transparency, such as fractal geometry already makes possible, with digital zoom effects that are nothing other than computer-generated *synthetic lighting*. The passages and their 'trans-appearance' signal the innermost constituents of the form-image, *shape of that which has no shape, image of that which has no image* (Lao-Tse) – a figure for the dynamic of emptiness, similar to the void of sub-atomic physics for which Oriental thought long ago paved the way.

But let us return to the city, the 'light-city' that has been home to all historical illuminations from the Fire of Rome through the pyrotechnics of the Age of Enlightenment to the laser displays of recent times. Since illumination is synonymous with the unveiling of a 'scene', with revelation of a transparency without which appearances would be nothing, only a narrow conception could still talk of light simply in terms of the lighting of places. For how can one fail to see, behind those dazzling electro-optical displays, that the public image is on the way to replacing public space, and that the political stage will not be able to do without indirect lighting, any more than it has been able to do without direct artificial lighting? With its origins in the city-theatre organized around the public spectacle of agora, forum or parvis, then in the *cinecittà* of Western modernity, the contemporary '*telecittà*' today establishes the *commutation of perceptible appearances* through the feats of satellites, Hertzian networks and optical fibre cables. In its respective time, each of these 'urban representations' has known how to use the spectacle of transparency, of public illumination, to develop its culture and collective imagination.

An exceptional situation may serve to illustrate this point. In the spring of 1989, between May and June, Beijing students decided to demonstrate for 'democracy'. They gathered and gradually took over Tiananmen Square, not setting any time limit to their occupation – an old practice which goes back, not to the sit-ins of the 1960s (as some have suggested), but to the Greek City where the public space of the agora was the guarantee of the citizens' political unity against the threat of a tyrant.

At the time of Gorbachev's arrival on 14 May, they numbered three hundred thousand, and three days later a million. Profiting from the fact that most of the international agencies had sent their cameras and reporters, and even such top editorial writers as Dan Rather, to cover the reconciliation of the two Communist giants, the Chinese students demanded live coverage of the Tiananmen events so that pictures of the country's most famous public square should be broadcast not only to the world but, above all, to Shanghai, Canton and everywhere else in China.

This demand was rejected by the authorities, and the eventual introduction of martial law was accompanied by a massacre of the population of Beijing by the tanks of the People's Liberation Army. What had already happened in Czechoslovakia after the Prague Spring, or in Poland with the decree establishing an 'internal state of war', was now being reproduced in Asia. The people's army was crushing the people.

But let us return to the 'illumination' of these events by the world's press agencies. Aware that the presence of fifteen hundred journalists in Beijing was of extreme political importance, the students repeatedly showed signs of collusion with their far-off TV 'viewers' by writing banners in French or English, by deploying exotic symbols such as the 'statue of liberty' beneath the portrait of Mao Tse-tung, or by making frequent references to the French Revolution. Formerly, the surface of the agora or the parade ground of a garrison town corresponded to the 'surface area' of the men under arms: citizen-soldiers in Ancient democracy or enlisted troops of fortified towns. 'March separately, strike together': this infantry maxim also fitted the gathering of citizens on the public square; the adjoining streets enabled them to fly to where the public power was identified with the crowd united in the face of external aggression or civil war.

Curiously enough, with the public image of Tiananmen Square broadcast all over the world, we saw both an infinite extension of that surface area (thanks to the real-time interface of the television screen) and a miniaturization of it in the shape of a 51 cm cathode screen that did not seriously convey any depth of field. Hence the importance of the fact that in Hong Kong during that crucial period, not only private television but *the giant screen in the city stadium* was used to unite people collectively with what was taking place at the heart of the Chinese capital.

This was a kind of 'teletopia'[6] in which real-time continuity made up for the absence of real-space contiguity. For a time, the stadium and giant screen in Hong Kong became inseparable from Tiananmen Square, as the square already was from millions of television viewers around the world. However much the forbidden city may ban it, things at one end of the earth are made visible, accessible, at the other end, thanks to the energy of a *living light*, at once electro-optical and acoustic, whose effects on society will be incomparably more important than those of electrification were more than half a century ago.

Real time, delayed time, two times, two 'movements'. On 15 May 1989, the students gathered on Tiananmen Square demanded *live* news coverage – a fruitless effort on their part.

After the tragic events of 7 June in Beijing, Chinese television constantly broadcast *recorded* material, shot by automatic police surveillance cameras, of certain excesses against isolated vehicles and soldiers – always without showing the peaceful occupation of the square or the massacre of its occupants by the People's Republic of China. The choice of image or, to be more precise, the *time* of the image chosen determined China's current political reality – as if, in the end, the country's vast expanse and the huge numbers living in it counted for less than the instant in time chosen to speak of it, to show what was really happening there; as if the real time and real space of the Tiananmen events disturbed the Chinese leaders so much that they had to temper its effects through a *replay*.

It is a strange politics when public images shown with calculated delay are supposed to staunch the disastrous consequences, as the ramparts of the public space and the laws of the city used to block the threat of subversion or aggression. Not only is the day and hour of *concrete* action chosen as before; now there is a decision to obscure the immediate event *temporally and temporarily*, while the actors, the students on Tiananmen Square, are subjected to physical repression.

The events may well be described as a 'siege', a new kind of 'state of siege': not so much an army encirclement of city-space as a *temporal siege*, a siege of the real time of public information. The key element is no longer the familiar censorship preventing disclosure of things that the state wishes to keep secret; it is *the replaying of recorded material*, the retarded ignition of the living light of events.

This 'war over real time' finally shows how right Louis-Ferdinand Céline was at the end of his life, when he said in disillusion: 'For the moment only the facts count, and not even they for very long.'

That moment has now passed, in China as in the wider world: what is done can be undone by means of interactive telecommunications; a 'tele-topian' reality has the upper hand over the topical reality of the event. On 9 June 1989, Chinese television solemnly announced that the Army would fire without warning upon anyone carrying a camera or other photographic device.

The mutation currently under way is confirmed by another, final aspect: namely the crisis of the household car or, more precisely, its symbolic decline to the advantage of other objects, more eccentric vehicles. 'The car will be the last of your worries' – a slogan placed above the Ford stand at the Paris motor show in 1988 – was a wonderful illustration of this process. For it is a decline which, as always, adorns itself with a maximum of useless accessories, rather as the event itself changed its name to the 'World Motor Show'.

In fact, what is really global today is live television; a particular car, whether for sport or transport, is never more than a local object. This explains the recent success of the all-weather vehicle, the famous 4 × 4 which tries to escape the rut of the beaten track. It is an eccentric trial indeed – an attempt to leave the way, the motorway, at any cost.

As we have seen, the image is now the only high-performance vehicle, the real-time image which is supplanting the space where the car still moves from one place to another. In the end, the crisis of the household car is rather like the crisis of the neighbourhood cinema. How many of those dark halls found themselves turned into garages or service-stations, before these in turn became supermarkets or, more recently still, recording studios or newspaper headquarters!

As Fellini put it a short time ago: 'I no longer travel, I only have fits of moving around.' For as fever or energy occupies and possesses us, we no longer dwell in the motive energy of any 'means of transport' – hence the major risk posed by the various 'speed' drugs.

The cinema, Alfred Hitchcock used to say, is armchairs with people inside. Even if the saloon-car bucket seats are for the moment less empty than the cinema armchairs, we should not have any illusions. How much longer will we accept the tedium of the motorway journey?

In Japan television has already invaded taxis and high-rise lifts. Just as dogs are banned from garden squares, cars no longer enter pedestrian zones in some central areas; they go into exile on Paris's ring boulevard while awaiting completion of the super-ring boulevard, or the ultra-rapid underground laser system in which cars will think they are the Metro.

How to make a journey without actually moving from one place to another? How to vibrate in unison? These questions should soon lead to different means of transport and transmission, quite unrelated to the domestic contraption that still serves us today.

Let us look more closely. We no longer turn a switch on our radio or television set; we touch a control or press a key on our remote-control pad. Even our quartz watches have a digital display instead of hands that move around.

'This will replace that', wrote old Victor Hugo referring to book and cathedral. Will it not be the same tomorrow with screen and limousine? Until when will we *really* keep moving from place to place?

Was it not again the Japanese who recently invented the *bo-do-kahn*, a vibrating pillow that allows you to listen rhythmically to a Walkman? Even the rising sun no longer casts its moving rays upon Japanese apartments bathed in sunlight by optical fibre.

Moreover, the people in charge tell us that in the Osaka conurbation, with a population of twenty million, cable networks are already being implanted beneath the motorways so that images can travel through the cars' subsoil. Listen to the Formula One world champion Alain Prost: 'Real speed is to approach obstacles with the impression that you are moving in a slow-motion film.' And the former rally-driver Bernard Darniche stated soon after retiring from competition: 'For me, the ideal car is a mobile video-control.'

Why try to hide it? The only way of saving the private car is to fit it with a temporal video-image compressor: a *turbo-compressor of the real-time image*.

The talking car that warns drivers of engine trouble is a mistake, once *road simulators* for motoring schools are on sale for a hundred thousand francs (the price of a new vehicle). What is needed is a car that actually sees other vehicles *over the horizon*, so that car speed and audiovisual speed are rendered compatible. Maybe the Prometheus project that unites twelve European companies within the framework of Eureka is actually working on such an idea. After all, the 'travel pilot' devised by the Blaupunkt corporation is already just an obsolete guidance system, given that electronic chips of less than one micron will soon each contain the equivalent of the whole US road network.

At a time when a single videodisc can depict all the different journeys in a town – Aspen, Colorado, as it happens – how can there not be attempts to give motoring a new 'perspective' in which the temporal depth of the electronic image prevails over the spatial depth of the motorway network?

Recent advertising for the Thomson washing-machine described this household object as a 'washing-computer'. So how can one fail to grasp that tomorrow's transport machine will first of all be a 'driving-computer' in which the audiovisual feats of the electronic dashboard will prevail over the optical qualities of the field beyond the windscreen?

Just as parachute exercises are moving more and more in the direction of 'relative flight', so will car travel develop from a means of absolute physical transport to a means of 'relative transport' associated with instantaneous transmission, the kinematic energy of the video-computer image advantageously replacing the kinetic energy of engine capacity.

As higher speeds progressively disentitle all others, the TGV and the ultrasonic aeroplane will not change anything. The *time-reducing machine* is no longer the motor-car but audiovisual and real-time technologies.

A few years ago, the Cartier Foundation for Contemporary Art exhibited a superb collection of Ferraris, a veritable symposium of coupés, saloons and convertibles. But this luxury display in the Jouy-en-Josas park merely illustrated the evolution of 'aerodynamics', a science as antiquated in the age of computer-assisted design and driving as the aesthetics of old antique furniture has long since been.

Translated by Patrick Camiller

Notes

This article is extracted from *Polart Inertia*, due to be published in October 1999 by Sage Publications.

1. Symbolically enough, this electronic surveillance system is operated from the basements of the Paris City Hall.
2. See Jules Romain, *La Vision extra-rétinienne et le sens paroptique*, Paris: Gallimard, 1964.
3. See Gilles Cohen-Tannoudji and Michel Spiro, *La Matière-espace-temps*, Paris: Fayard, 1986.

4. A harbinger of such eccentricity appeared in the 1930s with the sudden surge of aerial advertising. 'Skywriting' was then quite a common practice.

5. On 19 October 1987, the computerized Wall Street crash gave us a preview of the negative effects of that instantaneous link-up of financial markets which is commonly known as the Big Bang.

6. See in this connection the plan for 'decentralization of the capital of Europe' which I submitted to the Élysée Palace on 14 July 1988.

Virilio and Architecture

Neil Leach

A GROWING NUMBER OF philosophers and cultural theorists of the
20th century have turned their attention to aesthetic questions, and
to architectural issues in particular. It is as though there has been an
aesthetic turn which parallels and echoes the earlier literary turn. Among
these theorists, Paul Virilio stands out as the one who has engaged most
comprehensively with the world of architecture. An artist by background
and a self-styled urbanist, he has consistently colonized the space of
architecture as a platform from which to develop his cultural theory.

Virilio's interest in architecture even led to his involvement in an
architectural practice. In 1963 Virilio formed the 'Architecture Principe'
group with Claude Parent. The two remained partners until they fell out over
differences of opinion on the events of May 1968, in which Virilio took an
active part. In the reforms following those events, Virilio became involved
with teaching, and in 1972 was appointed co-director (alongside Anatol
Kopp) of the École Spéciale d'Architecture in Paris.

Virilio continues to explore architectural ideas, but the focus of his
research has now shifted. His research concerns may be divided into two
distinct phases. Virilio's early interests lay in questions of space, and his
more recent interests relate to the problem of time. It is a shift which he
himself describes as being from 'typology' to 'dromology'. With this shift
Virilio has gone on to pursue more abstract theoretical enquiries, and to
interrogate the way in which we perceive the environment around us. Yet,
while this more recent work resists a concrete engagement with architectural form, it always circles around the question of space and spatiality, and
remains highly relevant to architecture. This article will attempt to offer an
overview of Virilio's engagement with the world of architecture, acknowledging the positive contribution that he has made to that realm, but also
exposing the negative aspects of his work.

One of the problems in assessing Virilio's work is that he often comes

■ *Theory, Culture & Society* 1999 (SAGE, London, Thousand Oaks and New Delhi),
Vol. 16(5–6): 71–84
[0263-2764(199910/12)16:5–6;71–84;009959]

across as a somewhat inconsistent thinker. It is difficult to construct any unified position out of Virilio's thought and, by extension, equally difficult to assess its contribution. Indeed, one of the perverse questions that seems to arise from the work of Virilio, no less that that of Fredric Jameson and Jean Baudrillard, is that it always appears to be double-edged. Even when he appears as an outspoken critic around certain issues, he displays a marked fascination with those issues, which seems to betray an underlying interest in precisely what he is criticizing. His criticism always threatens to falter, and to fold into some form of acquiescent support.

One way to explain this might be to surmise that he has been seduced by his prey, as Baudrillard has suggested is typical of theorists in general through the analogy of Sophie Calle and her *Suite Vénitienne* (1988). Theorists are prone to become trapped by that which they are themselves attempting to stalk. Alternatively one might recognize that every intellectual position is defined by what it is not, and that the positive bears the imprint of the negative. A critical outlook will therefore often reveal the trace of its own repressed other. With Virilio, it is almost as though there is something he recognizes within himself which he wishes to suppress, and which he therefore projects on to some external object in order to criticize it. At certain strategic moments, then, it is profitable to read Virilio against Virilio as a theorist *for* rather than *against* what he is critiquing. This, at any rate, is the strategy adopted here. But it is clear that, however the double-edged nature of Virilio's position might be explained, the inconsistencies in his thought ensure that any attempt to offer an overview of his work must be compromised, and can only constitute a provisional undertaking.

Phase One: Virilio and Typology

The first phase of Virilio's research – his interest in typology – was centred around two principal projects, his archaeological work on wartime bunkers on the Atlantic coast, which was published in *Bunker Archeology* (1975) and his theoretical work on the function of the 'oblique', which was published mainly in the journal *Architecture Principe* (Virilio and Parent, 1996), which he had co-founded with Parent. Virilio was also directly involved in the design process, and co-designed a building with Parent, the church of Sainte-Bernadette du Banlay in Nevers, which, with its bunker-like forms and tilted floors, to some extent fuses these two interests (Virilio, 1996).

Bunker Archeology reads as a very personal exploration of the physical remains of the German Atlantic fortifications abandoned after the Second World War. Virilio had been brought up during the war. Life could not have been easy for a young boy in occupied France, especially one whose surname betrayed an obvious connection with 'fascist' Italy. If the war left a deep impression on Virilio, such that war and the weaponry of war echo throughout his work like some sort of constant refrain, the physical traces of war in the form of these all too concrete remains constitute an architectural version of this obsession. In *Bunker Archeology* Virilio presents an archaeo-logical survey of these forms. Alongside his own exquisite photographs of these bunkers, he includes drawings, documents and his own written reflections. It is the photographs, however, that catch one's attention. These are hauntingly sublime images of the now silent relics of war, set against the natural beauty of the Atlantic coast. And it is clear that their sublime beauty has captivated Virilio. He quotes Rainer Maria Rilke: 'The beautiful is just the first degree of the terrible' (Virilio, 1975: 139). It is here that we can begin to recognize an obsession with the sublime taking root, an obsession which, we shall see, will emerge as the Achilles' heel of Virilio's thought.

In *Bunker Archeology* there is a curious echo of Le Corbusier. In Virilio's textured images of these massive concrete forms, with their crude imprints from the wooden shuttering, one senses a fascination that parallels Le Corbusier's passion for *baton brut*, the conscious use of these imprints, that became a form of architectural signature. And if the great grain elevators of the American Midwest inspired Le Corbusier in his architectural design, so these pure, functional forms with their simple aesthetic, disappearing into the dunes, seemed to have fired the imagination of Virilio. Certainly, one can see the influence of these forms in the church at Nevers.

Through the 'theory of the oblique', meanwhile, Virilio explored the possibility of a non-orthogonal architecture. In this he rejected the two fundamental principles of Euclidean space, the horizontal and the vertical, and argued for a third alternative, the 'oblique'. His approach was based on Gestalt theory and the phenomenology of perception of Maurice Merleau-Ponty. Space was to be experienced not through the perception of the eyes, but through the movement of the body exploring new modes of habitation suggested by the possibilities of the oblique. In effect Virilio harnessed the work of Merleau-Ponty for a new dynamic model of dwelling. Whereas in traditional building there had been a split between dynamic zones of circulation and static areas of dwelling, Virilio sought to fuse the two to create circulation as a form of dwelling. This was underpinned by a concern to develop forms which would promote a sense of disequilibrium and instability. As he explains:

> The objective of our research was to challenge outright the *anthropometric precepts of the classical era* – the idea that the body is an essentially static entity with an essentially static proprioception – in order to bring the human habitat into a dynamic age of the body in movement. In our work, the *traditional stability* (habitable stasis) of both the rural horizontal order and the urban vertical order gave way to the Metastability of the human body in motion, in tune with the rhythms of life. (Virilio, 1996: 13)

This challenging of a static anthropometric approach to architecture reflected a broader questioning of the social order at a cultural level. Virilio recognized that there had been a change in humanity, 'a metamorphosis of consciousness', and the function of the oblique was to respond to the 'new plane of human consciousness'. In this there are echoes of the Situationist position, which looked for an architecture to fire the imagination and allowed for a richer ontological experience that broke free of the reified relationships of the society of the spectacle. Indeed, the forms of Virilio and Parent do not differ widely from those of Situationist-inspired architects. Prominent among these was the Dutch architect, Constant, whose New Babylon projects, although not fully embraced by the movement, remained the most comprehensive attempt to translate the Situationists' ideals into architectural forms (Andreotti and Costa, 1996). In these projects Constant pursued themes such as 'disorientation' and 'dynamic space'. Anxious to avoid the limitations of the static spaces of utilitarian society, he promoted the concept of the 'dynamic labyrinth', one that accepted that the liberation of behaviour requires a labyrinthine space, but one which allowed that space to be continually subject to modification, according to the 'ludic' imagination. While Virilio's work on the oblique allowed little scope for modification, he clearly shared a common concern with Constant for the principle of 'dynamic space'.

The theory of the oblique has also been considered influential in the origins of the architectural movement that has been termed 'deconstruction' or 'deconstructivism'. In challenging the authority of ideas such as stability and vertical equilibrium, and by introducing the unstable and the oblique, Virilio's work resonates with that of later architects, such as Bernard Tschumi, who likewise challenged the hegemony of concepts such as rectilinearity, order, symmetry and compositional hierarchy, some of the basic tenets of traditional architectural aesthetics. Tschumi has been concerned to establish a new architecture for a new age. It is, perhaps, in the displaced, fragmented, angular forms of Tschumi's pavilions at the Parc de la Villette in Paris, and in the tilted ground plane of his video pavilion in Groningen, Holland, that we find the logical inheritance of Virilio's ideas.

Phase Two: Virilio and Dromology

With time, however, Virilio himself began to realize the limitations of his theory. Oblique forms were difficult to build and impractical to use. Moreover, Virilio's design collaboration with Parent had come to an end. Increasingly Virilio became preoccupied with more abstract questions of time. His interests began to shift from spatial considerations to spatio-temporal ones. Out of a theory of movement through architecture there began to emerge a theory of architecture in an age of movement. The focus of his research changed from typology to 'dromology', which he defines as 'the study and analysis of the impact of increasing speed of transport and communications on the development of land-use' (Virilio, 1996: 13).

Virilio's interest in dromology can be traced through a number of publications, of which *Speed and Politics* offers the most direct engagement with the subject (1986). Here, Virilio analyses the effect of speed within the contemporary city, which is read as a machine whose streets act as channels for rapid communications. Through these veins of the city course the 'dromomaniacs', the mobile revolutionaries of the modern age. These dromomaniacs – from *sans culottes* to brown-shirts – reveal how speed is the essence of political change. Beyond this they offer a model for change on an international scale through the medium of war. Modern warfare, Virilio notes, with its emphasis on mobility and surprise, depends on speed. Not only this, but speed becomes an issue of propaganda: 'Speed is the hope of the West, it is speed that supports the armies' morale' (Virilio, 1986: 55). *Speed and Politics* amounts to a panegyric of speed and the possibilities which it affords, written with a certain Futuristic fervour.

Similar themes underpin Virilio's more recent publications, but it is in *Lost Dimension* that Virilio addresses these questions within a more obviously architectural framework (1991). Here Virilio offers a number of takes on a similar theme, the consequences of the collapse of the significance of spatial distance within an era of considerable technological advances. Again speed becomes the key theme, whether it is the speed of instantaneous information transfer or the speed of ballistic missile capabilities. Virilio explores the consequences of this in the context of domestic, urban, national and international scenarios.

From an architectural perspective, one of the key ideas to emerge out of this later work has been that of the erosion of the hegemony of the physical, or, as Virilio calls it, the 'exhaustion' of the physical. Virilio questions whether or not we now exist in a condition of 'post-architecture', whereby the way in which we engage with traditional constraints imposed by architectural elements such as walls has shifted as a result of advances in technology. Emblematic of this has been the change in how the city is entered. It is no longer the port or the railway station, but the airport that is the chief entry to the city. With that the importance of city gates as the symbolic entrance to the city has been replaced by invisible forms of control embodied in electronic surveillance systems. Virilio's message is clear enough. Physical constraints, such as city walls, have been superseded by other, more sophisticated methods of control. This has a marked impact upon the urban. Not only has the development of new technologies reduced the need for physical proximity and therefore precipitated a process of de-urbanization, but these technologies have challenged the very necessity of physical presence. Once personal interaction can be displaced into the realm of the virtual, all that is associated with the world of the physical loses its hegemony. This is the point at which the urban begins to wane, and the post-urban takes over.

Moreover, advances in informational systems and transportational networks have had a significant impact on traditional modes of perception. And it is by engaging with these shifts that Virilio, who is above all a theorist of speed and time, has made so many penetrating observations. For it is by observing how the acceleration of various operations and, in particular, the development of systems of instantaneous information transfer, have come to distort our conception of time, that Virilio highlights the influence of these developments on our perceptions of place. In an age when the window of the cathode ray tube comes to displace the actual window of

the physical enclosure as the site of immediate and instantaneous information transfer, we find ourselves in a location without a location:

> Thanks to satellites, the cathode-ray window brings to each viewer the light
> of another day and the presence of the antipodal place. If space is that which
> keeps everything from occupying the same place, this abrupt confinement
> brings everything precisely to that 'place', that location that has no location.
> The exhaustion of physical, or natural relief and of temporal distances
> telescopes all localization and all position. As with live televised events, the
> places have become interchangeable at will. (Virilio, 1997: 385)

This 'instantaneity of ubiquity' further challenges the hegemony of physical
space. We must now understand the world not in terms of spatial dimensions, but in terms of spatio/temporal dimensions: 'Speed distance obliterates the notion of physical dimension' (Virilio, 1997: 385) It is no longer a
question of how far away a place is. Now it is simply a question of how long it
takes to reach it. With the advent of supersonic transportation, for example,
it can take less time to cross the Atlantic by plane than to traverse a single
European city by foot. Physical distance gives way to temporal distance as
'the loss of material space leads to the government of nothing but time'
(Virilio, 1997: 385).

Evaluating Virilio

What, then, is the significance of Virilio's contribution to a debate about
architecture? The significance of his early work is easy enough to appraise.
In particular, the stylistic indebtedness of later architects to his work shows
the not inconsiderable influence of the 'theory of the oblique' on shifts in
architectural expression. Likewise, his *Bunker Archeology* has left its legacy
in a more recent publication by Diller and Scofidio (1994) on links between
tourism and war on the French Atlantic coast. But it is Virilio's later work,
which arguably has the greatest potential impact.

   In particular, Virilio points towards a way of theorizing virtual reality.
He recognizes that the key to understanding virtual reality is not to grasp the
purely instrumental opportunities afforded by new technologies, but to
apprehend the ways in which these affect our patterns of consciousness. If
technology will never actually replace consciousness, it will at least influence it in ways that are only now becoming apparent. It is as though the
concept of the 'tele-' – the 'far' – and all that is associated with the previous,
modernist paradigm have to be radically rethought. By adapting Merleau-
Ponty's theory of perception, Virilio argues for a tele-perception as a new
mode of operation. A theory of cyberspace, such as begins to emerge from
Virilio's work, draws upon the notion of telekinesis, of the capacity of the
body to operate in any corner of the universe through some form of
prosthetic interactive device. The principle of traditional prosthetics, such
as the walking stick or the artificial limb, as a mechanism for extending the
motility of the body, is itself expanded to include techno-prosthetics, such

as the virtual reality glove, which enlarge the body's sphere of operations indefinitely. As such the paraplegic confined to the wheelchair paradoxically offers a model of how the limitations of the body can be overcome, and how, in a virtual world, human beings may soon be able to access the far corners of the universe. Distance becomes no object. The body can operate as easily using this mechanism on the next planet, as it can in the next room.

Yet while distance is obviated, a new depth is created. Operating through technology introduces a new anonymity already witnessed in telephone conversations. Persons communicating from adjacent VDU consoles correspond as though they are miles apart. Telecommunications, in dissolving the 'here' and 'now', serve both to break down distance, physical distance, and to create psychological 'distance'. While Virilio seems to prophesy the Internet with his observations that the screen has become the city square, 'the crossroads of all mass media', he equally highlights a new *manner* of communication, where technology introduces both a distance and an anonymity (Virilio, 1997: 389). It is in the new telephone dating systems and the frankness and openness that they engender, that the decisiveness of Virilio's comments becomes apparent.

Virilio's work can be understood as an enquiry over the primacy of place in formulating ways of grounding the self. As such it offers a direct riposte to the work of Heidegger, whose concept of 'dwelling' has become something of a dominant paradigm within recent architectural theory amid calls for a regionalist architecture and celebration of the concept of *genius loci*. This concept has been pursued further by those who have developed Heidegger's thought – architectural theorists such as Christian Norberg-Schulz (1980) and philosophers such as Gianni Vattimo (1995: 74–7). It is against Heidegger's static model of 'dwelling' that the potential of a more dynamic model of existence becomes apparent. Even prior to the technological advances that Virilio considers so significant, one might perhaps challenge Heidegger's assumption on other accounts, and question whether such a place-specific mechanism for grounding the self could *ever* have been applied universally. One only has to consider nomadic tribes or, indeed, ethnic or religious groups such as gypsies and Jews, who traditionally – whether voluntary or otherwise – have led the life of the 'wanderer' to understand that, even within traditional societies, Heidegger's concept of 'dwelling' might have had certain shortcomings. But the important point, as Virilio realizes, is that more recent developments in material circumstances have influenced patterns of consciousness, so that even if Heidegger's outlook may once have been valid, its application can be seen as correspondingly less relevant today. Indeed, one might even argue that to a large extent the paradigm of the dynamic 'wanderer' has replaced that of the static 'dweller'.

In an age in which human beings are constantly mobile, the importance of place – place of origin, place of birth, etc. – as a mechanism for grounding the self is diminished. Even the home has been redefined as a 'property' exchangeable within the marketplace. In a world dominated, in

Marc Augé's terms, by 'non-places', individuals now begin to constitute their identity through more transitory phenomena, such as jobs and possessions (Augé, 1995). These possessions may include even technological objects, such as cars and computers. All this has undermined the role of place as a mechanism for constituting one's identity. This is further exacerbated by the reduction in status of the physical and the increased reliance upon the virtual within our contemporary world. In short, the whole thesis of the link between building, dwelling and thinking needs to be revised. This is where Virilio has much to offer. Virilio as a theorist of non-presence and omnipresence, as a theorist of the erosion of physical space and the increasing importance of virtual space, begins to suggest a model of dwelling as virtual dwelling, which feeds off the technological and absorbs it productively, and identifies new imaginative possibilities emerging from this situation. Furthermore, by engaging, seemingly positively, with technology, Virilio transcends the limitations of Heidegger's thought, and opens up the possibility of thinking of new, less place-specific, ways of grounding the self.

It is as though Virilio develops Merleau-Ponty's notion of the primacy of perception into a notion of simulated perception, that echoes in some way Baudrillard's arguments for a notion of hyperreality over traditional notions of reality. Just as in Baudrillard's terms we have come adrift from any sense of referent in the real world, as we now read the world through the image of the world, so too, for Virilio, we have lost touch with 'authentic' perception, and we experience the world increasingly through simulated perceptions. 'It seems that the *reality effect*', Virilio observes, 'replaces immediate reality' (1997: 389). Virilio's vision is therefore a cinematographic one, a vision of the world in which Hollywood provides the model for our contemporary paradigm: 'So, more than Venturi's Las Vegas, it is Hollywood that merits urbanist scholarship' (Virilio, 1997: 389–90).

Problematizing Virilio

Virilio's futuristic outlook must be read, however, with some caution. On occasion his thought appears to lack a sense of the dialectic. Thus, while Virilio appears to identify a shift which undermines the significance of place, and which promotes instead a space of appearances, one might argue that this shift seems to anticipate its opposite in a mechanism of reciprocal presupposition. In other words, the very overcoming of a sense of place seems to invite a renewed interest in the importance of place. The possibilities opened up do not introduce a total placelessness. Indeed, it is precisely because physical space does not constitute such an obstacle for the contemporary office with its faxes, Internet, telephones and so on, that choice of *actual* space becomes a significant concern. No longer is it necessary for offices to be trapped in congested, grimy cities. It is not therefore that physical space is irrelevant. Rather, traditional constraints in the way that physical space is perceived are now becoming less relevant.

For example, the flexibilities introduced by instantaneous information transfer now allow imaginative use of different time zones – and hence different spaces – for a new generation of technological servicing industries. Information can now be sent from New York at the end of the day to be processed overnight by others, say in Africa, operating during the day of their own time zone, so as to deliver the fully processed product back to New York for the following morning. Such strategies have the potential of exploiting not only differential time zones, but also differential labour markets. While the world becomes the potential office, the specific site of the individual workstation emerges as an increasingly important consideration.

Equally, one might introduce a sense of the dialectic to the opposition between the body and the virtual. The condition of cyberspace has the effect of obviating the body, while at the same time privileging the body. Not only is it that such conditions make one aware of the corporeality of one's own body by way of compensating for the erosion of the importance of the physical, but they also seem to highlight the body itself as a means of grounding these new perceptions. For it is only against the actual body in actual space that perceptions of the virtual body in virtual space can be gauged. To be fair, this is a conclusion that Virilio himself hints at. For while the notion of some ecstatic experience – an experience, that is, which is 'outside' the body – might provide some sense of temporary escape from the body, this can only be a provisional move. 'While spatial escape may be possible', notes Virilio, 'temporal escape is not' (Virilio, 1997: 386). Just as, for Virilio, there can be no escaping time, ultimately, one might surmise, there can be no escaping the body, since the body, like time, operates as a form of datum point, the baseline against which to measure all experiences. One might lose track of time, but one is always in time. One might lose sense of the body, but one is always in the body. To this extent virtual reality must always remain virtual.

Another way to reflect on the limitations of Virilio's thought is to contrast it with that of Michel Foucault and Gilles Deleuze on the progressive erosion of the importance of physical constraints. Foucault had first commented on the capacity for architectural form to condition behaviour in his essay 'Of Other Spaces: Utopias and Heterotopias' (1997a). Here architecture was employed as a form of institutionalized demarcation of structures of power. In *Discipline and Punish*, Foucault develops this thesis within a more fluid, post-structuralist framework. He becomes concerned with the relationship between architectural form and more diffuse ways in which power is exercised (Foucault, 1997b). The panopticon provides a model which encapsulates the characteristics of a society founded on discipline. It embodies a system in which surveillance plays a crucial role, and in which knowledge is inseparably bound to power. The very architectural layout of the panopticon affords various techniques of control, which, Foucault thought, would in themselves assure almost automatically the subjection and the subjectification of the inmates.

In his 'Postscript on the Societies of Control', however, Deleuze observes that disciplinary societies have now given way to societies of control (1997: 313). There has been a shift in mechanisms of control as visible constraints are superseded by invisible ones. This is reflected in the development from factories to corporations, and from machines to computers. Physical discipline has been replaced by more gaseous systems of control, where the credit card has supplanted the gaze of the foreman. This leads to a situation in which humankind is no longer constrained by physical space, but forever trapped by debt, ensnared in a system of limitless postponement. 'The burrows of the molehill' have been replaced by the complex 'coils of the serpent' (Deleuze, 1997: 309–13). For Deleuze, then, we must step beyond the Foucault of panopticism. Power is no longer linked to space, and architectural forms have little control over human behaviour.

This thesis echoes that of the 'exhaustion' of the physical in Virilio. But whereas Virilio looks at this condition invariably as an abstract consequence of technological developments, Foucault and Deleuze consider the question within a specifically political context. Space is always seen as political space, as the space of political agency. Their concern throughout is for the politics of use of a space, and how that use might affect the freedom of the individual. No such concern appears in Virilio, who offers little comment on the control of the technological world of which he speaks. Nor indeed does he ever seem to engage fully at any point with the social and economic problems posed by late capitalism. In short, the political – in both the specific and the most general senses – is seldom addressed. This is all the more surprising, given the purportedly political focus of Virilio's writings, and his own political activities.

How might we begin to explain this? One way would be to consider the extent to which Virilio's critique remains essentially an aesthetic one. The problem, it would appear, is that in any aesthetic discussion of form, the question of political content is all too easily elided, and while we might wish to refrain from a simplistic understanding of the relationship between aesthetics and politics, we might recognize that within the aestheticization of politics a certain complex restructuring of the relationship between the two occurs, whereby the political comes to collude with the aesthetic (Hewitt, 1993). But whatever the precise mechanism of interaction between the aesthetic and the political, it is clear that aestheticization leads if not to a rinsing of the political, then at least to a form of camouflaging. This is the guilty secret that haunts all engagements with the aesthetic.

Virilio, one might suppose, ought to be especially cautious when he deals with issues that touch upon such terrain. Given his own background against the events of May '68, and his undoubted familiarity with debates which served to fuel those events, such as Guy Debord's critique of the 'Society of the Spectacle', one would imagine that Virilio should have been only too aware of the issues at stake with the question of aestheticization. Yet the problem seems to be deeply ingrained in Virilio's whole project, and is evident in two early works, the publication, *Bunker Archeology* and the design for the church of Sainte-Bernadette du Banlay in Nevers. From these we can trace the emergence of a problem that is to haunt Virilio throughout his work.

It is precisely in his handling of architectural form in *Bunker Archeology*, where Virilio charts the German Second World War fortifications on the Atlantic coast, that the problem first appears. It is questionable enough – despite the accompanying text which is dressed up in the language of concern – for Virilio to publish a book full of exquisite photographs of bunkers, photographs that themselves fall prey to the trap of turning emblems of war into haunting, seductive images. But the problem becomes more deep-rooted when – with Parent – Virilio reproduces these forms in his design for the church of Sainte-Bernadette du Banlay. It is at this point when forms borne of war are reproduced in churches and other buildings, that the principle that Walter Benjamin had so incisively recognized in Marinetti's aesthetic celebration of war are replayed within an architectural forum (Benjamin, 1973: 234–5). And if Marinetti is to be criticized for proclaiming that war is beautiful, is not Virilio to be reprimanded for celebrating the aesthetic images of war, rinsed of their original meaning and recycled as abstract architectural forms? And even if Virilio had been attempting, however unsuccessfully, to reclaim these forms and harness them towards a Christian agenda, is it appropriate to attempt this in the first place?

All this hints at the Achilles' heel of Virilio's thought. His outlook remains essentially an aesthetic one, abstracted from political or any form of social concerns. While he addresses shifts in patterns of consciousness that arise from the implementation of new technologies, unlike Foucault or Deleuze he fails to interrogate the full political ramifications of these developments. It is this that allows him to distance himself from the sinister potential of these technologies, and to claim so seemingly naïvely, as he does with the Tactical Mapping Systems, that the functions of eyesight and weaponry 'melt into each other' (Virilio, 1997: 390). It is this that allows him to celebrate the 'dromomaniac' as a type, without distinguishing adequately the *sans culottes* of the French revolution from Hitler's brown-shirts, and without addressing the political ends to which his subject matter tends (Virilio, 1986: 20). And it is this that allows him to dwell so extensively and seemingly uncritically on themes such as 'war' and 'speed'.

It is through the figure of Marinetti, perhaps, that we might best understand the trajectory of Virilio's thought. Virilio is above all a champion of speed as an *aesthetic* gesture, and with that the same problems that afflicted Marinetti's celebration of speed echo throughout his work. It is speed and the machinery of speed that Virilio promotes. And it is against the backdrop of his own questionable obsession with war and the paraphernalia of war that we see further traces of this recurrent problem. *Speed and Politics* is less a manifesto for a general political agenda, than an enquiry as to how speed might facilitate one all too obvious particular agenda. 'Speed is the essence of war', notes Virilio, citing Sun Tzu. But in failing to distance himself from the problem, Virilio appears to condone this position, and to accept war as an almost necessary corollary of greater speed and mobility in contemporary society.

Virilio and Parent were once greeted with a phalanx of Nazi salutes when they gave a paper at a conference on avant-garde architecture at Folkestone in 1966. It has been suggested that this was a response to the monumental scale of their designs, that also led them to be branded 'Prix de Romists of cosmic thought' by left-wing students at the Ecole des Beaux-Arts (Ockman, 1993: 409). But perhaps those who offered the Nazi salute recognized only too clearly that there is more than a little of the Futurist mentality in their work, and that the whole criticism of the aestheticization of politics, raised by Benjamin, might equally be levelled at them. 'All efforts to render politics aesthetic', noted Benjamin, 'culminate in one thing: war' (Benjamin, 1973: 234). In this context it is perhaps no coincidence that Virilio himself should be so obsessed by war.

How might this obsession with war be manifested within an architectural scenario? An obvious example lies in the work of Lebbeus Woods. In his book, *War and Architecture*, Woods clearly finds the death and destruction in Sarajevo a deeply aesthetic experience. 'War is architecture, and architecture is war!' he proclaims (Woods, 1993: 1). What is most alarming about this equation of architecture with war is not the attempt to see architecture as a form of war, for inevitably architecture will involve some war-like destruction, in that the very process of construction presupposes the destruction of whatever had previously belonged to the site. It is, rather, the tendency to see war as a form of architecture. The destruction of the physical fabric of Sarajevo provides the aesthetic impulse for new forms of architecture. These forms are generated in response to the destruction of the buildings but, more importantly, in their jagged, torn aesthetic, they complement and draw inspiration from the mutilated buildings. As such they constitute an aesthetic celebration of destruction. The work of Woods therefore provides an obvious example of the potential consequences of Virilio's aestheticization of politics.

If we are to find fault with Virilio, we should look beyond the pseudo-scientific language which Alan Sokal and Jean Bricmont criticize so simplistically, failing to recognize the essentially romantic nature of his futuristic vision (Sokal and Bricmont, 1998). Rather, we should focus on the problem of aestheticization. With the aesthetic bias of Virilio's project, the political is too often elided. There is a form of anaesthesia at work which 'numbs' the concern for the political. Just as Albert Speer's sublime stage-sets for Nazi rallies recast a highly unsavoury political agenda as an intoxicating spectacle, so too Virilio's celebration of the exhilaration of 'speed' seems to overlook the political consequences of what is being celebrated. While 'speed' may offer many positive advantages, it may equally have negative ones. All this is lost in Virilio's empty, aphoristic slogans, such as, 'The speed of violence becomes the violence of unsurpassed speed' (Virilio, 1997: 138). And the intoxication of Speer's sublime stage-sets is matched by the intoxication of speed – the 'high' of high speed, as Virilio describes it (Virilio, 1986: 27). And it is perhaps no coincidence that the term 'speed' is also used for various drugs. Virilio's celebration of the exhilaration of 'speed' and 'war' seems to appeal to a culture dominated by a desire for the sublime and for ecstatic escapism.

In the aesthetics of disappearance, it would seem, it is not the aesthetic which disappears, but the political. Yet in reality the political never fully disappears. For what lurks beneath the veneer of the aesthetic is a more insidious, reactionary form of politics: a politics of acquiescence.

All this points to a deeper underlying problem. If Virilio's work is so popular today, what does this say about contemporary culture? In an age in which, according to Baudrillard, everything has become aestheticized, is it surprising that a writer who holds such a viewpoint should prove so appealing? For it is in a culture where politics is reduced largely to a matter of mere images that Benjamin's formulation of the link between aesthetics and politics is replayed within a specifically postmodern constellation. Perhaps, then, rather than worry about the sinister implications of Virilio's work, we should be concerned about the culture in which it seems to command such appeal. For in a culture where 'speed' and 'war' become fashionable slogans, violence will always threaten to reappear.

References

Andreotti, Libero and Xavier Costa (eds) (1996) *Situationists: Art, Politics, Urbanism*. Barcelona: Actar.

Augé, Marc (1995) *Non-Places*, trans. John Howe. London: Verso.

Benjamin, Walter (1973) 'The Work of Art in the Age of Mechanical Reproduction', in *Illuminations*, trans. Harry Zohn. London: Fontana.

Calle, Sophie (1988) *Suite Vénitienne*, trans. Danny Barash and Danny Hatfield. Seattle, WA: Seattle Bay Press.

Deleuze, Gilles (1997) 'Postscript on the Societies of Control', in Neil Leach (ed.) *Rethinking Architecture*. London: Routledge.

Diller, Elizabeth and Richard Scofidio (eds) (1994) *Back to the Front: Tourisms of War*. Basse-Normandie: FRAC.

Foucault, Michel (1997a) 'Of Other Spaces: Utopias and Heterotopias', in Neil Leach (ed.) *Rethinking Architecture*. London: Routledge.

Foucault, Michel (1997b) 'Panopticism', in Neil Leach (ed.) *Rethinking Architecture*. London: Routledge.

Hewitt, Andrew (1993) *Fascist Modernism*. Stanford, CA: Stanford University Press.

Norberg-Schulz, Christian (1980) *Genius Loci: Towards a Phenomenology of Architecture*. London: Academy Editions.

Ockman, Joan (ed.) (1993) *Architecture Culture 1943–1968*. New York: Rizzoli.

Sokal, Alan and Jean Bricmont (1998) *Intellectual Impostures*. London: Profile.

Vattimo, Gianni (1995) 'The End of Modernity, the End of The Project?', trans. David Webb, *Journal of Philosophy and the Visual Arts*. London: Academy Editions.

Virilio, Paul (1975) *Bunker Archeology*, trans. George Collins. Paris: Les Éditions du Demi-Cercle.

Virilio, Paul (1986) *Speed & Politics*, trans. Mark Polizotti. New York: Semiotext(e).

Virilio, Paul (1991) *Lost Dimension*, trans. Daniel Moshenberg: New York: Semiotext(e).

Virilio, Paul (1996) 'Architecture Principe', in Pamela Johnston (ed.) *Theory of the Oblique*. London: Architectural Association Documents.

Virilio, Paul (1997) 'The Overexposed City', in Neil Leach (ed.) *Rethinking Architecture*. London: Routledge.

Virilio, Paul and Claude Parent (1996) *Claude Parent and Paul Virilio 1955–1968*. Paris: Éditions de L'Imprimeur.

Woods, Lebbeus (1993) *War and Architecture*. Princeton, NJ: Princeton Architectural Press.

Neil Leach is Reader in Architecture and Critical Theory at the University of Nottingham. He is author of *The Anaesthetics of Architecture* (Cambridge, MA: MIT Press, 1999) and *Millennium Culture* (London: Ellipsis, 1999). He is the editor of *Rethinking Architecture* (London: Routledge, 1997) and *Architecture and Revolution* (London: Routledge, 1999). He is also co-translator of *L.B. Alberti, On the Art of Building in Ten Books* (Cambridge, MA: MIT Press, 1988).

Paul Virilio's Bunker Theorizing

Mike Gane

> If man has no need for the machine to live in his natural environment, he
> needs the machine to live in a hostile one. (Virilio, 1994 [1975]: 41)

> We must get inside pure war, we must cover ourselves in blood and tears. We
> mustn't turn away. (Virilio, in Virilio and Lotringer, 1997 [1983]: 108)

Introduction

PAUL VIRILIO'S WORK has a curious status today. On the one hand
his name is still absent from leading social theory commentaries. On
the other he is widely cited – I note even in today's *Guardian*, Adrian
Searle writes that Seurat's painting *The Bathers* has a 'kind of stillness we
have nearly lost. And with its loss, we ourselves are in danger of disappearing. This is the kind of dark thought Paul Virilio warms his hands over of an
evening' (*Guardian, G2* 30 Dec. 1997: 13). This is precisely the kind of
reference Jean Baudrillard's work was receiving ten years ago (*Guardian*, 21
Sept. 1988: 27). The two writers are often associated as the pre-eminent
French postmodern theorists (see Kroker, 1992; Ritzer, 1997).[1] Both writers
refer to the other in friendly terms, but admit some profound differences.
Virilio: 'I have a friendly relationship with Baudrillard, even if I don't
always agree with him' (in Rötzer, 1995: 98); Baudrillard:

> We have worked together . . . without any problem . . . His analysis of the
> cyberworld is intransigent, inexorable, fatal I might dare say, and I find it
> beautiful and remarkable . . . [but] he puts himself in the position of the anti-
> apocalypse prophet, having been persuaded that the worst can come about.
> On this point we have ended up going our separate ways. I do not believe in

■ *Theory, Culture & Society* 1999 (SAGE, London, Thousand Oaks and New Delhi),
Vol. 16(5–6): 85–102
[0263-2764(199910/12)16:5–6;85–102;009960]

> his real apocalypse ... it is the coming of the virtual itself which is our apocalypse, and this deprives us of the real apocalypse. (1997b: 46–7).

Virilio:

> There's a neonihilism in him that I don't like. (in Rötzer, 1995: 98)

Baudrillard:

> Virilio takes a position which is very clearly moral.... Ultimately his analysis is more radical than mine. (1997b: 80)

These cryptic remarks refer in fact to something of a major divergence, and it is highly instructive to follow through the logic of this particular difference of opinion. In this article I attempt to do this by examining Virilio's part in the exchange by tracing the theme of the bunker through his writings, and the way his thinking seems to be caught in an unresolved dilemma.

Bunker Archaeology

> My relation to the war machine has always had a kind of mythic dimension.
> (Virilio, in Virilio and Lotringer, 1997 [1983]: 7)

A selection of Virilio's earliest writings has recently been re-published (in Parent and Virilio, 1996), including material which makes it possible to reconstruct to some extent the first phase of Virilio's work. Born in 1932, he was brought up in war-time Nantes in France. He was educated at the École des Metiers, Paris, and trained to become an artist in stained glass, working eventually with Braque and Matisse. He followed courses by Jankelevitch, Merleau-Ponty, Wahl and Aron at the Sorbonne. He has been close to Abbé Pierre, and the worker priest movement, having joined the Catholic movement in 1950 (Petit, in Virilio, 1996). In 1958 he was on vacation at Saint-Guenole (Virilio, 1994: 10) when he noticed a German-built war bunker. He wrote up his reflections in a short piece called 'Bunker Achaeology' (1958, included in Parent and Virilio, 1996: 71). In this essay he reported: 'Using the techniques of archaeology, I have explored the subterranean world of one of the esoteric forms of times: the blockhouse. The plan of the blockhouse is strangely reminiscent of that of an Aztec temple' (Parent and Virilio, 1996: 71). From 1958 to 1965 he made a study of the bunkers around the western and northern coasts of France. An exhibition of his photos with explanatory text was later presented by Virilio in 1975–6 at the Museum of Decorative Arts in Paris and published in translation as *Bunker Archeology* (1994). The first period of Virilio's thought goes through to about 1978 and we can trace this through texts collected in *L'Insecurité du territoire* (1993 [1976]).

In the decade 1958–68 Virilio passed from being an artist specializing in stained glass, to architect under the guidance of Claude Parent, though apparently Virilio had no technical qualification in architecture (who needed this in 1968?). Virilio became a teacher at the École Speciale d'Architecture (ESA) in 1969, a co-director with Anatole Kopp in 1972 (Parent and Virilio, 1996: 13) its General Director, 1975, and President in 1990 (Virilio, 1994: 213). His relationship with Parent, 1963–8 was thus pivotal. Parent was an experimentally minded architect using concrete. Virilio's studies of the bunkers formed a natural point of convergence of ideas and interest. But Virilio was also interested in the structural characteristics and philosophy of space, what he called topotonics. Having investigated bunkers that had toppled over in the sand, he had become fascinated with the potentialities of inclined planes as a resource. In what appears today as a frighteningly naïve vision, he sought to combine bunker style with oblique planes in order to revolutionize the habitable space of cities. The revolution would involve a rejection of conventional room design – he stigmatized such spaces as 'micro-ghettoes' – to continuous 'habitable circulation' on slopes made possible by the technology of reinforced concrete. Curiously, Virilio and Parent wore smart black suits at this time in contrast to the 'psychedelic ensembles favoured by most architects' and when they presented their ideas for 'oblique cities unfolding across the landscape' at a conference at Folkstone in 1966, 'the audience rose up *en masse* and gave them a Hitlerian salute' (Crompton, cited by Migayrou, in Parent and Virilio, 1996: 63). Others, according to Claude Parent, compared the oblique spaces proposed by Virilio 'to the prisons of the Bolshevik police, which had skewed cells and ceilings so low that it was impossible to stand' (Parent and Virilio, 1996: 55).

Transforming the Bunker

> ... to say that the positive phenomenon of technology came in large part from the arsenal and war is.. hard for people to accept. (Virilio, in Virilio and Lotringer, 1997: 24)

Though no large-scale project of this kind was ever realized, Virilio was able to win a commision through his Catholic contacts for a new church in Nevers, the church of Sainte-Bernadette du Banlay. The church indeed looks like a concrete bunker and has inclined floors. It also has stained-glass windows (see Parent and Virilio, 1996: 20–31), though Parent detested them 'they weren't my idea, and I never show them in photographs' (Parent and Virilio, 1996: 52). Clearly Virilio's radical architecture was transformative: to make military architecture, as it condensed social energy and revealed new functions, serve other functions, a theme he was to develop at some length in essays on critical space. But in the mid-1960s Virilio seemed to be fascinated by the idea of a 'repellent' brutal architectural style which would force users to question conventions in a mode similar to that adopted in Situationism (see Migayrou, in Parent and Virilio, 1996: 62), adding alienation to alienation. At this juncture he promoted a revolutionary and expansive conception of space, a style of intervention within critical modernism. In the journal which functioned as their manifesto, *Architecture Principe*, Virilio wrote 'we have never before witnessed a change in humanity itself. We are now on the brink of such a metamorphosis – a metamorphosis of our consciousness ... a radical transformation of the notion of dimensions' (1966, in Parent and Virilio, 1996: 65). In a radical but obscure utopianism, Virilio wrote:

> ... urbanism will in future have much more to do with ballistics than with the partition of territories. In effect, the static vertical and horizontal no longer correspond to the dynamics of human life. In future, architecture must be built on the oblique, so as to accord with the new plane of human consciousness. (1966, in Parent and Virilio, 1996: 65)

Virilio stressed the importance of bodies in circulation or, as he called it, 'habitable circulation', indeed the 'conditions are ripe for the emergence of a civil architecture, for this spatial art to pass from the private to the public realm and, in so doing, to accede to its true role – the invention of society' (1996: 68). His vision was precise, the new oblique architecture would change the nature of the city, which now would become 'an enormous projector, a torrent of every kind of activity, every kind of fluidity' (1996: 68). The emphasis was insistent: conventional architecture had condemned humanity to horizontality and therefore to stasis. The vision was one of transforming 'static space' into a habitat 'mobilized by the function of the oblique' and liquid technology (1996: 45, 68). The new structures of urban development would not grow in static concentric rings, but would be 'mediated structures' and 'would form interlinked assemblages that would develop and spread out over regions, along the vital arteries of a territory'. Virilio saw this use of the incline, and the curve, as necessary 'when alienation has become commonplace' (1996: 71).

In the seventh issue of *Architecture Principe* (1967), he republished the article he had written on 'Bunker Archaeology' in 1958 in which he noted that the geometry of these bunkers 'is no longer affirmatory, but eroded, worn. The right angle is reduced, suppressed, in order to make the structure resistant to capture.' The effect of ballistics on structure was clear, the oblique had been invented for essential, practical not aesthetic reasons. These monuments also had a different relation to the earth for 'the mass is no longer grounded ... but centred upon itself, independent, capable of movement and articulation' (1958, in Parent and Virilio 1996: 71). As Migayrou has pointed out, this meant for Virilio that the 'bunker expressed fluidity, building without foundation – the Corbusian ideal of the ocean liner' (1996: 62). Life in these bunkers, in Virilio's view, was 'an exercise in becoming more subtle' (1996: 71). Bunkers heralded he argued, without irony, 'a new architecture that is founded no longer on man's bodily proportions, but on his capacity for thought' (1996: 71).

Claude Parent, crucial agent for the transformation of Virilio from master painter on glass to novice architect of the oblique, was interviewed in

1995 about his early relation with Virilio. Parent met Virilio in 1963. Parent's background – decisively influenced by Andre Bloc (see Migayrou, in Parent and Virilio, 1996: 59f), neo-plasticism and geometric abstraction-ism – naturally aligned itself with Virilio's study of bunkers (1996: 51). 'After a while, he began coming to the office for a few hours each day', and he:

> ... brought a couple of jobs into the office: the church of Sainte-Bernadette and the Thompson-Houston Aerospace Centre. I was responsible for drawing up the initial designs and plans (he lacked the technical know-how), but then ... [we would] discuss how the project should evolve ... (Parent and Virilio, 1996: 51)

Thus in the project for the church 'it was Virilio who said that we should put a slope on the floor planes ... the challenge of working together on a real, concrete project inspired a fundamental breakthrough – the first application of the function of the oblique' (1996: 51). The military aspects of the project was seen in a purely technical light, for what interested Virilio was not ·simply the war functioning in terms of a system of antagonistic blocs, but that the 'D-Day landings consolidated the whole of the industrial might of the United States' (1996: 51). Virilio 'admired that in the same way that he admired the super-organized Panzer divisions and the autobahn system' (1996: 52). There was considerable opposition to these ideas: 'Virilio insisted that the general resistance to the oblique derived from a resistance to anything new. In the early days of the automobile, people were afraid that they would suffocate if they went above thirty kilometres an hour' (Parent, in Parent and Virilio, 1996: 55).

Virilio's theoretical ambitions were restated in a retrospective essay of 1996:

> The objective of our research was to challenge outright the anthropometric precepts of the classical era – the idea of the body as an essentially static entity ... In our work, the traditional stability (habitable stasis) ... gave way to the metastability (habitable circulation) of the human body in motion ... The space of the body became mobile. (Parent and Virilio, 1996: 13)

The project was not a success however and 'after a few years the overwhelm-ing difficulties of building an oblique habitat led us to abandon this work' Virilio admitted (1996: 13).

In 1975–6 Virilio was able to stage his photos of the bunkers in an exhibition at the Museum for Decorative Arts in Paris. His text for the exhibition (orig. 1975) has been republished with a new preface and after-word (Virilio, 1994). The preface recounts the moment of discovery of the bunkers and the way in which they exercised their fascination: passing under a tympanum a 'companion piece to the porch of a religious building' and through this entrance to a 'low, small room, round or hexagonal ... and having, at its centre, a socle quite similar to a sacrificial altar. Trap doors open in the cement floor, through which access to the crypt is gained.' Virilio talks of 'the crushing feeling' experienced within this monumental structure, 'the visitor in this perilous place is beset with a singular heaviness' (1994: 15–16). The text suggests that it is war, or the war machine which is at the origin of industry and industrialization, indeed Virilio argues that it is war which is at the origin of civil and religious social forms (1994: 43–4). The bunker is the precursor of the survival machine, where the crypt is a form 'that prefigures resurrection', a 'vehicle that puts one out of danger' an 'ark that saves' (1994: 46). The 'Afterword' gives a concise overview of the changes in the character of the world's military situation from 1945 to 1990 and it is clear that for Virilio a remarkable reversal has taken place, a reversal which his writings through the 1970s and 1980s charted in detail. He sums this up in the following way: 'the supremacy of arms of communication . . . over arms of massive destruction . . . became a reality, bringing about a mutation in real warfare as important as the mutation brought long ago by the supremacy of light arms of destruction' (1994: 202). It seems clear that even by the time the *Bunker Archeology* exhibition was held in Paris in 1975–6, Virilio had already reorganized his own position well beyond abandoning the idea of 'habitable circulation' for purely technical reasons.

Out of the Bunker, Briefly

> May '68. . . the place was packed. I heard a guy . . . say '. . ."imagination comes to power" that's not true, it's the working class!' I answered: 'so comrade, you deny the working class imagination. . .' (Virilio in Virilio and Lotringer, 1997: 82)

Something else had also happened: the events of May '68 in Paris. As Claude Parent recounts, it was the dramatic politicization of Virilio in those events which was to lead to the break-up of their relationship. In the early part of 1968 Parent and Virilio were preparing to build a structure at the University of Nanterre called 'The Pendular Destabilizer'. This was a purely experimental double oblique structure (rather like two bunkers joined together side by side in the form of an X) elevated 12 metres above the ground and isolated from the rest of the world : 'there was no telephone, no post, no means of communication – except for a little hole in the wall that we could talk to each other through' (Parent and Virilio, 1996: 55). The events of May '68 ended the experiment. Virilio joined the student occupation of the Odéon. Parent remained convinced that the oblique was aesthetic not political, Virilio regarded it as essentially aesthetic and political; the friendship and the partnership came to an end in 1970. What Virilio encountered and explored through 1968 is developed through the idea of 'critical space' which can be read as a very specific recasting of his idea of 'habitable circulation'.

Virilio's new ideas emerge over the period 1969–75 in journals *Esprit*, *Cause Commune* and *Critique*, essays collected together in *L'Insecurité du territoire* (1993 [1976]).Virilio reports the joy of having been able to sleep in a lecture theatre at the Sorbonne (after making the intervention in the Richelieu Amphitheatre reported in Virilio and Lotringer, 1997: 80) have breakfast in a box at the Opéra, eat lunch in a director's office, find a nursery in the library, find a games room in the Renault showroom, indeed of having been able to find France, its stations, airports, schools, shops, as a space to be occupied, thereby reversing the alienated state of everyday life (Virilio, 1993: 86–7): just as there is a need for freedom of speech so there is also a need for freedom of movement. A barricade, he wrote, is not simply a territorial limit but a construction of a new kind of liberated space, a 'new mode of the appropriation of space and time' (1993: 89). Although Virilio uses the experience of May '68, in these years, he does not adopt Marxist language or ideas (with the possible rare exception of an observation that his work concerns the primacy of a revolution in the 'means of destruction' rather than 'means of production' [Virilio and Lotringer, 1997: 105]). What interests him is the experience of space in the changing character of the overall strategic situation in its military aspect, and increasingly the logic of mass communications which he sees as its inevitable counterpart.

Volte Face: **Back to the Bunker**

> We're in a system in which military order dominates ... no matter if that order is socialist, capitalist or anything else. (Virilio, in Virilio and Lotringer, 1997: 96)

Virilio's reflections on the failure of May '68 are now worked through the theme of speed, not of economics or politics. The leading body of capitalist civilization has become a 'jet set' which no longer resides in traditional and expected locations in time and space. This counter-revolution succeeds through an escalation to 'hyper-communication' transforming the terrain of struggle. Fundamental innovations and technical revolutions put an end to any hope of a genuine revolution in 'habitable circulation'. Indeed, his former position which depended on a critique of the stasis of bourgeois society is inverted. He charts the emergence of nuclear deterrence, 'total peace', not as stasis but as absolute war (1993 [1976]: 71), another reversal in the logistical order. He concludes his study in *L'Insecurité du territoire* by outlining the unexpected consequences brought in the wake of this new order (1993: 243–70). The old communism equated progress with speed but speed is no longer the sign of progress, quite the opposite, since speed is where the enemy to progress resides (1993: 266–70).

Speed and Politics (1986 [1977]) and *Popular Defense* (1990 [1978]) register the scope of the vast change in Virilio's position. The problematic shifts from space to time, and from an expansive politics of mobilization and liberalization, to a defensive and conservative politics of resistance to acceleration and to a defence of the social. Responding to the appeals of theologians like Bonhoeffer, Virilio begins to warn of the dangers implied in the new state of the world, dangers to the experience of space of the city and of democracy, and of the new possibility of apocalypse brought about by new technologies and strategies available to and adopted by the military elite. In a sense the essay *Speed and Politics*, with its theory of power through control of movement a 'dromocracy' (1986: 70), was the culmination of an analysis applicable to a world already passing away. If the proletariat still thinks in terms of the control of streets and physical movement (1986: 103), the military thinks otherwise: it thinks logistically in relation to new meeting points such as airports, highways and telecommunications (1986: 104). Communism died, fascism survives (1986: 117) and has adapted. In this world, available in instantaneous communication and immediate information, a new permanent state of emergency is created which brings a sharp end to struggles in relative speed (1986: 149).

Virilio draws out these conclusions more dramatically in his book *Popular Defense*:

> If... civilians could have resisted the assault of the war machine, gotten ahead of it, by creating a defence without a body, condensed nowhere, it is quite evident that today they don't even realize that technology has surpassed this kind of defence. (1990: 71)

This is because: 'There is no need for an armed body to attack civilians, so long as the latter have been properly trained to turn on their radios or plug in their television sets' (1990: 71). In these conditions the political state declines, and where 'hyper-communicability' exists there grows totalitarian power (1990: 64–6). The right of armed defence by citizens is lost, while on the other hand 'from now on' the military power is so 'shapeless' it can no longer be identified as it installs itself in a regime of generalized security: an important and irreversible shift from a state of political and civil justice, to a state of logistical and military discipline (1990: 75). This is achieved through the systematic destruction of all the major forms of social solidarity which previously offered real resistance to the state: particularly the family, conceived by Virilio as essentially a combat unit. The liberation of women effectively weakens the solidarity of the family as a defensive form against the state. The resort to terrorism by ultra-left-wing groups again only serves to strengthen, not weaken, the war machine (1990: 88). This creates a paradox: the possibility that the revolution can succeed through control of the streets has been lost yet 'there is no more revolution except in resistance' (1997: 82). Virilio returns to his bunker.

Symbolic Exchange and Death

> As soon as the civil detaches itself from death, denies it ... we fall body and soul into the militaristic interpretation. (Virilio, in Virilio and Lotringer, 1997: 129)

It is instructive at this point to compare Virilio's experience with that of Baudrillard, with whom he began to collaborate on the journal *Traverses* from 1976. Both Virilio and Baudrillard reversed their positions on the meaning of the events of May 1968, coming in the mid-1970s to a common point of view that the political situation had rendered a simple commitment to revolution and progress untenable. The points of departure were, however, very different. Baudrillard's background in literature, anthropology and sociology was in marked contrast with Virilio's background in craftwork, theology and military architecture, but the convergence was strong and condensed around the acceptance of a new social condition marked by the success of material consumerism, the dominance of mass communication in a condition of political stasis (theorized by Virilio as a paradoxical situation of pure war). There were, however, clear differences of opinion. As Virilio was later to remark (in Virilio and Lotringer, 1997: 125), Baudrillard's key text, *Symbolic Exchange and Death* (1993) developed no discussion of the war machine (for take-up of this idea one has to go to Deleuze and Guattari); Baudrillard, if anything, moved to a pagan position of symbolic exchange which saw the Christian forms adhered to by Virilio as the very source of modern simulacra. And while Virilio sought a base in the social for retrenchment of resistance to ongoing technological transformations, Baudrillard notoriously announced the 'end of the social'. Baudrillard's essay on the architecture of the Pompidou Centre ('L'Effet Beaubourg: implosion et dissuasion', 1994a [1977]) stands in remarkable contrast with Virilio's *Bunker Archeology* (1994 [1975]). Just as Virilio had described the bunker as a dead animal, so Baudrillard began his essay on the Beaubourg by defining it as a 'carcass of flux and signs' (1994a: 61) and 'an imperial compression – figure of a culture already crushed by its own weight – like moving automobiles suddenly frozen in a geometric solid' (1994a: 63). Instead of celebrating the idea of polyvalent space in the interior of the new building, Baudrillard is scathing in his contempt for the idea of 'circulation' in this space, with its 'immense to-and-fro movement similar to that of suburban commuters'. The paradox is, he said, people search for a 'corner which is precisely not one, (and so) exhaust themselves secreting an artificial solitude ... the ideology of visibility, transparency, of polyvalency' (1994a: 62). It leads Baudrillard to a famous formulation: from now on the vision of a possible revolutionary explosion has to be replaced by that of implosion; and the same is true of the city itself: 'fires, war, revolutions, criminal marginality, catastrophes: the whole problematic of the anticity, of the negativity internal or external to the city, has some archaic relation to its true mode of annihilation' (1994a: 70–1). Baudrillard reflects that the events of 1968 have to be rethought: 'something else began ... the violent involution of the social' (1994a: 73).

Baudrillard's position in the mid-1970s is to pit 'culture', in the anthropological sense, against the regimes of simulacra. Baudrillard's critical essay only works, in fact, on the basis that he can say what this opposition between them is. Culture is at this moment in his thought an ordered structure, 'a site of the secret, of seduction, of initiation, of a restrained and highly ritualized symbolic exchange' (1994a: 64). While the Beaubourg Centre is 'nothing but a huge effort to transmute [the] famous traditional culture of meaning into the aleatory order of signs, into an order of simulacra (the third) that is completely homogeneous with the flux and pipes of the facade' (1994a: 65). But what about a concrete bunker? It is strange that Virilio sought to find, and did find in his concrete bunkers, a sacred altar, a place of initiation, a crypt. But the very fact that concrete is a liquid medium is for Baudrillard, against Virilio, important in its own right. In *Symbolic Exchange and Death* Baudrillard refers to the 'old cook' who lived in the Ardennes who sculptured everything in that 'single polymorphous material: reinforced concrete' (1993: 52). Everything modelled in concrete, and Baudrillard lists them: chairs, sewing machines, an entire orchestra. Baudrillard notes, that this project is:

> ... not so far removed from the stucco builders of Baroque art, nor very different from projecting an urban community onto the terrain of a large contemporary group ... it is already aiming at control of a pacified society, cast in a synthetic substance ... a project which aims at political and mental hegemony, the fantasy of a closed mental substance. (1993: 53)

In this analysis concrete plays the same role as stucco, a primitive medium for simulacra (of the first order), but Baudrillard already notes its second-order industrial potentialities. The essential nature of this project is identified as belonging to the counter-reformation, conceived in detail by the Jesuits in a new type of reactionary elite and state organized around a homogeneous theology (1993: 52). Stucco is 'an apparatus of the same order' and the concrete of the Ardennes cook is a 'mental substance' (1993: 52–3).

Baudrillard's analysis here was developed as part of what he called a theory of 'orders of simulacra' (1993: 50–88), a topic taken up as the feature of a special issue of the journal *Traverses* (no. 10, *Le Simulacre*) in February 1978. Baudrillard's contribution was the essay 'La Precession des simulacres' (orig. 1978: 3–37, trans. in 1994: 1–42), and Virilio wrote 'La Dromoscopie ou l'ivresse des grandeurs' (orig. 1978: 65–72) which was also published in an expanded version in the journal *Critique* (vol. 34: 324–37, as 'La Dromoscopie ou la lumière de la vitesse', this version reproduced as chapter 6 of *L'Horizon negatif* [1984: 143–55]). It is not surprising to find that Virilio's discussion starts with the statement that 'movement commands the event' (1984: 143) which we find later is derived from Napoleon (1984: 161). Virilio's idea sees simulacra as phenomena closely linked to those of command posts, control consoles, cockpits. He develops the idea that with moving vehicles like cars the travellers see the world in a new way, a double reduction: of the time-distance of the voyage and the new screen vision of the world. He calls this the dromoscopic simulation (1984: 146). Thus Virilio's idea of simulation is quite different from that of Baudrillard and

closer to that of McLuhan (who theorized the new vision of the world
produced by the speed of trains). Virilio's thesis is that the driver in such a
position of simulation in the dromocratic order maintains the dictatorship of
movement (1984: 148).Virilio traces the idea of the 'conductors' of peoples
behind the 'dromoscopic screen of absolute power' before passing to the
motorcyclist and 'conductors of families who reproduce in their little everyday movements (*evasions*) the dromocratic order of great invasions'(1984:
154–5). The discussion suggests that now it is the earth itself which is the
vehicle, and all perception of the movement of the sun, moon and stars is
equivalent to perception of 'the real' through a panoramic screen (1984:
159). The way is open for new means of teleguidance or what he calls
'dromovisual apparatuses' (1984: 160). But against McLuhan he argues that
the significant developments here cannot adequately be seen as or reduced
to the technological, the crucial effects concern the new levels of rapidity of
communication between interlocutors: the violence of speed is not a simple
technological phenomenon. Here the motor has been war, with industrial
civilization its transformed effect, and the new acceleration producing the
condition of pure war (1984: 161).

   Virilio's 'simulations' are representations of the real world, representations which are substituted for one another as technology develops.
Baudrillard's conception of these relations is more complex: the real is not
a brute given, but a historically and socially evolved form of appropriation
of the world (and replaces other forms through their constant and systematic destruction). For Baudrillard, then, '[r]epresentation stems from the
principle of the equivalence of the sign and the real' whereas simulation,
'on the contrary, stems... from the radical negation of the sign as value,
from the sign as reversion ... of every reference.' In this new situation
'there is no longer a Last Judgement to separate the false from the true'
(Baudrillard, 1994a: 6). As Baudrillard had noted in his essay on the
Pompidou Centre in Paris the 'Beaubourg illustrates very well that an
order of simulacra only establishes itself on the alibi of the previous order'
(1994a: 64).[2] What separates Baudrillard and Virilio at this point in time,
is not just Christianity (where Baudrillard takes a Nietzschean position
which is anathema to Virilio, (see Virilio and Lotringer, 1997: 133), but
essentially a dispute about the theory of the real as a referent for simulation, and particularly the social as referent. The different emphasis given
by Virilio to the theory of war could be seen as providing a relatively
specialized zone which ensures that theoretical topics do not come into
direct contact, and which allows theoretical exchanges between him and
Baudrillard to occur.

   Both Virilio and Baudrillard follow McLuhan in their own way: the
medium is the message. The development of the mass media, tele-technolo-
gies, brings about the ecstasy of communication and the hegemony of the
screen, the vision machine. As I have noted, Virilio made this transition in
his writings over the period 1969–75 (in *L'Insecurité*) with his thesis that
acceleration is generalized through communication. This becomes a

decisive new step in his account of dromocracy: at the end of *Speed and Politics* Virilio concludes with the observation that with the advent of nuclear war and the new means of communication 'the war-machine becomes (thanks to the reflexes of the strategic calculator) the very decision for war' (1986 [1977]: 139–40). Preparation for war is part of war itself, and creates 'extreme proximity of parties in which the immediacy of information immediately creates the crisis' (1986: 143). Virilio suggests this realizes what was most feared by Clausewitz, the 'full discharge' of total war (1986: 151). The Red Brigades in Italy called in February 1978 for all militants to 'act militarily in order to act politically against the "bunkers in which the agents of counter-revolution hide"' (Virilio, 1990: 42). Virilio, stung to reply wrote a resolute critique of this aim: it is too late for any assault, only popular defence is possible. But it is clear this creates a crisis at the heart of Virilio's position: there are three kinds of resistance – first, to struggle against the war-machine by declaring war on it or, second, to enter its body and divert its effect or, third, simply to act defensively where possible forms of solidarity arise and to build up these solidarities where possible. The former seems outmoded by the 1970s, but the question which haunts Virilio's project of popular resistance is what forms it would take and whether they are effective. Even more pressing is the question of what happened to the work of transforming the technological developments brought about by the military machine?

Bunker Visions

I believe in the peace of Christ. (Virilio, in Virilio and Lotringer, 1997: 122)

Virilio's most mystical text, *The Aesthetics of Disappearance* (1991a [1980]), followed on from Baudrillard's own rather strange text *Seduction* (1990 [1979]). Virilio's work might well be considered an attempt to counter Baudrillard's Nietzschean fatal theory with a statement of Christian meditation on seduction and evil. Virilio's argument relies heavily on a range of bizarre mystical texts and positions including that of Saint Bernadette of Lourdes. He has no hesitation in claiming that her witness to the Virgin is as valuable as any work of the German romantics and idealist philosophers. Indeed, he sees a profound unity between the 'simple story' of a young seer, and the 'elaborate tales of the transcendental poets' (1991a: 42). One finds here he says a 'sort of para-optic aesthetics of the real world, an unusual activity of the senses, usurping their function by chance' (1991a: 42). Bernadette's visionary experience is cited as primary evidence of the experience of time:

> I saw poplars beside the torrent and brambles in front of the cave quiver as if the wind was shaking them, but all around nothing moved and suddenly I saw something white ... a white girl no bigger than me. She greeted me, bowing... (1991a: 38)

Virilio is bitterly critical of the way children are now deprived of their apparitions. Bernadette said of her experience 'for that moment you'd give a whole lifetime', and Virilio records 'this is exactly what she does by hiding in a convent at Nevers where she dies at age 35' (1991a: 39). Nevers is now marked by Virilio's Bunker church. Virilio has subsequently noted the similarity of the experience of being in the grotto at Lourdes and being in a bunker (Virilio and Brausch, 1997: 35).

At the end of this book Virilio muses on the mystery of the bunker. 'As a young man I wondered about the aesthetics of war machines ... I found myself often contemplating a bunker or the silhouette of some submarine seen at a distance, wondering why their polished forms were so inscrutable', he writes. His first reflections related these forms to:

> ... zoomorphism, to metamorphism, but all of that was comparison, imitation and could not satisfy me. Then I believed these forms were inscrutable because they all related to speeds that were different, excessive... But the over-production of movement implied by war changed the way things looked; the motor, since it relates directly to the state of paradoxical wakefulness replaced the causal idea – that was its revolution; the motor proceeds from the soul. (1991a: 103)

The deepest threat is the systematic elimination of genuine religious consciousness (Virilio and Lotringer, 1997: 124). In his *L'Horizon negatif* (1984) Virilio specifies the nature of this threat and the military as false priesthood. It is a struggle between two temporalities: the 'instant' is the warrior, the 'eternal' the priest (1991a: 291). The condition of nuclear pure war sees the emergence of the cult of military-scientistic objects, a millenarianism founded as a cargo cult of the arsenal. It is the evocation of a mystical apocalypse through the 'adoration of vehicles'. It is 'the nuclear faith' (1991a: 305), a pure parody of religion. Virilio is fighting the war of a new virtual Christian priesthood.

Bunkers in the Desert

> ... the apocalypse is here. It could happen at any moment ... [it] is hidden in development itself, in the development of arms – that is, *in the non-development of society.* (Virilio and Lotringer, 1997: 139)

What happens to the bunker in the 1980s? In the key essay of *L'Horizon negatif* he suggests pure speed and pure war are desert forms, devoid of human life and historical events. The desert as the negative horizon; the desert as 'the last figure of the bunker' (1984: 210). It is one of the effects of a series of important transformations: capital accumulation is to be understood as the accumulation of wealth and wealth as condensation of speed. But speed is above all transport and as transportation structures accelerate it becomes clear that what occurs is above all a revolution in the transportation of messages, to the radical dematerialization of carriers: pure communication and the dramatic disappearance of man, cities, citizens. This radical situation makes even more significant the new value of the simple act of presence: in the Latin American case, a visible protest, a witness to the disappearance of individuals. With the emergence of the speed of the new media all peoples are exposed to a similar process, and also tend to disappear, 'as if by magic' (in Rötzer, 1995 [1986]: 101–2).

When pure war changed gear and the Gulf War broke out in 1991, Virilio was keen to locate and analyse, just like Baudrillard, its new logic, in the light of theorizing over 25 years. Virilio's analysis, in *L'Ecran du desert* (1991b) concluded that a shift had indeed taken place and this was the first 'post-modern war' (1991b: 177) in the sense that it was now clear, as had been foreseen, many of the temporal and spatial aspects of war had been completely transformed by communication and other technologies (see the commentary on this transition in Bogard, 1996: 78–97). This war was, for Virilio, a world war 'in miniature', and deserved to be known as World War III 'in reduction' (1991b: 162), where the military vision machine proved itself sovereign. The instantaneity of decision-making through information produced at an unprecedented speed meant that space–time relations were fused in a total 'electromagnetic environment' (1991b: 165). Much has been made of the apparent difference between Baudrillard and Virilio on the Gulf War, indeed the difference appeared sharp at the time. Yet Virilio introduced the spectre of the '4th front': the speed of communication and information is so rapid and decisive it rules out at a stroke effective responsibility and democratic control. It creates the paradoxical elimination of the distinction between true and false, the fusion of object and image, even of defence and attack (1991b: 182). And Baudrillard wrote at the time:

> ... in confronting our opinions on the war with the diametrically opposed opinions of Paul Virilio, one of us betting on apocalyptic escalation and the other on deterrence and the indefinite virtuality of war, we concluded that this decidedly strange war went in both directions at once. (Baudrillard, 1995: 49)

But this conclusion is superficial. For Baudrillard the crucial point was that the separation between war and peace was dissolved into virtual transpolitical forms. Virilio, on the other hand requires the separation of the two terms in order to perform his critique. We can say, therefore, that Virilio noted something Baudrillard did not: a new situation of the bunker. Unlike the bunkers on the Atlantic Wall, Saddam's bunkers were hidden and disguised, resembling other 'furtive' phenomena of this new type of war (1991b: 119). These bunkers were hidden in the desert, a modern Atlantis. Thus Virilio, from a Baudrillardian point of view, seems to have taken at face value the war machine's own propaganda (see Keeble, 1997: 166–87, esp. 180), a further absolute reversal had taken place. The destructive arms were now exposed, but the defensive infrastructures were disguised (1991b: 121). The new bunkers were proof against nuclear attack and designed to maintain hundreds of soldiers in a new kind of hostile environment with sophisticated air filtration systems (1991b: 121). On the other hand one of the great 'errors' of the allies was to have bombed a civilian bunker less well disguised than others (1991b: 189, 185–6), compounded, paradoxically, by the problem of an inability to assess accurately the effect of its attacks, even with all the immense panoply of sophisticated spying apparatuses. These seemed able only to give precise information about position, not to be able to play any significant qualitative role in the verification of damage inflicted.

Grey (Bunker) Ecology

> ... a pollution no longer atmospheric or hydrospheric but dromospheric. (Virilio, 1997: 64)

Virilio has often complained that people do not understand his position, that: 'war and not commerce is the source of the city, as they don't accept the negativity of technology' (1997: 24). Thus we must be clear: war and peace are not simply opposite states. They do not figure as unique categories, but are transformed into each other: the priest transforms war into peace, the warrior transforms peace into war. Virilio models himself, however, not on a Christian example, but on a pagan example: the Greeks brought politics and citizenship into existence out of war. In the Agon the individual dies for the city. He exchanges this death for a new life. But in the new situation the 'military man is a false priest because the question of death doesn't interest him. He's an executioner, not a priest. A new inquisitor' (Virilio and Lotringer, 1997: 49).

Virilio is also fascinated by the emergence of a new type of inertial mode of being, and in particular Howard Hughes, who 'ended up a technological monk in the desert of Las Vegas, without getting out of bed' (Virilio and Lotringer, 1997: 73). All he did was to watch films. He saw *Ice Station Zebra* 164 times: 'he never stopped watching a film that represented exactly that same inertia in a polar city...' (Virilio and Lotringer, 1997: 73). 'What fascinated me about Howard Hughes ... was the fact that he managed to foreshadow a mass situation' (Virilio and Lotringer, 1997: 74). But, asks Virilio: 'Who are these people fascinated by their electronic windows?' This interests him since here 'we have a phenomenon of inertia and death on the spot ... a sedentariness in dead time' (Virilio and Lotringer, 1997: 74). So: pure war which is infinite in its preparation (Virilio and Lotringer, 1997: 92), has an ineluctable but paradoxical logic. The increase in the rate of acceleration of communication leads to the elimination of the world's dimensions: point, line, surface, volume. For Virilio this is the supreme pollution, the pollution of space–time: 'there is no longer any "here", everything is "now"' (Virilio and Lotringer, 1997: 144).

Conclusion

> Virilio ... the last and best of all the saints. (Kroker, 1992: 44)

Virilio conceives the bunker occupant in this new situation as being 'encapsulated in the arrow of cosmic time, cut off from local time by his very travels, the extra-worldly navigator (or worldly televiewer) is the victim of an unprecedented inertia' (1997: 128). The cybernaut is an atrophied body 'whose safety takes precedence over all activity, to the point where, for him, the concrete environment has only a single point left, the point' (1997: 128). But it is clear that Virilio is unable to find any way he can enter and divert this machine (unlike Baudrillard's analyses of the virus, etc.). Virilio does not seek to introduce a pathology, the problem for Virilio is that pathology, in the shape of an accident, is all too likely to become general (1997: 69ff). The earnest and humourless logic of Virilio's position is quite different therefore from that of Baudrillard. Virilio in essence has a theory of the relentless and accumulative dromocracy, while if Baudrillard's 'orders of simulacra' appear accumulative (since they abolish previous orders) in the end they occupy a curved space and are subject to reversibility, for the last judgement has already occurred ('might it not perhaps be necessary to replace Paul Virilio's dromology with a palindromology?' asks Baudrillard wickedly [1994b: 122]). Virilio tries to specify a 'grey ecology' a new kind of resistance (it has no means) to a new pollution (it is 'omnipolitan') (Virilio, 1997:143). For Baudrillard, Virilio's 'attempt to escape the apocalypse of the virtual, is. . . the last of our utopian desires' (1994b: 117).

We should return, finally, to the basic dilemma Virilio finds himself facing. If 'we must get inside pure war . . . cover ourselves in blood and tears' (Virilio and Lotringer, 1997: 108), he has failed to discover from his high-tech bunker window any mode of entry to the machine. If he fights a battle for the real against the virtual, presenting a resisting distance, even from a low-tech bunker (no television or computer screen, no fixed or – horror! – mobile telephone, fax, a kind of Non-pendular Stabilizer) he remains a prophet of the last utopia arising on the lost horizon of the social. But in the new situation pure war brings a new obstacle to exchange: polar inertia, so that eventually every 'city will be in the same place – in time' (Virilio and Lotringer, 1997: 61). Every Bunker will be in the same place. Virilio now outlines his strategy:

> Proximity, the single interface between all bodies, all places, all points of the world – that's the tendency. And I push this tendency to extremes. It's not science fiction. Science and technology develop the unknown, not know-ledge. Science develops what is not rational. That's what fiction is. (Virilio and Lotringer, 1997: 62)

To pass from fiction into the 'real', however, he must at some point, come out of his bunker. He is profoundly furtive about his capabilities on this front: 'I have no solution to offer', and he adds: 'if there's a salvation it lies in the humility of philosophical, scientific and political thinking ... a radical scientific and philosophical humility. We are nothing' (in Rötzer, 1995: 103–4). The perfect disguise.

Notes

Versions of this article were read at the Universities of Nottingham and Warwick. Many thanks to those who took part in the discussions and to the two anonymous referees who read the article.

1. It is not uncommon to find their names associated with the same publications (e.g. at one time on the French journal *Traverses*, through numerous Semiotext(e) publications), at the same conferences (e.g. the *Looking Back on the End of the World* collection, Kamper and Wulf, 1989), interviewed for the same publication series by Sylvère Lotringer for Semiotexte (see Baudrillard, 1987, and Virilio's discussions with Lotringer in *Pure War*, 1997), by Rötzer – a chapter each for Boer Verlag (Rötzer, 1995 [1986]), and both interviewed at book length by Philippe Petit for Grasset: Virilio in *Cybermonde, la politique du pire* (1996) and Baudrillard in *Le Paroxyste indifférent* (1997a).

2. It is interesting to note that in a recent interview Virilio remarks that the Beaubourg was 'already a symptom of the mobilization of architecture' in a way which paralleled the acceleration of the real (Virilio and Brausch, 1997: 74).

References

Baudrillard, J. (1987) *Forget Foucault*. New York: Semiotext(e).

Baudrillard, J. (1990 [1979]) *Seduction*. London: Macmillan.

Baudrillard, J. (1993 [1976]) *Symbolic Exchange and Death*. London: Sage.

Baudrillard, J. (1994a) *Simulacra and Simulation*. Ann Arbor: University of Michigan Press.

Baudrillard, J. (1994b) *The Illusion of the End*. Oxford: Polity.

Baudrillard, J. (1995) *The Gulf War Did not Take Place*. Sydney: Power Publications.

Baudrillard, J. (1997a) *Le Paroxyste indifférent*. Paris: Grasset.

Baudrillard, J. (1997b) 'Interview: Jean Baudrillard', *Dazed and Confused* June: 80–3.

Bogard, W. (1996) *The Simulation of Surveillance: Hypercontrol in Telematic Societies*. Cambridge: Cambridge University Press.

Kamper, D. and C. Wulf (eds) (1989) *Looking Back on the End of the World*. New York: Semiotext(e).

Keeble, R. (1997) *Secret State, Silent Press: New Militarism, the Gulf and the Modern Image of Warfare*. Luton: University of Luton Press.

Kroker, A. (1992) *The Possessed Individual*. London: Macmillan.

Parent, C. and P. Virilio (1996) *The Function of the Oblique*. London: Architectural Association.

Ritzer, G. (1997) *Postmodern Social Theory*. New York: McGraw-Hill.

Rötzer, F. (1995 [1986]) *Conversations with French Philosophers.* New Jersey: Humanities Press.

Virilio, P. (1984) *L'Horizon negatif.* Paris: Galilée.

Virilio, P. (1986 [1977]) *Speed & Politics.* New York: Semiotext(e).

Virilio, P. (1990 [1978]) *Popular Defense & Ecological Struggles.* New York: Semiotext(e).

Virilio, P. (1991a [1980]) *The Aesthetics of Disappearance.* New York: Semiotext(e).

Virilio, P. (1991b) *L'Écran du desert.* Paris: Galilée.

Virilio, P (1993 [1976]) *L'Insecurité du territoire.* Paris: Galilée.

Virilio, P. (1994 [1975]) *Bunker Archeology.* Princeton, NJ: Princeton University Press.

Virilio, P. (1996) *Cybermonde, la politique du pire.* Paris: Grasset.

Virilio, P. (1997) *Open Sky.* London: Verso.

Virilio, P. and M. Brausch (1997) *Voyage d'hiver: entretiens.* Paris: Parentheses.

Virilio, P. and S. Lotringer (1997 [1983]) *Pure War.* New York: Semiotext(e).

Mike Gane is Reader in Sociology in the Department of Social Sciences at Loughborough University. His main interests are in the development of social theory and he has published widely on Durkheimian sociology, on Baudrillard, and he has edited two collections on Foucault. His recent writings have concerned Comte, Marx, Durkheim, Mauss, Lyotard, Canguilhem, Baudrillard and Derrida. He is a member of the editorial board of *Economy and Society* and *Durkheimian Studies*.

Virilio, War and Technology
Some Critical Reflections

Douglas Kellner

P AUL VIRILIO IS one of the most prolific and penetrating critics of the drama of technology in the contemporary era, especially military technology, technologies of representation, computer and information technologies, and biotechnology. For Virilio, the question of technology is *the* question of our time and his life work constitutes a sustained reflection on the origins, nature and effects of the key technologies that have constituted the modern/postmodern world. In particular, Virilio carries out a radical critique of the ways that technology is transforming the contemporary world and even the human species.

Yet I want to argue in this study that Virilio has a flawed conception of technology that is excessively negative and one-sided, thus missing the empowering and democratizing aspects of new computer and media technologies. My argument is that his vision of technology is overdetermined by his intense focus on war and military technology and that this optic drives him to predominantly technophobic perspectives on technology per se as well as the new technologies of the contemporary era. I contend that Virilio's project is essentially conservative, wishing to preserve the human body and natural life against the assaults of what he sees as a demonic technology which he regards as having a highly destructive impact on nature, human beings and socio-political life. However, it is precisely the extremely critical discourse on war and military technology, as well as his penetrating reflections on war, cinema, technologies of representation and vision machines, and biotechnology, that constitute valuable aspects of his work.

Consequently, in the following pages I will follow Virilio in pursuing what he calls the 'riddle of technology' and interrogate his critique of technology, the normative position from which he assails technology and

■ *Theory, Culture & Society* 1999 (SAGE, London, Thousand Oaks and New Delhi),
   Vol. 16(5–6): 103–125
   [0263-2764(199910/12)16:5–6;103–125;009961]

the limitations of his project. Nowhere does Virilio directly theorize technology in any systematic or sustained way, although reflections on it permeate his analyses, hence I will survey a broad expanse of his works to elucidate his perspectives. Thus, I want to probe Virilio's work on technology to determine the extent of his insight and use-value, and to indicate what I see as problematic in his writings. In this reading, Virilio emerges as one of the major critics of war, technology and vision machines in our time, albeit with excessively hypercritical and even technophobic proclivities.

Speed, Politics and Technology

> We must take hold of the riddle of technology and lay it on the table as the ancient philosophers and scientists put the riddle of Nature out in the open, the two being superimposed. (Virilio and Lotringer, 1983: 30)

> Totalitarianism is latent in technology. (Virilio, 1995a)

In *Speed and Politics* (1986 [1977]), Virilio undertakes his most sustained attempt to delineate the importance of accelerated speed, of the impact of technologies of motion, of types of mobility and their effects in the contemporary era. Subtitled 'Essay on Dromology', Virilio proposes what he calls a 'dromomatics' which interrogates the role of speed in history and its important functions in urban and social life, warfare, the economy, transportation and communication, and other aspects of everyday life. This book sets up the basic terms of Virilio's problematic which is to measure how technologies alter our sense of space, time and the body, and have an impact on social, political and human life in destructive ways.

'Dromology' comes from the Latin term, *dromos*, signifying race, and dromology studies how innovations in speed influence social and political life. The 'dromocratic revolution' for Virilio involves means of fabricating speed with the steam engine, then the combustion engine, and in our day nuclear energy and instantaneous forms of warfare and communication. Speed vectors constitute the trajectory of various technologies along a fixed length and direction, but from no fixed point. Vectors describe any trajectory along which goods, money, information or military apparatuses can flow, including roadways, airwaves and communication and military circuits. Territory is the space across which speed, technology, politics, economics and urban and everyday life traverse, via vectors of transportation, commerce, war, social interaction, communication and information. From a political and military perspective, territory is the space of human habitation, it is a space to be defended and secured, or to be invaded and colonized. Within modern societies, the nation-state was the territory that defined politics and the city, with its public spaces and institutions, served as a key site of modernity. In the contemporary world, however, Virilio argues that the city has been displaced by technologies of speed and power, and the spaces of politics are being usurped by the forces of technology.

Virilio was initially an urbanist who describes the city as a dwelling place organized by channels of communication and transportation, penetrated by roadways, canals, coastlines, railroads and now airports. Each crossing has its speed limits, its regulations, and its systematic enclosure and spaces within a system of societal organization. The city itself is in part a conglomeration of these roads, a stop-over for travel, and a system of 'habitable circulation' (Virilio, 1986: 6). City life unfolds in the spectacle of the street with its progressions and movements, its institutions and events, mobilizing and moving flows of traffic and people. Likewise, politics unfolds in the streets and in urban sites of debate, demonstrations, revolt and insurrection.

For Virilio, the city and its institutions have military origins. In his view, the medieval cathedral and early modern fortified cities were military sites. In Virilio's words: 'Before it became the throne of totality, the Christian sanctuary was a stronghold, a bunker, a fortified church for those who remained within it; all their powers and capacities were deployed and strengthened *in, through and as combat*' (1986: 38). Likewise, although Virilio himself does not make this point, the early Christian missions in the Americas were military fortifications used by the colonizing powers as defense and control mechanisms.

In the military sphere, the city no longer serves as a break against military conquest and as a site of protection of its citizens when instantaneous violence can assault it from hidden spaces (airplanes, nuclear submarines and missiles). With politics occurring through media and information circuits, the time of deliberation and consensus is obliterated. Space and time are thus overwhelmed by technologies that travel at ever faster speeds and as new technologies instantaneously circulate images and information across space.

Dromology also involves analysis of the forces that brake or diminish speed as well as those forces that accelerate it. War, for instance, involves both offensive attempts to rapidly control space and territory contrasted to defensive efforts to slow down the attack, to decelerate the offensive, just as laws and rules brake or slow down certain actions deemed destructive to the community. Virilio claims that the acceleration of speed dramatically increased in the 19th century with the combustion engine to electric telegraphy, a period in which first transportation is greatly speeded up and then communication takes place instantaneously over great distances, thus obliterating traditional barriers of time and space. Consequently, the generation of modernity involves transition from the age of the brake to that of the accelerator (Virilio and Lotringer, 1983: 44f), as intensification of speed generates new economic, political, social and other forms.

Virilio argues that the role of speed had been previously overlooked in the organization of civilizations and politics and that speed is crucial, as well, to the production of wealth and power. Rejecting the forms of economic determinism associated with Marxism, without ignoring economic conditions, Virilio's dromology focuses on those instruments that accelerate and intensify speed and that augment the wealth and power of those groups who control them. In his vision, it is groups like the military, the state and the corporation which control speed and become dominant societal powers. This situation produces an accelerating decline of the public sphere and democratic politics, and increasing power of the military, which, for Virilio, becomes a key force in politics and society whose importance he believes is often underestimated.

Virilio thus makes important conceptual connections between technology, speed and war. In Virilio's view, the importance of warfare in understanding human history had been grossly undervalued. For Virilio, the need for defense and the preparation for war was at the origins of the foundation of cities,[1] while logistics, the preparation for war, begins the modern industrial economy, fueling development of a system of specialized and mechanized mass production. War and logistics require increased speed and efficiency, and technology provides instruments that create more lethal and effective instruments of war. The acceleration of speed and technology, in turn, create more dynamic industry, and an industrial system that obliterates distances in time and space through the development of technologies of transportation, communication and information. The fate of the industrial system is thus bound up with the military system which provides, in Virilio's vision, its origins and impetus.

Hence, on Virilio's optic, cities, cathedrals, the economy, politics and other key aspects of the modern world are products of military and technological mobilization and deployment. In his view, war technology serves as a constitutive force of history, producing many calamities. For Virilio, the system of deterrence in the Cold War nuclear stalemate created a situation in which technological development channels technology into military forms and technocratic political domination. In this situation, 'Weapons and armor constantly need to be strengthened. Technological development thus leads to economic depletion. The war-machine tends toward societal non-development' (Virilio and Lotringer, 1983: 5). With more and more resources going to the military and military imperatives dominating production, government and the evolution of science and technology in the Cold War and beyond, societal development is undermined and social underdevelopment becomes a defining mark of contemporary societies.

This process culminates in what Virilio calls 'pure war', which is 'improperly named "deterrence" by the apologists of nuclear conflagration', and marks 'the emergence of a cult, the institution of a *military scientific messianism*' similar to primitive cargo cults (1998a: 90 [1984]). Pure war advocates salvation through armament, faith in nuclear deterrence, submission to a system of mass destruction in the hopes that it will provide protection and security. Appropriately named MAD, such 'mutually assured destruction' constitutes for Virilio the insanity of the Cold War, the arms race and the erection of systems of mass destruction in which contemporary societies mobilize for the perpetual possibility of war, thus existing in a condition of 'pure war'.

In addition, for Virilio, the acceleration of events, technological development and speed in the current era designates 'a double movement of implosion and explosion', so that 'the new war machine combines a double disappearance: *the disappearance of matter in nuclear disintegration and the disappearance of places in vehicular extermination*' (Virilio, 1986: 134). The increased speed of destruction in military technology is moving toward the speed of light with laser weapons and computer-controlled weapons systems constituting a novelty in warfare in which there are no longer geo-strategic strongpoints since from any given spot we can now reach any other, producing what Virilio calls 'a strategy of Brownian movement through geostrategic homogenization of the globe' (Virilio, 1986: 135). Thus, '*strategic spatial miniaturization* is now the order of the day', with microtechnologies transforming production and communication, shrinking the planet and preparing the way for what Virilio calls 'pure war', a situation in which military technologies and an accompanying technocratic system come to control every aspect of life.

In Virilio's view, the war machine is the demiurge of technological development and an ultimate threat to humanity, producing 'a state of emergency' in which nuclear holocaust threatens the very survival of the human species. The ever increasing diminution of the time of reaction in nuclear crisis situations, the fatal 'one minute', takes issues of war and peace out of the hands of deliberating bodies and the public, putting the fatal power in the hands of techno-elites and their machines. This involves a shift from a 'geo-politics' to a 'chrono-politics', from a politics of space to a politics of time, in which whoever controls the means of instant information, communication and destruction becomes a dominant socio-political force. For Virilio, every technological system contains its specific form of accident and a nuclear accident would, of course, be catastrophic. Hence, in the contemporary nuclear era, in which weapons of mass destruction could create a world holocaust, we are thrust into a permanent state of emergency that enables the nuclear state to impose its imperatives on ever more domains of political and social life, disciplining and regulating populations to submit to the authority and dictates of the state and military.

Politics too succumbs to the logic of speed and potential catastrophe as increased speed in military violence, instantaneous information and communication and the flow of events diminishes the time and space of deliberation, discussion and the building of consensus that is the work of politics. Speed and war thus undermine politics, with technology replacing democratic participation and the complexity and rapidity of historical events rendering human understanding and control ever more problematical. Ubiquitous and instantaneous media communication in turn makes spin-control and media manipulation difficult, but essential, to political governance. Moreover, the need for fast spin control and effective media politics further diminishes the space and role of democratic political participation and interaction.

For Virilio, technology drives us into new modes of speed and motion, it carries us along predetermined trajectories. He believes that the question:

> 'Can we do without technology?' cannot be asked as such. We are forced to expand the question of technology not only to the substance produced, but also to the accident produced. The riddle of technology we were talking about before is also the riddle of the accident. (Virilio and Lotringer, 1983: 31–2)

Virilio contends that every technological system generates its specific form of accident: with the invention of the ship, you get the shipwreck; the plane brings plane crashes; the automobile, car accidents and so on. For Virilio, the technocratic vision is one-sided and flawed in that it postulates a perfect technological system, a seamless cybernetic realm of instrumentality and control in which all processes are determined by and follow technical laws. In the real world, however, accidents are part and parcel of technological systems, they expose technology's limitations, they subvert idealistic visions of technology. Accidents are consequently, in Virilio's view, an integral part of all modes of transportation, industrial production, war and military organization and other technological systems.[2]

Virilio further argues that new technologies alter our mode of perception and experience, change the way we see and encounter the world, and that in particular technologies of speed have produced an increasingly fragmented, discontinuous and transhistorical mode of experience that grasps instances, fragments and partial relations rather than whole fields. In his view, technological time has invaded the time and space of the city and other sites of habitation, creating new rhythms and modes of interaction that dramatically transform social and everyday life. Virilio describes what he calls 'endo-colonization' in which the state and technology colonize their own urban spaces and come to increasingly colonize the mind and body, as the eruption of new 'vision machines' and information technologies create autonomous realms of experience and perception.

Technology and Representation: From Vision Machines to Information Technologies

> These new technologies try to make virtual reality more powerful than actual reality, which is the true accident. The day when virtual reality becomes more powerful than reality will be the day of the big accident. Mankind never experienced such an extraordinary accident. (Virilio, 1997a: 43)

With *War and Cinema* (1989 [1984]) and his subsequent writings such as *The Vision Machine* (1994 [1988]), *Polar Inertia* (1998b [1990], *The Art of the Motor* (1995d [1993]), *Open Sky* (1997b [1995]) and *Cybermonde* (1996), Virilio focuses more on the relation between war, speed, technology and the means of representation, particularly vision machines and the logistics of perception embodied in cinema, computers and new virtual reality machines. War, Virilio suggests, has long been dependent on the logistics of representation, on providing accurate depictions of the enemy's troop and weapons deployment. As technologies of pictorial surveillance progressed, cinematic representation became more salient to military strategy although, more recently, informatics, computer simulation and satellite imaging have become more central.

From approximately 1904, accelerating in the First World War, and until the recent high-tech explosion, the apparatus of cinema was deployed as part of military strategy, involving lighting the terrain of battle and enemy forces, accurately representing their strength and movement, and instantaneously perceiving the actual battlefield itself as a dynamic field of motion, all of which were crucial to military strategy. Cinema, too, followed a certain military logic, with great directors serving as dictators and authoritarian orchestrators of cinematic spectacle, leading Virilio to conclude that: 'War is cinema, and cinema is war' (1989: 26).

Cinema has long been part of Virilio's imaginary and his reflections on cinema and war cover a vast expanse of modern history, providing a unique take on the history of cinema and the ways that modes of cinematic representation are also crucial to war and society. Virilio's theme is the progressive dematerialization of warfare in high-tech and virtual war, in which technologies progressively replace human beings:

> What the video artist Nam June Paik calls the triumph of the electronic image over universal gravity has carried this [dematerialization] still further. The sense of weightlessness and suspension of ordinary sensations indicates the growing confusion between 'ocular reality' and its instantaneous, mediated representation. The intensity of automatic weaponry and the new capacities of photographic equipment combine to project *a final image of the world*, a world in the throes of dematerialization and eventual total disintegration, one in which the cinema of the Lumière brothers becomes more reliable than Junger's melancholy look-out who can no longer believe his eyes. (1989: 73)

This passage refers to the tendency of technology to displace modes of human perception and representation in military planning and execution, as computer programs replace military planners and computer simulations replace charts and maps of the territory. On the level of the battlefield itself, human power is replaced by machines, reducing the soldier to a cog in a servomechanism. Virilio comments:

> The disintegration of the warrior's personality is at a very advanced stage. Looking up, he sees the digital display (opto-electronic or holographic) of the windscreen collimator; looking down, the radar screen, the onboard computer, the radio and the video screen, which enables him to follow the terrain with its four or five simultaneous targets; and to monitor his self-navigating Sidewinder missiles fitted with a camera of infra-red guidance system. (1989: 84)

With *The Vision Machine* (1994 [1988]) and Virilio's subsequent reflections on information and computer technologies, the epistemological turn to focus on modes of representation and the logistics of perception decenter, to some extent, Virilio's intense focus on war, though his interconnection of the themes of war, technology and representation give a unity and coherence to his otherwise highly fragmentary and elusive thought.

In the concluding chapter of *The Vision Machine* (1994), Virilio distinguishes between painting as the age of the image's *formal logic*, photography and film as the age of the image's *dialectical logic*, and video recording, holography and computer graphics as the beginning of an age of *paradoxical logic*: the latter emerges 'when the real-time image dominates the thing represented, real time subsequently prevailing over real space, virtuality dominating actuality and turning the very concept of reality on its head' (1994: 63). In this situation, images and representations replace the real, the object of representation declines in importance, and a domain of images and digital representation replaces reality. Culturally, this involves the proliferation of new vision machines that generate an artificial realm of data, images and information that constitute a novel realm of experience. In war, it involves new modes of weapons based on the annihilation of time (just as nuclear technology involved the disintegration of matter and space). Just as computers and new image machines dramatically transform the nature of culture, so too do new laser technologies, modes of surveillance, and new forms of image warfare, disinformation and high-tech military spectacle change the nature of war (1994: 66f), as was evident in the Gulf War.

The Vision Machine did not, however, explore in any great detail the new forms of information technology, multimedia or high-tech warfare, providing instead an introduction to the ways that vision machines influence perception and representation. It is in *Polar Inertia* (1998b [1990]), *The Art of the Motor* (1995d [1993]), *Open Sky* (1997b [1995]), and many interviews and articles of the 1990s that Virilio interrogates the new information technology. His central insight is that new information, communication and transportation technologies are taking us out of this world, beyond the limits of space and time, outside of nature and the material world into a new dimension with its own temporality, spatiality and modes of being. Virilio fears that this journey will take us out of our bodies, minds, nature and world as we have experienced and known them into a terrifying new sphere that will cause disastrous, possibly fatal, mutations of mind, body and experience.

For Virilio, the astronauts are harbingers of a new experience beyond the familiar space and time coordinates of material existence. Shot into outer space beyond the laws of gravity and earth's spatial and temporal coordinates, the astronauts found themselves in a no-place and no-time continuum without fixed coordinates or dimensions. In this new dimension, some experienced a vertigo of intense disorientation and collapsed into madness after their return, or into strange metaphysical musings. Virilio's comments here, however, are somewhat anecdotal and serve more as metaphorical and rhetorical devices to dramatize the strangeness of outer space travel and the displacement of our scientific and conceptual schemes in this new dimension than a serious scrutiny of the effects of space flight on human beings. Such statements are typical of his propensity to exaggerate negative effects, fixing on as examples extreme cases (i.e. madness after space flight) of the negative effects of new technologies, rather than sorting out positive and negative features and carrying out sustained investigations of the actual effects of technologies.

Cyberspace, Virilio claims, supplies another space without the usual space–time coordinates that generates a disorienting and disembodying form of experience in which communication and interaction takes place instantaneously in a new global time, overcoming boundaries of time and space. It is a disembodied space with no fixed coordinates in which one loses anchorage in one's body, nature and social community. It is thus for Virilio a dematerialized and abstract realm in which cybernauts can become lost in space and divorced from their bodies and social world.

In addition, Virilio analyzes and denounces what he calls 'a pernicious *industrialization of vision*' (1997b: 89) and what he fears is a displacement of vision by machines. Virilio is afraid that vision machines are increasingly seeing for us, ranging from cameras to video to satellite surveillance to nanotechnology which probes the body (and next the mind?). He fears that media like cinema and television train and constrain vision, leading to degradation of vision and experience:

> If, according to Kafka, cinema means pulling a uniform over your eyes, television means pulling on a straitjacket, stepping up an eye training regime that leads to eye disease, just as the acoustic intensity of the walkman ends in irreversible lesions in the inner ear. (1997b: 97)

But even more, he fears that the 'standardization of vision feared by Kafka' will:

> ... make way for a sort of *electro-ergonomic suppressant*, in which design of the pathways of waves and their sequential aesthetic will replace the movie theatre for the viewer armed with an audiovisual helmet that relays the eyeball's *mis en scène*, the optic nerve irradiated by laser beams reproducing on the screen of the occipital cortex that fine line of light once produced by the old movie projector. (1997b: 94)

In other words, he fears that substitution of audiovisual helmets in virtual reality devices will replace the previous emphasis on natural sight, creating a new technological aesthetic and new mechanization of sight:

> There is no need to look for any further reasons for the decline of the film industry: following on from the innovation of the earlier vision machines of photography, film or video, we are already seeing the beginnings of a true 'mechanization of perception', whereby the intrusion of optoelectronic

devices right inside the nervous system partly explains the abandonment of projection rooms which have also become smaller and smaller. (1997b: 94–5)

Moreover, Virilio fears that we are increasingly subjected to bombardment by images and information and thus by 'a discreet pollution of our vision of the world through the sundry tools of communication' (1997b: 96). Virilio thus demonizes modern information and communication technologies, suggesting that they are doing irreparable damage to the human being. Sometimes over-the-top rhetorical, as in the passages just cited, Virilio's 1990s comments on new information technology suggest that he is deploying the same model and methods to analyze the new technologies that he used for war technology. He speaks regularly of an 'information bomb' that is set to explode (1995a, 1995b, 1995c, 1997a, 1997b), evoking the specter of 'a choking of the senses, a loss of control of reason of sorts' in an explosion of information and attendant disinformation.

Deploying his earlier argument concerning technology and the accident, Virilio argues that the information superhighway is just waiting for a major accident to happen (1995a, 1995b, 1997a, 1997b), which will be a new kind of global accident, affecting the whole globe, 'the accident of accidents' (Epicurus):

> The stock market collapse is merely a slight prefiguration of it. Nobody has seen this generalized accident yet. But then watch out as you hear talk about the 'financial bubble' in the economy: a very significant metaphor is used here, and it conjures up visions of some kind of cloud, reminding us of other clouds just as frightening as those of Chernobyl . . . (1995b)

In a 1995 interview with German media theorist Friedrich Kittler (1995c), titled 'The Information Bomb', Virilio draws an analogy between the nuclear bomb and the 'information bomb', talking about the dangers of 'fallout' and 'radiation' from both. In contrast to the more dialectical Kittler, Virilio comes off as exceedingly technophobic in this exchange and deploys an amalgam of military and religious metaphors to characterize the world of the new technologies. In one exchange, Virilio claims that 'a caste of technology-monks is coming up in our times', and 'there exist monasteries (of sorts) whose goal it is to pave the way for a (kind of) "civilization" that has nothing to do with civilization as we remember it'. These monks are avatars of a 'technological fundamentalism' and 'information monotheism', a world-view that replaces previous humanist and religious world-views, displacing man and god in favor of technology.

> [This world-view] comes into being in a totally independent manner from any controversy. It is the outcome of an intelligence without reflection or past. And with it goes what I think is the greatest danger (of all), the derailment, the sliding down into the utopian, into a future without humanity. And that is what worries me. I believe that violence, nay hyperviolence, springs out of this fundamentalism.

Virilio goes on to claim that fallout from the 'information bomb' will be as lethal for the socius as nuclear bombs, destroying social memory, relations, traditions and community with an instantaneous bombardment and overload of information. Thus, the technological 'monks' who promote the information revolution are guilty of 'sins in technical fundamentalism, of which we witness the consequences, the evil effects, today'. One wonders, however, if the discourse of 'sin', 'evil' and 'fundamentalism' is appropriate to characterize the effects and uses of new technologies which are, contrary to Virilio, hotly and widely debated, hardly monolithic and, in my view, highly ambiguous, mixing what might be appraised as positive and negative features and effects.

Yet Virilio is probably correct that the dominant discourse is largely positive and uncritical, and that we should be aware of negative aspects and costs of the new technologies and debate their construction, structure, uses and effects. Virilio is also right that they constitute at least a threat to community and social relations, as previously established, though one could argue that the new communities and social relations generated by use of the new information and entertainment technologies have positive dimensions as well as potentially negative ones – an issue that takes us to the question of Virilio's normative perspectives on technology.

Disappearance and Loss: Virilio's Critique

We now have the aesthetics of the disappearance of a numerical, unstable image of fleeting nature, whose persistence is exclusively retinal. (Virilio, 1991a: 36)

In his recent writings, Virilio engages the ways that new technologies are penetrating the human body and psyche, taking over previous biological, perceptual and creative functions of human beings, making humans appendages of a technological apparatus. He writes: 'I am a materialist of the body which means that the body is the basis of all my work' (Virilio, 1997a: 47). In his early work, Virilio spoke of the body as 'a vector of speed' and 'metabolic vehicle' in which increased speed and velocity overwhelmed the human sensorium and empowered technologies of speed over humans (1986). These reflections on technology, speed and war, recall Walter Benjamin who pointed out that the human body simply could not absorb the speed and lethality of modern war (1969).

In more recent work, Virilio has described the body as a planet, as a unique center around which objects gravitate, and criticizes an increasing derealization of the body in cyberspace and virtual technologies (1997a, 1997b). He also critiques biotechnology that is invading the body and reconstituting the human being (1995d). In *The Art of the Motor*, Virilio claims that 'The technology question is inseparable from the question of *where* technology occurs', noting 'the very recent advent of nanotechnological miniaturization' promoting 'biotechnology's physiological intrusion into, or insemination of, the living organism' (1995d: 99). Recent progress in technoscience, Virilio claims, 'has today resulted in the gradual colonization of the organs and entrails of man's *animal body*, the invasion of the microphysical finishing off the job that the geophysical invasion began' (1995d: 100). Such biotechnology 'leads to the *intraorganic intrusion of technology and its micromachines into the heart of the living*' (1995d: 100).

Virilio fears here a 'postindustrial metadesign' of the human being, in which the 'transplant revolution', biogenetic engineering and nanotechnology will generate a new species of being, 'hyperactive man' which he sees as a caricature of Nietzsche's 'superman'. This analysis in conjunction with his critique of information technology discloses a conservative desire to preserve life and human beings as they are, positing technology as a demonic threat to life and the human. Virilio thus operates with a Manichean value system, rooted in materialist phenomenology, that contrasts a positive 'life' and the human to a negatively interpreted technology. This normative position, never spelled out but implicit throughout his writings, constitutes an optic in which technology is seen as a dire threat to human life itself.

Virilio is thus in part a materialist humanist and phenomenologist who is disturbed by the invasion of the human body by technology and the substitution of the technological for the human and lived experience. His project is to describe the losses, the disappearances, the substitutions and the invasions of new technologies, noting how technology displaces human faculties and experience, subjecting individuals to ever more powerful modes of technological domination and control. Virilio criticizes the discourses of technophilia, that would celebrate technology as salvation, that are totally positive without critical reservations, but he himself is equally one-sided, developing a highly technophobic and hypercritical discourse that fails to articulate any positive aspects or uses for new technologies, claiming that critical discourses like his own are necessary to counter the overly optimistic and positive discourses. In a sense, this is true and justifies Virilio's predominantly negative discourse, but raises questions concerning the adequacy of Virilio's perspectives on technology as a whole and the extent to which his work is of use in theorizing the new technologies with their momentous and dramatic transformation of every aspect of our social and everyday life.

There is a strong convergence on some themes between Virilio and Jean Baudrillard concerning the radical breaks and ruptures in the contemporary technological world with past modes of social organization, as well as significant differences in theorizing this rupture. For Baudrillard, postmodernity means the end of reality, the end of being able to distinguish between the real and unreal, the end of being anchored in and living in a real material world. On Baudrillard's optic, we dwell increasingly in the realms of hyperreality: broadcast media, the cyberspace of computer interaction, video and computer games, and a range of mass-mediated worlds – film, music, multimedia and VR devices. Moreover, it becomes increasingly difficult to distinguish between the real and hyperreal, leading to a dissolution of the real. Thus, as Virilio notes, 'The question of *modernity* and *postmodernity* is superseded by that of *reality* and *post-reality*' (1994: 84).

Yet Virilio differs from Baudrillard in his theorizing of contemporary technological society. In an interview with John Armitage published in this issue, Virilio says that he disagrees with Baudrillard over the issue of simulation, seeing simulation not as an obliteration of reality, but instead as substitution, in which a technological reality replaces a human one, as photography substitutes itself for real life, or film substitutes the static representation of the real with 'moving pictures', or, in our day, when virtual reality substitutes itself for 'real life'. Consequently, unlike Baudrillard, Virilio believes reality does not disappear, but is rather displaced by another mode of reality, a virtual reality: 'Thus, there is no simulation, but substitution. Reality has become symmetrical. The splitting of reality in two parts is a considerable event which goes beyond simulation' (Virilio, 1997a: 43). Thus, whereas for Baudrillard reality disappears in hyperreality, for Virilio new technologies provide a substitute reality, a virtual reality which becomes more powerful and seductive than ordinary reality.

While Virilio focuses intensely on speed and a simultaneous eruption of a dialectic of implosion and explosion, both he and Baudrillard theorize inertia and the crisis of the subject and the political in the contemporary moment, evoking the end of history and politics. More than Virilio, who often expresses his own political and religious passions, Baudrillard more neutrally describes, accepts, perhaps even affirms, the end of politics and history, in the 'catastrophe of modernity'. Virilio, by contrast, wants to preserve and expand the social and politics against pure war and the military, opposing a transpolitics which denies the continued relevance of modern politics.[3]

Both Virilio and Baudrillard describe the loss of key human capacities and powers in the contemporary world under the influence of always accelerating technology, while Virilio, in *The Lost Dimension* (1991b [1984]) and other works, deals with the decline of the city, its decentering and displacement in the information and postindustrial society. For Virilio, the city is decentered in relation to the rise of suburbs and then telecommunications and new sites of work and interaction in a postindustrial society. Virilio's 'overexposed city' is penetrated by media and advertising, information technology, and what Debord called the 'Society of the Spectacle', overwhelming urban space and life.[4] In Virilio's vision (1991b: 9ff), the urban walls and gateways have given way to a plethora of openings to media channels, information and communication networks and diverse new technologies. Each technology is a window to the outside world, and new cybertechnology obliterates urban boundaries and spaces in favor of the geo-political channels of the global world and atopic cyberspace. Exposed to global culture and communication, the city loses its specificity and city life gives way to technological cyberlife, an aleatory, heterogeneous and fractured space, and a world-time that enables individuals to experience events simultaneously from every time zone in the world.

Henceforth, fragmentary images derived from diverse sources constitute one's 'image of the city', rather than the grids of maps or personal experience. Virilio is analyzing a momentous shift in the image and imaging of the world, of what he calls a 'morphological irruption', of an 'iconological disruption' mutating from perception to quantitative representation and then to digitization. This shift in experience progressively volatilizes the real and obliterates the object of lived experience into technological modes of representation, that constitute a derealization and dematerialization of the object. That is, whereas the object of lived experience was once an object of perception, an object seen and handled by the bodily subject, the objects of cyberspace and virtual reality – as well as the objects of contemporary scientific theory – are abstract and immaterial, generating a new form of technological idealism.

For Virilio, theories of light and speed replace time and space, as a new immateriality and 'new illuminism' comes to dominate contemporary scientific thinking. Virilio believes that, as with the notions of critical mass or temperature, when states of affairs break up and become radically other, space too becomes 'critical' (Virilio, 1997b: 9ff). The notion of 'critical space' refers to the breaking up and dissolution of previous configurations of lived space and time under the impact of technology. For Virilio, telecommunication that eradicates all duration and extension of time in the transmission of messages and images, as well as interactive computer technologies that decenter urban or lived space, all constitute threats and dissolutions of previous configurations of experience as space becomes virtual and takes on new modalities. Lived space and time are replaced by time–light (i.e. the time of the speed of light) and a new 'lumiocentrism' (1997b: 5f, 14f), in which the instantaneous flow of information ruptures past organizations of time and space, requiring new concepts to describe the parameters and processes of the emergent worlds of technology and technological experience.

For Virilio, developments in science and technology are thus obliterating both modern and common-sense views of the world *and* producing new objects and spaces that cannot be explained by modern conceptual schemes. The 'physics of the infinitesimally small' and the cosmological speculations on outer space produce novelties and puzzles that put in question the facts of perception and the realm of experience, while pointing to novel, unperceived and imperceptible entities, which confound common sense and current scientific schemes (Virilio, 1991b). Moreover, new technologies are producing both new domains of experience (i.e. cyberspace, virtual reality, etc.) and new modes of perception and representation (i.e. fractal geometry, computer-generated representations of external and internal realities, etc.) that themselves require new modes of thought and cognition. Such shifts in modes of perception and representation began with cinematic photography that captured motion and phenomena not visible to the naked eye, increased with developments in microscopes and telescopes, and proliferated new modes of perception and representation with computers and new virtual technology.

In short, Virilio is mourning the loss of the object of ocular perception in the emergent forms of technological vision and representation, the displacement of the dimension of direct observation and common sense (1991b: 111), and thus the loss of the materiality and concreteness of the objects of perception constituting the realm of appearance and lived experience. In other words, Virilio mourns the loss of the phenomenological dimension that privileged lived experience. Always a phenomenologist, as he affirms in his interview with John Armitage in this issue, Virilio roots his thought in concrete experience of objects, people and processes in the observed and experienced worlds of everyday life and the natural and social worlds. The new technological worlds, for him, constitute a break and rupture with ordinary experience and thus shift the locus of truth, meaning and validity to, for Virilio, an abstract and enigmatic virtual realm.

His commitment to phenomenology is evident in the text in *Polar Interia* (1998b [1990]: 117f) in which Virilio undertakes a reading of Husserl's analysis of the body and ego as the fixed locus of experience and perception, which he contrasts to the volatilization of the body and subject in contemporary science and philosophy and the experiences of cyberspace and virtual reality. While noting some ways in which Husserl is outdated, Virilio nonetheless shows his commitment to philosophical perspectives committed to the primacy of the body, subjective experience and concrete relations to the earth that he sees as being undermined in both technological experience and contemporary theories which deconstruct experiences of the body and subject.

Virilio's complaint is that 'new technologies of instantaneous inter-activity' – as well as space travel – cause a detachment from our body, other people and our habitual experiences of time, space and the lived environment (1998a: 129). These technologies 'exile us from ourselves and make us lose the ultimate physiological reference: the ponderous mass of the locomotive body, axis, or more exactly seat of comportmental motility and of identity' (1998a: 129). Contemporary science and technology for Virilio are thus producing new forms of experience, new modes of perception and representation, and new objects of experience that decenter the human subject, that replace human cognition with technological vision, and displace human labor power in favor of automated technological production. Losing control over its world, the human subject becomes a mere recording device and the human body is reduced to functions in a technological system. Material reality is decentered and a new technological idealism generates concepts increasingly distant from common sense, the body and material world, the conceptual systems of the past and lived experience.

In addition to the loss of the concrete object of perception and the material reality of the body, Virilio mourns the disappearance of the city, the community and the end of politics in the new globalized technopolis.

Just as computer-aided production and a new virtual form of automation displace human labor power, so too do 'flexible accumulation' (David Harvey), the new global division and organization of production, and international financial markets, databases and simultaneity of information transmission, communication and video representation obliterate previous experiences and concepts of time and space, producing a grave new world of transnational global corporations, political organizations and cities, displacing the national firm, the city, the nation-state, and previous forms and sites of modern politics.

Indeed, for Virilio part of the 'lost dimension' is the end of politics in a world of increased speed and virtualities. This is most evident in the realm of military technology in which the complexity of weapon systems creates ever shorter response times for humans to react to frightening computer-generated information concerning military threats and in which military technology itself can autonomously generate catastrophes ranging from 'friendly fire' incidents to nuclear apocalypse. But the loss of stable referents of the political – the city, state, nation – in the deterritorialized and dematerialized virtual and global spaces of the new information economy and polity, also render human participation in politics perplexing and perhaps futile.

This vision of technological domination, of technology displacing human beings, has echoes of the theories of 'autonomous technology' (Winner) developed by Heidegger, Ellul and other totalizing critics of contemporary technology. Virilio cites Heidegger positively on technology, although he also suggests critiques of Heidegger and totalitarianism, specifically his affiliation with German National Socialism (1986: 90, 113f, passim, and Virilio and Lotringer, 1983: 23f). Thus, while Virilio is quasi-Heideggerian in his perspective on technology, seeing technology as the enframing demiurge of the modern world, as the matrix in which human practice unfolds, he is clearly anti-totalitarian, and might be seen perhaps as a left-Heideggerian. Further, in the light of his Christian religious beliefs, he has certain affinities with Jacques Ellul's radical critique of technology, that sees technology as an autonomous force that is coming to dominate the contemporary world, effacing human freedom and meaning.[5]

Certainly, there are echoes of Ellul's technique, of a totalitarian tendency toward domination and destruction from technological development, running throughout Virilio's work, although he uses more concrete models of war machines, or vision machines, to characterize technology, is less overtly totalizing than Ellul and is more muted in his religious perspectives. Yet there are similar themes of the demise of human autonomy and creativity in a world in which technique and technological development impose their imperatives on human beings, and both have a predominantly negative and critical take on what they see as the totalitarianism of modern technology. Like Ellul, Virilio denies the technological imperative and affirms the dignity and sovereignty of human life and experience against the world of technology and things.

Against all forms of economic determinism and idealist humanism, Virilio posits an autonomous force and power of technology and describes the ways that it constrains economic and social life. Yet in place of Marxian economic determinism, Virilio arguably substitutes a form of military-technological determinism. In his view, the military organization and deployment of people is the origin of proletarianization and pre-dates capitalism; military mobilization is exploited by political, economic and military forces to augment their power; and the result is the ever more sophisticated and lethal development of a war machine, a destructive apparatus that is increasingly automated, lethal, fast, effective and removed from human control or values, producing 'a state of emergency' in which the very fate of the earth and humanity is at stake.

Summing Up: Virilio, War and Technology

> I don't claim to define the situation, I try to reveal tendencies. And I think I've revealed a number of important ones: the question of speed; speed as the essence of war; technology as producer of speed war as logistics, not strategy; war as preparation of means and no longer as battles, declaration of hostilities. (Virilio and Lotringer, 1983: 157)

This passage provides a fair summary of Virilio's major themes up to the point where he began critiquing new information technology, multimedia and biotechnology. Indeed, his sustained interrogation of the virulence and power of military technology constituted a strong contribution, but his work's limitation results from using the model of military technology to interrogate technology as such, and particularly the new information technologies. Virilio was justly distressed by the specter of total war, by the forces of military-technological domination, by the inexorable growth of power and the danger of the military-industrial complex during the Cold War.[6] During this era, the propagation and growth of the military-industrial complex and military state capitalism was the fundamental project and the organizing force behind the development of science, technology and the allocation of public resources. More money was spent on this project than any other domain of existence and military priorities helped determine the mode of science, technology and industry that developed in the Cold War period.

Military capitalism helped produce Big Government, Big Corporations and a Big Military that deployed a tremendous array of manpower, weapons and resources. Computers were largely developed from military imperatives, producing large, centralized calculating machines and information machines, including the so-called 'information superhighway' which had its origins in the defense industry (see Edwards, 1996). The military, big government and giant corporations also controlled scientific and technological research and development, with the military-industrial complex dominating the post-Second World War Cold War economies (see Melman, 1965, 1974).

New information technologies, personal computers, new multimedia and other microtechnologies, however, have a different trajectory, history and, arguably, effects than those technologies criticized by Virilio. While his earlier works stress the connection between the military and technology, he does not engage the corporate forces that are producing the new information and entertainment technologies; that is, while Virilio criticizes the state and the military that developed military technology of vast destruction, he does not focus on the political economy of the mode of information, the corporate forces behind this development, or its imbrication in a global restructuring of capitalism (compare Castells, 1989, 1996, 1997, 1998).

Thus, Virilio's recent books seem to blame the woes of the present moment and dangers emerging from new technologies on technology itself, rather than specific forces like capitalism, the state and corporations. Moreover, he misses a key component of the drama of technology in the present age which involves a titanic struggle between national and international governments and corporations to control the structure, flows and content of the new technologies in contrast to the struggle of individuals and social groups to use the new technologies for their own purposes and projects. Such an optic posits technology as a contested terrain, as a field of struggle between competing social groups and individuals trying to use the new technologies for their own projects. Despite his humanism, there is little agency or politics in Virilio's conceptual universe and he does not delineate the struggles between various social groups for the control of the new technologies and the new politics that they will produce (compare Kellner, forthcoming; Best and Kellner, forthcoming). Simply by damning, demonizing and condemning new technologies, Virilio substitutes moralistic critique for social analysis and political action, reducing his analysis to a lament and jeremiad.

Hence, Virilio has no theory of justice and no politics to counter, reconstruct, reappropriate or transform technology, as well as no counterforces that can oppose technology, other than critical intellectuals like himself. He grounds his politics of technology in a rhetorical critique and condemnation, rather than engaging in a project of examining and carrying out reconstructions of technology that will serve human purposes, reinvigorate a democratic politics and help produce a more egalitarian and just society (compare Feenberg, 1991, 1995, 1999). Instead, his politics are basically conservative, attempting to conserve 'life' and the human against the juggernaut of technology.

While Virilio's take on technology is excessively one-sided and technophobic, his work is still of importance in understanding the great transformation currently under way.[7] Clearly, speed and the instantaneity and simultaneity of information are more important to the new economy and military than ever before, so Virilio's reflections on speed, technology, politics and culture are extremely relevant. Yet he seems so far to have inadequately conceptualized the enormous changes wrought by an infotainment society and the advent of a new kind of multimedia information-entertainment technology. If my hunch is correct, his view of technology and speed is integrally structured by his intense focus on war and the military, while his entire mode of thought is a form of military-technological determinism, which forces him not only to downplay the important role of capital, but also the complex ambiguities, the mixture of positive and negative features, of the new technologies now proliferating and changing every aspect of society and culture in the present era.

Virilio thus emerges as a astute theorist of the post-Second World War and Cold War era of the military, with the domination of military technology and military capitalism, but is without an adequate analysis of the complicity of capitalism and those economic forces that use technology for power and profit, instead putting all blame for contemporary problems on technology and its deployment by the military and perhaps the state. But, against Virilio, it should be recognized that new technologies are part of the capitalist project, that capital recognizes, along with Marx, that surplus value is gained by productive deployment of new technologies, and that technology provides powerful weapons of profit and social control. Yet, to spin the dialectic in another direction, such technology can be appropriated, reconfigured and deployed in a multiplicity of ways so that it is a mistake to reject new technologies out of hand, as does Virilio, because of its allegedly nefarious nature and effects.

By eschewing critical social theory, Virilio does not have the resources to theorize the complex relations between capital, technology, the state and the military in the present age, substituting a highly elusive and evocative method for systematic theoretical analysis and critique. Virilio himself acknowledges his rhetorical approach to writing, noting:

> I don't believe in explanations. I believe in suggestions, in the obvious quality of the implicit. Being an urbanist and architect, I am too used to constructing clear systems, machines that work well. I don't believe it's writing's job to do the same thing. I don't like two-and-two-is-four-type writing. That's why, finally, I respect Foucault more than I like him. (Virilio and Lotringer, 1983: 38–9)

Indeed, Virilio's style is extremely telescopic, leaping from topic to topic with alacrity, juxtaposing diffuse elements and themes, proliferating images, quotes and ideas which rapidly follow each other, often overwhelming the reader and making it difficult to grasp the thrust of his argument. His work is fragmentary and disruptive, deploying collage methods of assembling pieces of quotes, examples and analysis, while quickly moving from one topic to another.

One could argue, in fact, that the speed which Virilio so well theorizes enters into the very fabric and substance of his writings. Virilio's texts move along quickly, they catch their topics on the run, they overwhelm with detail, but rarely develop a topic in systematic and sustained fashion. His style thus reflects his themes with speed, fragmentation and complexity the warp and woof of his work. One wonders, however, whether a critic of speed, war and technology should not occasionally slow down and more carefully and patiently delineate his theoretical position.

To some extent, Virilio exemplifies Walter Benjamin's (1969) method of illuminations and fragments, which creates constellations of ideas and images to illuminate specific phenomena and events. Like Benjamin, Virilio circles his prey with images, quotes, often startling and original ideas, and then quickly moves on to his next topic. Virilio believes in the virtue of breaks and interruptions, of gaps and absences, eschewing systematic theorizing. But although Virilio pursues some of the same themes as Benjamin, deploys a similar method and cites him frequently, there are major differences. Whereas Benjamin, in the spirit of Brecht, wanted to 'refunction' new technologies to make them instruments of progressive social change and to develop political strategies to exploit the potentially progressive features of new technologies, Virilio is relentlessly critical, eschews developing a technopolitics and nowhere speaks of using or refunctioning technology to serve positive ends.

Thus, Virilio is highly one-sided and does not develop a dialectical conception of technology or a progressive technopolitics. So far, Virilio has produced no master oeuvre that will pull together his ideas and perspectives, that will provide a synthetic vision. His long interviews with Sylvère Lotringer (1983) and John Armitage (in this issue) contain the best overviews of what I take to be his most valuable work, but it remains to be seen whether he will attempt to develop a critical theory of technology for the present age. In addition, as a critical philosopher, Virilio is quite ascetic, never articulating the normative position from which he carries on such a sustained and ferocious critique of technology. He seems to assume something like a philosophical humanism, that human beings are significant by virtue of their capacity for speech, reason, integral bodily experience, morality, political deliberation and participation, and creative and spiritual activity, while technology is seen as undermining these human capacities, taking over human functions and rendering humans subservient to technological rationality. Virilio himself, however, does not adequately articulate the humanist or religious dimension of his critique and, as noted, describes himself as a materialist and abstains from developing the normative perspective from which he carries out his critique.

But first and foremost his critique of technology has echoes of Heidegger's and Ellul's complaints concerning the totalitarian ethos of modern, and we would now add postmodern, technology, the ways that its instruments and instrumentality dominate human beings and create a novel world in which things and objects increasingly come to rule human beings. To the extent that Virilio's works illuminate the great transformation that we are currently undergoing and warn us of its dangers, too often ignored by the boosters and digerati of the new technologies, he provides a useful antidote to the uncritical celebrations of the coming computopia. But to the extent that he fails to provide critical perspectives which delineate how new technologies can be used for democratization, human empowerment and to create a better world, he remains a one-sided critic rather than a philosopher of technology who grasps the full range, effects and possibilities of the high-tech adventure that we are currently undergoing.

Notes

1. His early text *Bunker Archeology* (1975) explores this theme; see also Virilio (1986: 3ff) and Virilio and Lotringer (1983: 2f).

2. Virilio suggests that in science a Hall of Accidents should be put next to each Hall of Machines: 'Every technology, every science should choose its specific accident and reveal it as a product – not in a moralistic, protectionist way (safety first), but rather as a product to be "epistemo-technically" questioned. At the end of the nineteenth century, museums exhibited machines: at the end of the twentieth century, I think we must grant the formative dimensions of the accident its rightful place in a new museum' (Virilio and Lotringer, 1983: 35). English novelist J.G. Ballard actually staged an exhibition of wrecked cars in London in 1966, described in his 1970 novel *The Atrocity Exhibition*, while an apocalyptic vision of Western civilization's systems of control and circulation erupting in proliferations of car wrecks informed Ballard's 1973 novel *Crash* and the 1996 film directed by David Cronenberg based on the novel.

3. In an interview with Sylvère Lotringer, Virilio states that: 'For me, trans-politics is the beginning of the end. That's where my understanding of it radically differs from Jean Baudrillard's; for him it's positive. For me, it's *totally* negative. I fight against the disappearance of politics. I'm not saying that we should revert to ancient democracy, stop the clock and all that. I'm saying that there's work to be done . . . in order to re-establish politics' (Virilio and Lotringer, 1983: 28). One might argue, however, that Baudrillard does not see the end of politics, or 'trans-politics', as 'positive', but rather as inevitable in an era in which politics, aesthetics, sexuality and culture implode; see Baudrillard (1994).

4. On Debord and the Situationist International, see Best and Kellner (1997: Chapter 3, and forthcoming).

5. When asked if Ellul or Christian existential philosopher Gabriel Marcel influenced his thought, he affirmed the influence of Ellul while denying the impact of Marcel. See Virilio's interview with John Armitage published in this issue and Virilio (1997b: 139f).

6. Virilio well captures the political-military insanity of the 1980s in texts like *L'Horizon negatif*, excerpted in Virilio (1998a: 73–94).

7. Virilio sometimes denies he is a technophobe and said in the interview with John Armitage that he is for Apple computers against IBM and in an interview with James Der Derian (1998a: 6), he claims that he 'is in love with technology', but these comments are a smokescreen to hide his virulent technophobia, for the overwhelming thrust of his major works is harshly negative and hypercritical.

References

Baudrillard, Jean (1994) *The Illusion of an End*. Oxford: Polity.

Benjamin, Walter (1969) *Illuminations*. New York: Schocken Books.

Best, Steven, and Douglas Kellner (1997) *The Postmodern Turn*. New York: Guilford Press.

Best, Steven, and Douglas Kellner (forthcoming) *The Postmodern Adventure*. New York: Guilford Press.

Castells, Manuel (1989) *The Informational City: The Space of Flows*. Oxford: Basil Blackwell.

Castells, Manuel (1996) *The Rise of the Network Society*. Oxford: Blackwell.

Castells, Manuel (1997) *The Power of Identity*. Oxford: Blackwell.

Castells, Manuel (1998) *End of Millennium*. Oxford: Blackwell.

Edwards, Paul (1996) *The Closed World: Computers and the Politics of Discourse in Cold War America*. Cambridge, MA: MIT Press.

Feenberg, Andrew (1991) *Critical Theory of Technology*. New York: Oxford University Press.

Feenberg, Andrew (1995) *Alternative Modernity*. Berkeley: University of California Press.

Feenberg, Andrew (1999) *Questioning Technology*. New York and London, Routledge.

Kellner, Douglas (forthcoming) 'Toward a Radical Democratic Technopolitics', *Angelaki*.

Melman, Seymour (1965) *Our Depleted Society*. New York: Holt, Rinehart and Winston.

Melman, Seymour (1974) *The Permanent War Economy: American Capitalism in Decline*. New York: Simon and Schuster.

Virilio, Paul (1975) *Bunker Archaeology*, trans. George Collins. Paris: Les Éditions du Demi-Cercle.

Virilio, Paul (1986 [1977]) *Speed & Politics*. New York: Semiotext(e), Foreign Agents Series, Autonomedia.

Virilio, Paul (1989 [1984]) *War and Cinema: The Logistics of Perception*. London: Verso.

Virilio, Paul (1991a [1980]) *The Aesthetics of Disappearence*. New York: Semiotext(e), Foreign Agents Series, Autonomedia.

Virilio, Paul (1991b [1984]) *The Lost Dimension*. New York: Semiotext(e), Foreign Agents Series, Autonomedia.

Virilio, Paul (1994 [1988]) *The Vision Machine*. Bloomington: University of Indiana Press.

Virilio, Paul (1995a) 'Global Algorithm 1.7: The Silence of the Lambs: Paul Virilio in Conversation', in *C-Theory* [www.freedonia.com/ctheory].

Virilio, Paul (1995b) 'Speed and Information: Cyberspace Alarm!', in *C-Theory* [www.freedonia.com/ctheory].

Virilio, Paul (1995c) 'The Information Bomb: A Conversation between Paul Virilio and Friedrich Kittler', translated and forthcoming in John Armitage (ed.) *New Cultural Theory and Techno-Politics*, *Angelaki* 4(2).

Virilio, Paul (1995d [1993]) *The Art of the Motor*. Minneapolis: University of Minnesota Press.

Virilio, Paul (1996) *Cybermonde, la politique de pire*. Paris: Textuel.

Virilio, Paul (1997a) 'Cyberwar, God and Television: An Interview with Paul Virilio', pp. 41–8 in *Digital Delirium*. New York: St Martin's Press.

Virilio, Paul (1997b [1995]) *Open Sky*. London: Verso.
Virilio, Paul (1998a) *The Virilio Reader*, ed. James Der Derian. Malden, MA and Oxford: Blackwell.
Virilio, Paul (1998b [1990]) *Polar Inertia*. London: Sage.
Virilio, Paul and Sylvère Lotringer (1983) *Pure War*. New York: Semiotext(e), Foreign Agents Series, Autonomedia.

Douglas Kellner is George Kneller Chair in the Philosophy of Education at UCLA and is author of many books on social theory, politics, history and culture, including *Camera Politica: The Politics and Ideology of Contemporary Hollywood Film* (co-authored with Michael Ryan), *Critical Theory, Marxism, and Modernity*, *Jean Baudrillard: From Marxism to Postmodernism and Beyond*, *Postmodern Theory: Critical Interrogations* (with Steven Best), *Television and the Crisis of Democracy*, *The Persian Gulf TV War*, *Media Culture, and the Postmodern Turn* (with Steven Best).

Virilio and New Media

Sean Cubitt

I T IS ALWAYS FLATTERING to read that you inhabit the ultimate moment in history, and that your own time witnesses the definitive crisis of your civilization. Much of the interest and attraction of Virilio's writings comes from his belief that we inhabit today a crisis of perception, precipitated through the militarization of perceptual technologies and the embedding of these technologies in the familiar environs of the street, the home and the architecture of daily life. This crisis of architecture, in which the solid geometry of buildings gives way to the fluid transparencies of media, he sees inaugurated in the time-lapse chrono-photographic experiments of Etienne Jules Marey (for example Virilio, 1994: 60–1; see also Ceram, 1965; Dagognet, 1992), precursors to cinema, and in any given text of Virilio's is seen as culminating in the latest upgraded and accelerated medium of transmission or recording. If much of his assertive and allusive, elliptical and epigrammatic writings are crowded with hyperbole and unsubstantiated assertions, yet the work seems to capture key elements of our awe before the new constellation of communicative technologies, our belittlement under the regime of contemporary mediated and networked societies. Yet Virilio's is a deeply liberal critique, formed not only in his Christian faith (see Virilio and Lotringer, 1997: passim) but in the centrality he affords to individuals. Faced with the collapse of the values he holds dearest, Virilio must recount the classical liberal scenario of Armageddon. Virilio's liberalism is in the lineage neither of Stirner's right-wing libertarianism, the deep subtext of much North American neo-liberal techno-utopianism, nor of Kropotkin and the agrarian utopianism that occasionally surfaces in contemporary writings critical of technological rationalism. Instead, it forms an anarchist mirror to the pessimistic Marxism of Adorno. But where Adorno is concerned to discover in the European past the roots of Nazism and authoritarianism, for Virilio the burning issue is a contemporary apocalypse. That catastrophe is ultimately ethical, since the progress of

■ *Theory, Culture & Society* 1999 (SAGE, London, Thousand Oaks and New Delhi),
Vol. 16(5–6): 127–142
[0263-2764(199910/12)16:5–6;127–142;009962]

media technologies leads to the destruction of the properly human will, the ground for ethical choice.

Virilio's epigrammatic, even ideogrammatic prose traces a media history, deeply informed by current media and communications scholarship, in the attempt to trace not so much the genesis as the trajectory of a historical process under whose wheels we are even now being crushed. According to his central thesis, the militarization of society at large, and the media in particular, produces an acceleration of communication which demands of us an accommodation to rapidly shrinking technological time-scales. This is the point in mediated perception into which Virilio inserts his concept of picnolepsia, the momentary lapse in consciousness which facilitates the invention of cinema, since it acclimatizes us to the production of continuities where there are none, and which ultimately will lead to 'the authority of electronic automatism, reducing our will to zero' (Virilio, 1991a: 104). Virilio spends little time analysing the films of the Lumière brothers, often seen as the originals of the documentary and realist traditions of cinema, and instead repeatedly returns to the illusionistic magical tableaux of Georges Méliès. Marey's chronophotography, Virilio argues, established a science of the invisible, revealing what the eye is too slow too catch. In the trick films of the 1890s:

> What science attempts to illuminate, 'the non-seen of the lost moments', becomes with Méliès *the very basis of the production of appearance* of his invention, what he shows of reality is what reacts continually to the absences of the reality which has passed. (Virilio, 1991a: 17)

The problem addressed here, of the ability of the eye to establish continuity between frames ('persistence of vision') and even more so the ability to effect the transition from shot to shot, have been central to the discussion of cinema since the earliest times. It forms the nub of the famous Kuleshov effect, an experiment in montage in which the audience reinterpret a single shot of the actor Mosjoukin according to whether the following shot is of a plate of soup, a coffin or a pretty girl (Kuleshov, 1973).

Film theory addresses this retrospective Gestalt in a number of ways, one of the most influential being the theory of suture advanced by Lacanian film analysts of the 1970s, according to which the closure of the film text depended on the responsibility assumed by the spectator to become the subject of that text, so completing its absences (marked by framing and editing) by becoming present as spectator (see Dayan, 1976; Heath, 1977/8; Oudart, 1977/8). As Rothman puts it, this view of film can be read as 'intrinsically tyrannical' (Rothman, 1976: 453); the question remains as to whether it is, as Rothman believes, the theory that is tyrannical, or the media. Suture played a crucial role in restoring a temporal dimension to screen-theoretical accounts of cinematic subjectivity, a major crux of structural analysis. Effectively, what the theory of suture argued is almost exactly the opposite of Virilio: that the viewer is constituted as a presence by the absences of the filmic text. Where the suture theory scores, contra Rothman, is in giving to this newly constituted subject in return an active role in the construction of the film. If, in the post-'68 fervour of film theory in France, Oudart sees this as a complicity in the oppression operated by Hollywood, it can also give us the grounds for a more mature understanding of the interactivity between audiences and texts now that media studies is more forgiving of popular pleasures and more interested in the audience's active participation in the construction of meaning.

Virilio's picnoleptic theory, by contrast, assumes the subordination of the viewer not to the textual production of the film, but to the apparatus of the cinema. Though this view too had its place in 1970s screen theory (see Baudry, 1975, 1985; Heath and de Lauretis, 1980), the specificity of the individual film was always a retardant on generalization about the medium as such. In Virilio's case, we come into contact with a media theoretical tradition for which, on the McLuhan principle, the medium rather than its individual instances is the message. This creates a crux in Virilio's thought, since to some extent, especially in *The Aesthetics of Disappearance* (1991a), he offers not only a sociological account of the powers of the militarized media, but the elements of a phenomenology of mediated experience. Where screen theory gave itself the task of understanding the production of subjectivity in the textual production of the reality effect, picnoleptic theory attempts to understand the abolition of subjectivity in the disappearance of reality. In a lucid summary of his earlier work, Virilio argues a distinction between the 'small' or 'passive optics' he associates with the geometries of our immediate environs and the 'big' or 'active' optics of wave-particle physics and the weapons and transmission media that operate at the speed of light. The former puns on *'grandeur nature'*, translatable as both 'life-sized' and 'natural grandeur', an experiential category of vision based on unmediated, immediate vision. The latter, 'big optics', is the optics of lasers, radar, television, to which materiality is transparent, and which reduces the human world at first to a tiny globe spinning in empty space and finally to a point disappearing into unreality. Founded in the irreality of quantum mechanics and technologically sourced outside the human perspective in satellites and aircraft, 'the *active* big optics of the speed of light are unleashed (from beyond any horizon) onto the intermittent perception of the SMALL WORLD made transparent by waves carrying their various signals' (Virilio, 1992: 88). The problem of intermittence still haunts perception, the more so, according to Virilio, as the photo-mechanical media, with their quasi-physiological pulse of 24 frames per second, are replaced by opto-electronic circuits of pure information. Where analogue media still claim at least a resemblance to actual objects and actual vision, the digital image is now entirely abstracted, converted into signal and number, circulated at speeds that defy the human sensorium. The picnoleptic moment becomes then an ontological quality of the mediation of appearances, which in their most recent manifestations as satellite observations or immersive virtual reality systems reveal the destiny which all mechanical mediation has pursued under the governance of militaristic modernity: the eradication of distance: 'how can you not', he asks, 'as of now dread the advent of a deep feeling of confinement of man locked in an environment at once deprived of horizon and of *optical depth?*' (Virilio, 1992: 88).

The governing theme of this discourse is clearly one of loss, summarized most apothegmatically as 'the more speed increases, the faster freedom decreases' (Virilio, 1986: 142) and, in a paraphrase of Kipling: 'the concept of reality is always the first victim of war' (Virilio, 1989a: 33). The implication – that freedom and reality are mutually dependent – of course begs the question of where such an innocent state of real freedom and free reality has ever existed. There seems to be some suggestion that this state exists in a divine time outside of human history, as an Ideal. Virilio rarely addresses the issue directly or positively, but by indirections amid the grim warnings concerning the accelerating degradation of human and material reality. Claiming his position as 'realist' (Oliveira, 1996: np), he nonetheless occupies an exclusively critical stance towards the technologies of transport and transmission which have, in his analysis, reformulated what it means to be human. In this way, as Kellner has proposed (Kellner, 1998: np), he follows in the phenomenological footsteps of Martin Heidegger (1977) and Jacques Ellul (1964) in offering an account of mass media as totalitarian, adding a specific spin concerning the loss of the local: as he expresses it to Oliveira, 'Globalization – and don't we have a paradox here? – also means the end of one entire world: the world of the particular and of the localized' (Oliveira, 1996: np). The human scale of perception is inundated by the sheer speed of communication, and in its place there arrives a fierce, inhuman view whose motive is assault and destruction, and whose mechanical delivery systems not only carry into daily life the imperatives of warfare but, replacing the human scale of face-to-face perception, deprive us of the bases from which we might resist its domination.

The position is summed in an essay dating from the mid-1980s:

The will-to-power of those industrial nations who, at the turn of the century, practised the techniques of total war, has now been replaced by the theoretical operations of a totally involuntary war, on the part of post-industrial nations investing increasingly in informatics, automation, and cybernetics. In these societies, the use of human labor-force and the direct responsibility of people has been displaced by the powers of 'anticipated' and 'deferred' substitution, the power of the system of auto-directed armaments, self-programmed detection networks, and automatic respondents who lead humanity to the confinement of a hopeless waiting. (Virilio, 1991b: 136)

Like Baudrillard in the same period (Baudrillard, 1994: 32–3), Virilio reads the armed stand-off of the Cold War as a mutual pact between the antagonists to guarantee that both can extend their power over their own territories, a process Virilio describes as 'endo-colonization'. But in the period since the fall of the Berlin Wall and the effective end of global bipartisan politics, the motive force of cultural change has shifted towards the imagined enemy, now dematerialized as potential or virtual, whose fictive character we had learned to delineate in the harshest years of nuclear deterrence.

In one sense, the Gulf War of 1991 was the last gasp of Cold War-fare, a war based on the attempt to deter the enemy from striking. But in another it foreshadowed what has occupied Virilio throughout the subsequent years, the nature, dimensions and impact of information war. Again like Baudrillard (1995), Virilio understands Desert Storm as a derealization of warfare, not only in terms of the news coverage (his book on the subject is called *Desert Screen*), nor exclusively in terms of the abstraction of the combatants from the results of their actions (an effect he traces back at least to 'the pressurized cockpits of US Superfortress bombers' which 'had become artificial synthesisers that shut out the world of the senses' at the end of the Second World War [Virilio, 1989a: 24]). Much more than either, the accumulated data on the battlefield had allowed US pilots and technicians to simulate battle in the Iraqi desert in computer models and ground-based flight-simulators for several years prior to the actual events. The upshot of this dematerialized mode of information warfare was the terrifying effectiveness of the US military machine in the Gulf. Moreover, the enemy in this instance occupied effectively a different historical period to the US, fighting for a territory in which they still believed, and in which they had a stake. For the information warrior, territory, according to Virilio, has no meaning whatsoever. It has been assimilated into the datastreams of battle computers, and has become immaterial.

Ironically, the automobile and the cinema alike produce an immobile spectator of action, not a mobile participant. From the first pan shot of 1896 to the broadcasting technologies of the post-war period, he argues in 'The Last Vehicle', travelling has been diminished, losing first the transit in the acceleration of trains, cars and planes, then the act of departure, substituting 'the primacy of arrival (which is momentary)' (Virilio, 1989b: 118). With the diminution of journeys, there arrives the possibility of the elimination of space. Global electronic information and transmission systems now provide the technological infrastructure not only for the destruction of space, but for its replacement with the 'time of light', the instantaneous transmission of data at the limit speed of the universal constant. But while Virilio, consistently and inaccurately describing transmission rates as 'instantaneous', argues for the triumph of time (speed) over space, he is also able to offer an insight into the changing nature of time. 'Today', he notes in *The Vision Machine*, ' "extensive" time has given way to "intensive" time. This deepens the infinitely small of duration, of microscopic time, the final figure of eternity rediscovered outside the imaginary of the extensive eternity of bygone centuries' (Virilio, 1994: 72). Clearly for Virilio technology and science are barely distinguishable, science acting as the discursive expression of technology's historical imperative. The advanced dematerialization he sees in quantum physics, as indeed in the fractal mathematics of emergence, is intrinsic to the opto-electronic technologies which are busily substituting for first-hand experience. Equally clearly, he goes against the flow of Anglo-Saxon postmodernism, with its emphasis on spatialization and the diffusion of history and temporality. Instead, he sees the inhabiting of the moment as the end of historical experience, an experience itself premised on spatial and especially local awareness. The picnoleptic moment has ceased to function as the motive inattention that permits the illusion of cinema, and instead has become the goal of new data-streaming technologies whose speed exceeds that of perception, and which therefore promote a permanent state of unawareness, of null experience, with all activity delivered over to the optical machine, and all passivity delivered to the immobilized passenger aboard Concorde or immersed in virtual reality.

One might forgive Virilio his typical use of 'final' and 'ultimate', the constant rhetorical companions of a certain journalistic urgency, were it not for the apocalypse which they so certainly announce. This vision, I would argue, derives from Virilio's misunderstanding of the nature of mediation in general and network communications in particular, a misunderstanding that limits his analysis to the existential position of the individual. 'The thing described takes over from the real thing' (Virilio, 1995a: 43) in the politics of disinformation, indeed the 'essential culture of disinformation' (Virilio, 1995a: 61). This substitution or commutation of virtual for physical proximity reduces to zero that distance which, for Virilio, is constitutive of human identity: the distance between observer and observed, subject and object. Disinformation is then the creation of a fiction in which the world is no longer object over against the subject, but simply a malleable and consumable entity, almost a Heideggerian 'standing-reserve'. But this analysis, once again like Baudrillard's, derives from a sense that the business of mediation is representation. When, as he believes, representation ceases to evoke a real world of immediate perception, the representational media also curtail the possibility of democratic representation.

Liberalism is a philosophy founded in individual identity. In Virilio's pessimistic liberal anarchism, the crisis of representation occurs in the essential subject–object relation though which identity marks itself off from the world and the others. But mediation is not representation: media serve to mediate, not between subjects and objects, but between subjects. This conclusion, already adumbrated in the theory of suture, provides us with the grounds for a social theory of mediation. Screen-theoretical work argues that identity, individuality and subjectivity are constructed, in a mediated society, through mediation. Individuality is then an end product of the mediation process, not its foundation. It is Virilio's imaginary embattled individual, clinging to identity in the face of technology, that grounds his more paranoid Jeremiads, and blinds him to the mutuality involved in media productivity. Where Virilio sees only the diminution and vanishing of subjectivity, the theory of suture allows us to understand subject formation as always already ephemeral, the always temporary and contingent structure of the self in the experience of media. What is being lost in the acceleration of communications media is only a historically specific mode of subjectivity, not subjectivity as such. It is only the individual – along with such perquisites as freedom and privacy – which disappears, faced with the new necessity for a blurred boundary between the public and, for lack of the private, the intimate sphere of what perhaps we can still refer to as the unconscious. This unconscious, however, is framed less by the individuation process of the bourgeois family, and more by the interactive, fluid subjectivities of online communities. In a rare moment of positivity, Virilio concludes a 1995 article by suggesting that:

> We have to acknowledge that the new communication technologies will only further democracy if, and only if, we oppose from the beginning the caricature of global society being hatched for us by big multinational corporations throwing themselves at a breakneck pace on the information superhighways. (Virilio, 1995b: np)

It is an unusual moment in which the possibility of political action is entertained,[1] and the opening up of this possibility comes from the equally unusual suggestion of a 'we': a community of the like-minded. It is also surprising to find Virilio recognizing that there are other agencies beyond self-activating technological change, and that the capitalization of online communications is, at least in the short-term, the major threat to the democratic capabilities of the net. The lack of such hopeful eschatologies among his major statements is a direct consequence of the grounding of his philosophical liberalism in the theory of representation.

I cited earlier Virilio's rewriting of Kipling, equating war's first casualty, truth, with the casualty reality. The slippage is effected, once again, by dependence on representation theory, in which the key function of signification is to establish referential links between subject and object. This surely sits well with the definitions of communication offered by contemporary cognitive science and information theory, for which the mathematics of communication systems and the metaphor of mind as computer both rely on the concept of signal as datum, byte or unit of information. But from the point of view of media theory, emphasis on reference ignores the centrality to mediated communication of the phatic, the establishment of social and cultural solidarity in dialogue, as when we ask almost content-free questions like 'How are you?' From the standpoint of a mediation theory, the history of the phatic mode includes the history of exclusions from communicative solidarity, the denial of their presence and the turn towards re-presenting them as objects external to the world of communication. In fact, I believe it is quite possible to argue that the phatic is the central function of communication, to the point that even the exchange of orders or information are modes of phatic solidarity. Emphasizing the phatic suggests that the truth-content of messages is not necessarily restricted to their content but to their address. It is curious in this context that Virilio, normally so attentive to shifting technologies, centres so much of his attention on production and transmission technologies, and so little on the structure of distribution. It is distribution which holds the key to the massification of the media, from the film exchanges that gave rise to the Hollywood studios (see Gomery, 1992) to the global ambitions of the Microsoft Channel. Distribution not only focuses on the address to audiences, both in marketing and in such day-to-day rhetorical truisms as 'We bring you live pictures' or 'Thank you for welcoming us into your home', with their implicit announcement of power relations, and also in the address characteristic of specific technologies like the Internet browser window or the layout of newspaper pages. It also draws us back to the relationships between people which appear, from Virilio's liberal point of view, as the magical relation between objects, specifically the vanishing world and the ever-more present media.

Virilio's theory of representation appears to rest rather specifically on a concept of truth as total and complete, and completely identified with the existence of a pre-existing world, a unity only ruptured by its communication. Virilio's position is not only liberal but humanist, a humanism arising from a Christian phenomenology curiously akin to that of realist film critic André Bazin. In *The Vision Machine*, Virilio addresses the intersection of militarization and representation in terms of 'the logistics of perception':

> It is a war of images and sounds, rather than objects and things, in which winning is simply a matter of not losing sight of the opposition. The will to see all, to know all, at every moment, everywhere, the will to universalised illumination: a scientific permutation on the eye of God which would forever rule out the surprise, the accident, the irruption of the unforeseen. (Virilio, 1994: 70)

War has changed, in the era of Stealth bombers and smart weapons, by a process of absolute acceleration, from the face-to-face struggle for occupation of physical space to a thoroughly mediated struggle for absolute surveillance. This absolute surveillance and its counter, camouflage and deception, are extended to the politics of the militarized state. In the meantime, visual media accelerated to the point of instantaneity have altered the terms of perception, through the ambition to emulate God, in the erasure of the contingent which marks the perception of reality.

In Virilio's terms, mediation eradicates first the substance, the immutable essence of objects and later, in a second movement from mechanical to electronic media, obliterates even the *accidence*, the material form in which substance presents itself to perception. The reality of an object's image is thus displacing the virtuality of its presence (Virilio, 1994: 64); that is, in transmission, even the materiality of the image is substituted in a process of virtualization in some ways the offspring of military dissimulation. We are then faced with the 'fusion of the object with its equivalent image' (Virilio, 1994: 68) tending towards 'an artificial reality involving digital simulation that would oppose the "natural reality" of classical experience' (Virilio, 1994: 76).

Here, as throughout his work, Virilio depends upon a belief in the wholeness of perception independent of cognition. This depends upon (1) a whole event or state of affairs in the world which is (2) simultaneous with (3) a whole perception of that state of affairs. This phenomenology of perception, which appears to derive from Husserl, shares Husserl's dilemma over the relation between perception, memory (retentions) and expectation (protensions). Immediate perception is allied, in both Husserl and Virilio, with temporal and spatial contiguity and with instantaneous and mutual wholeness of both perception and perceived. Yet the duration introduced by cognitive functions of retention and protension shatters the wholeness of both. Virilio correctly notes that mediated perception does not share this immediacy. However, since he does not believe that perception is in every case mediated, both by the phenomenal aspect that the perceived takes on in the moment of perception, and by the retentions and protensions of the perceiver, he understands mediation as a fall from grace, from a natural perception which, in its integration of human and world, provided the basis of human identity. He is therefore free to declare that higher degrees and velocities of mechanical perception are the phenomenal form of a collapse of both humanity and reality, 'as though our society were sinking into the darkness of a voluntary blindness' (Virilio, 1994: 76).

To turn Virilio on his head, it is sufficient to point out, as Derrida does in his critique of Husserlian phenomenology of perception (1973: 60–9), that consciousness has no present. Moreover, since the world itself is never self-present either, perception is already mediation. This is not to say that we should therefore embrace uncritically the loss of human identity, or that we should abandon the Bazinian project for a cinema in which 'life might . . . be the self into which film finally changes it' (Bazin, 1971: 82) . It does suggest, however, that we proceed beyond a state in which social relations appear in 'the fantastical form of relations between things' (Marx, 1976: 165). As Linda Brigham argued in the excellent Special Issue of the online journal *Speed* devoted to his work, like Habermas Virilio interrogates 'the social effects of media in terms of their relation to a prior social and perceptual condition' (Brigham, 1995: np). But communication is not about the recuperation of some prior truth of things, but rather a perpetual and mutual building and negotiation of truth, reality and subjectivity. Virilio's representation theory understands truth as an impossibly total content of communication: that is why it is perpetually disappointed, or forced to confront the human impossibility of rendering in mediated form the totality of truth associated with an object. But if instead we were to direct attention towards the distributive moment, with its extended labour performed on the materials of mediation, we find instead that truth is always partial, always postponed and always negotiated, while offering also an understanding of the strategic structural domination practised by the mega-corporations of the infotainment industries over the distributive media. If it seems niggling to correct Virilio's description of new computer-mediated communication as 'instantaneous', it is an important detail, most of all because the time needed to download a file is the temporal intervention into the mediation process of the labour time necessary to compose, store and decode its content. If it is a key job of commercial media to disguise the processes of their production, the very delay of distribution channels nonetheless bring back to us the labour involved in their making.

Without an understanding of the control structures of the media industries, Virilio is cast back on the meagre resources of the isolated individual, unsurprisingly now envisioned as the stunned receiver of a vast, unintelligible, real-time data-stream. At such a juncture, *'Vision, once substantial, becomes accidental'* (Virilio, 1994: 13; original emphasis). This slogan carries with it the double meanings of substance and accident, read in the light of Nicholas de Cusa (Virilio, 1997: 17). If, as appears here, the substance is the truth of the object, then the truth lost in digital representations is that ideal form that precedes and exceeds the limits of the mundane, while *accidence*, which is all that can be captured in photo-mechanical or opto-electronic media, is the merely ephemeral and worldly. Yet this ephemerality and worldliness are surely the most significantly material aspects of the object, not least because they give the lie to the thing-in-itself, and require us to speak of its appearance to some other, that is, its dependence on its subject or, in a mediated world, its dependence on its mediation. In this sense objects exist, as objects, only as mediations, only as they signify in relations between people

For Virilio, on the contrary, the triumph of ephemeral appearance is a sign of the abolition of the weight, mass, bulk and depth of truth. Their obdurate otherness, their truth, gave objects a position relative to subjects that they have lost in the instantaneity of transmission. Without that relative position, accident takes on its second meaning, of catastrophe. Ungoverned now by truth, rendered into the quantum fluctuations of hypermedia, appearances circulating at unheard-of speeds bring us to the brink of info-war and data-crash. Such is Virilio's account of the 1989 Black Friday crash, which he reads as the uncontrolled acceleration of machine-driven trading in derealized stocks and shares, rather than as a function of anarchic capital. Likewise, hacker hits on power supplies and databanks appear to him as the disaster which is always invented at the same moment as the vehicle, in the same way that derailments and wrecks are the necessary accompaniment of trains and cars. The 'general accident' (Virilio, 1997: 132) will prove Virilio right in the moment that it makes all statements of truth or probability impossible. The insubstantial will, in that moment of wreckage, ruin the substance of the world, homogenizing all differences previously guaranteed by the distance between objects and subjects.

If, however, we deny to Virilio his philosophical liberalism and his ontological substance, what can we draw from his poetics of transmission? Reversing his evaluation of the changing nature of mediation, we can take a conception of the new centrality of the ephemeral in human affairs. The true difference between computer-mediated communications and the older forms of print and photo-mechanical media is that the heart of computer media lies in distribution, not recording. The storage media associated with computers are notoriously liable to corruption and infection. The only hope for permanence is in proliferation of copies, that is, in the distribution of texts across a variety of media and machines. But even this belies the capacity of computer files to be overwritten: corrected, discussed, amended or erased. Like the death of privacy, the end of permanence is a frightening effect of new media, one that drives Virilio to distraction. Yet in that vertiginous impossibility of archiving the world's Internet traffic, we confront not the desecration of the temple of learning, but the avenue of escape from the Foucauldian archive. It is that archive, as much as the phenomenological *Umwelt*, that constitutes the horizon of the self, whose loss Virilio so greatly mourns, but which from a different viewpoint becomes a crucial act of emancipation.

We can also, I believe, abstract from his description of the collapsing gap between subject and object a vision of the increasing integration of subject with subject in the mediation of objects. Neither cognitive science nor phenomenology allows for the socialization of subjectivity in a mediated world: the challenge remains to provide such a social psychology and social phenomenology in the pursuit of a sociology of communication that recognizes its centrality, as Virilio does, but also permits intervention and creativity. The old liberal-anarchist tirades against state and technology cannot bring us a politics adequate to the new media formations. That task remains to be undertaken. But here again Virilio does give us some avenues to explore, most of all in his work on memory. Noting the movement from older theories of retinal retention to the theory of cognitive schemata in the formation of memory, he insists on 'the role of memorisation in immediate perception' (Virilio, 1994: 61). Such instantaneous memorization, demanded by the flicker of images at 24 or 25 frames per second, allows both for subliminal effects – a theory to which Virilio is almost alone in clinging – and an editing of vision in the breaks between frames, producing a virtual memory of virtual objects. On the one hand, this will lead Virilio to worry at the emergence of prospective simulations, computer models devised in order to foresee, such as Geographical Information Systems (GIS). This is a genuine fear: the purpose of computer simulations is an extension of business plans and Soviet 5-year plans: the administration of the future according to the dictates of the present. But Virilio also recognizes, on the other hand, that 'The weak light that allows us to apprehend the real, to see and understand our present environment, itself comes from a distant visual memory without which there would be no act of looking' (Virilio, 1994: 62). What now guides his anxiety is not the fact of memorization, which in any case shapes even direct perception, but the transfer of visual memory from the human sensorium to mechanical perception.

The loss of a guiding 'distant visual memory' might be likened to a process in which we lost the ability to recognize the picturesque, painting-like quality of a landscape. One of the guiding themes of modernist art, indeed, is the elaboration of visual and verbal strategies to provoke a renewal of habituated vision. One of the most important single works of modernism, Duchamp's *Large Glass* (also known as *The Bride Stripped Bare by her Bachelors, Even*) of 1917–22, works along this fault-line of modernist mediated vision in a particularly fascinating way, eroticizing the gaze between the bachelors in the lower half and the bride in the upper, mechanizing the look through the intervention of fantastic machineries of desire, and capturing the whole fantastical narration in a variety of media which, in their physical materials and their dependence on chance techniques, vividly capture the aporias of photography. One of the work's titles, *Delay in Glass*, can surely be read as a direct reference to glass-plate photography and the capture not only of light but of time, postponing its emergence back into the world. What Duchamp manages that Virilio does not, apart from his profound understanding of the implication of gender in visual technologies, is his readiness to surrender rational control. What, after all, is the purpose of GIS simulations if not rational control over the future environment? Duchamp, by contrast, demonstrates in a practical way the impossibility of exercising control even over the past. The apparatus for Duchamp as for Virilio takes on a life of its own. But in Duchamp's version, that life is one which can be respected as an authentic contribution to dialogue, the active participation of the machineries of mediation in the mediative process between humans. Where Virilio lives in terror of the mechanical take-over of human activities, Duchamp points us towards the necessary realization that we are already in dialogue with our devices.

Our machines, now more than ever, constitute our environment. Where Virilio imagines a pre-media innocence of perception, always already lost to mediated humanity, he projects a curiously passive relation into the monologue of self and object, in which the object addresses the self, throwing itself before it, seeking in the self a completion of its truth. The Duchamp perspective suggests instead that there is a partnership between us and our technologies, an assimilation of our conventions into the technologies, and of their conventions into us, but in a dialogue in which both are subject to constant negotiation and change. This is not to say that the military and commercial applications of technological research have not had immense repercussions on the nature and functioning of such familiar gadgets as the desktop computer: the crushing individualism of the design of the typewriter keyboard, mouse and graphical user interface in the interests of office automation rather than commonality of communication is a case in point. But it is also true that our relations with technologies are as complexly negotiated as our relationships with films, novels or philosophies; that we jury-rig our sense of minute-by-minute existence and our world-views out of the interactions we have with a world constituted as much by the materiality of the media as by the physical environment of which they form so salient a characteristic.

The spectacular eradication of distance is exactly that: spectacular.

And as with a Hollywood special effects blockbuster, our attention is split between the illusion and the spectacular craft that makes the illusion possible. That divorce is typical of our dialogue with the uncanny intelligence of machines (and of course their equally uncanny ability to go wrong). For Virilio, there is no dialogue, only resistance to media technologies that have become forces of history: 'How', he asks, 'can we resist this deluge of visual and audiovisual sequences, the sudden *motorization of appearances* that endlessly bombard our imagination?' (Virilio, 1997: 96). Subjectivity, once formed in relation to objectivity, is now constituted in relation to mediation. The process appears to him one-sided, with the techno-logic of militarization and endo-colonialism enforcing the ongoing, yet final process of dehumanization. The only alternative is to turn away from mediation, 'out of a concern to preserve one's integrity, one's *freedom of conscience*' (Virilio, 1997: 96), a term which in French means both moral standards and consciousness. One warms to his dogged refusal of cybertopian optimism, to his crying out against the abuse of power in the design and delivery of technologically mediated perception. But it is inadequate to refuse technologization, to appeal to a pre-technological 'ethics of immediate perception' (Virilio, 1997: 102), or to refuse that mediation which, in the contemporary world, is the material form taken by our solidarity with others in the interests of an imaginary free consciousness. For all its perversion in the interests of transnational capital and the imperialism of finance, mediation is the condition in which we live, and which in many respects has forced us, in the globalization as well as the mediation process, away from the philosophy of individual will into deeper mutual dependency, and a consequent surrender of individual freedom in the interests of a human ecology. In order to understand the processes through which we are living, and to develop tactical means for intervening in the macro-scale organization of communications in a critical moment of their evolution, more is required than philosophical nihilism.

To take an example where Virilio's analysis is extremely informative, the private automobile is without doubt the single most deleterious innovation of the last century, even more so than the military technologies deployed in wars too often begun to secure supplies of fuel for them. Motorists are careless of the ecological effect of the noxious fumes expelled by their vehicles, despite the fact that their own children suffer from the respiratory diseases they cause, just as they claim innocence for the oil spills attendant on the trade in petrol. The car instils in its driver and passengers that sense of right and invulnerability that is responsible for so many deaths. It inscribes in the motorist the expectation of surveillance. It travels far faster than the human sensorium can cope with. Few people would batter an animal to death in cold blood, but roadkill is considered an acceptable by-product of the right to speed. It is a device which isolates the driver from the world, transforming it into pure trajectory and removing all but the most rudimentary communication with others, consisting solely of signals concerning direction and velocity. The motorway, not the mediasphere, is the scene of picnolepsia, the suspended consciousness of auto-pilot driving. The non-space of the car's interior, underwritten by its isolating soundtrack of radio and recorded music, abstracts from the unplan-able environment of populations and weather. Inscribed in discourses as various as marketing campaigns and Chuck Berry songs as the individualist icon of freedom and mastery, the motor is in fact quite the opposite: a device for immobilization and subjection. Its reality is neither the open road nor the moment of arrival but the horizonless no-man's-land of the traffic jam. Yet it would be absurd to accept this nightmare as either historical necessity or unchallengably hegemonic. From Greenpeace to Reclaim the Streets, the incompetent ugliness of private cars is challenged globally. One can hope for its eventual demise.

Perhaps this ecological catastrophe is easier to fight than the process of mediation: more obvious, more dangerous, more tangible. In transport there is a single technology against which to rail: we are so interwoven in mediation that no act of sabotage can break our need to communicate. To develop beyond pessimism, we need not only the essayistic media theory of Virilio's vibrant gloom: we need the meticulous scholarship on which he draws, that analyses the detailed history of the new technologies as well as the old, work now being undertaken in the histories of radio, television and cinema but still in its infancy in terms of networked and digital media (though see Edwards, 1996, on Internet historiography and Curry, 1998: 59–86 for a critical history of an extremely germane digital technology). We need to understand the economic rationales and design philosophies that enter into the construction of new technologies. But most of all we need to grasp the nettle of principled analysis: that as the world changes, nostalgia for a lost innocence is no grounds for critique or politics. Virilio at the very least offers us the opportunity, indeed demands that we reflect upon the urgent necessity, for an ethical grounding of our coming to terms with the new media.

I have tried to show that Virilio's liberal humanism, his reliance on theories of representation and, most of all, his philosophical individualism, have hampered his ability to provide a telling analysis and prognosis in the new media field. But I hope that I have also shown that re-reading his scenarios of disempowerment and indifferentiation in the light of concepts of dialogue, communication and mediation can provide us with a way of drawing from his works a sense of the ethical demands placed on us by the technologization of community. Apocalypse is not the only possible future. Even if it were, we are ethically bound to act as if it were not. As the old revolutionary has it, pessimism of the intellect; optimism of the will.

Note

1. Virilio has been an active participant in anti-racist and homeless struggles in France: it is his writing which tends towards political quietism. Like many of his contemporaries, notably Deleuze and Guattari and Jean Baudrillard, Virilio tends to see the state as the villain of the piece, a view that normally denies him access to

analysis of the globalized capitalist enterprise as central player in new media technologies.

References

Baudrillard, Jean (1994) *Simulacra and Simulation*, trans. Sheila Faria Glaser. Ann Arbor: University of Michigan Press.

Baudrillard, Jean (1995) *The Gulf War Did Not Take Place*, trans. Paul Patton. Sydney: Power Publications.

Baudry, Jean-Louis (1975) 'Le Dispositif', *Communications* 23: 56–72.

Baudry, Jean-Louis (1985) 'Ideological Effects of the Basic Cinematographic Apparatus', trans. Alan Williams, pp. 531–42 in Bill Nichols (ed.) *Movies and Methods*, vol. 2. Berkeley: University of California Press.

Bazin, André (1971), 'Umberto D: A Great Work', trans. Hugh Gray, pp. 79–82 in *What is Cinema?*, vol. 2. Berkeley: University of California Press.

Brigham, Linda (1995) 'Transpolitical Technocracy and the Hope of Language: Virilio and Habermas', *Speed* 1(4) [http://proxy.arts.uci.edu/~nideffer/_SPEED_/ 1.4/articles/brigham.html].

Ceram, C.W. (1965) *Archeology of the Cinema*, trans. Richard Winston. London: Thames and Hudson.

Curry, Michael R. (1998) *Digital Places: Living with Geographic Information Technologies*. London: Routledge.

Dagognet, François (1992) *Etienne-Jules Marey: A Passion for the Trace*, trans. Robert Galeta with Jeanine Herman. New York: Zone Books.

Dayan, Daniel (1976) 'The Tutor Code of Classical Cinema', pp. 438–51 in Bill Nichols (ed.) *Movies and Methods*, vol. 1. Berkeley: University of California Press.

Derrida, Jacques (1973) *Speech and Phenomena*, trans. David B. Allison. Evanston, IL: Northwestern University Press.

Edwards, Paul N. (1996) *The Closed World: Computers and the Politics of Discourse in Cold War America*. Cambridge, MA: MIT Press.

Ellul, Jacques (1964) *The Technological Society*, trans. John Wilkinson. New York: Vintage.

Gomery, Douglas (1992) *Shared Pleasures: A History of Movie Presentation in the United States*. London: BFI.

Heath, Stephen (1977/8) 'Notes on Suture', *Screen* 18(4): 48–76.

Heath, Stephen and Theresa de Lauretis (eds) (1980) *The Cinematic Apparatus*. London: Macmillan.

Heidegger, Martin (1977) 'The Question Concerning Technology', pp. 3–35 in *The Question Concerning Technology and Other Essays*, trans. William Lovitt. New York: Harper and Row.

Kellner, Douglas (1998) 'Virilio on Vision Machines', *Film-Philosophy: Electronic Salon* 9 October [http://www.mailbase.ac.uk/lists/film-philosophy/files/kellner. html].

Kuleshov, Lev (1973) 'The Origins of Montage', pp. 67–76 in Luda Schitzer, Jean Schitzer and Marcel Martin (eds) *Cinema in Revolution: The Heroic Era of Soviet Film*, trans. David Robinson. London: Secker and Warburg.

Marx, Karl (1976) *Capital: A Critique of Political Economy*, vol. 1, trans. Rodney Livingstone. London: NLB/Penguin.

Oliveira, Carlos (1996) 'Global Algorithm 1.7: The Silence of the Lambs: Paul Virilio in Conversation', trans. Patrice Riemens, in *CTheory* [http://www.ctheory.com/ga1.7-silence.html].

Oudart, Jean-Pierre (1977–8) 'Cinema and Suture', *Screen* 18(4): 35–47.

Rothman, William (1976) 'Against "The System of Suture"', pp. 438–51 in Bill Nichols (ed.) *Movies and Methods*, vol. 1. Berkeley: University of California Press.

Virilio, Paul (1986) *Speed and Politics: An Essay in Dromology*, trans. Mark Polizotti. New York: Semiotext(e).

Virilio, Paul (1989a) *War and Cinema*, trans. Patrick Camiller. London: Verso.

Virilio, Paul (1989b) 'The Last Vehicle', pp. 106–19 in Dietmar Kamper and Christoph Wulf (eds) *Looking Back on the End of the World*, trans. David Antal. New York: Semiotext(e).

Virilio, Paul (1991a) *The Aesthetics of Disappearance*, trans. Philip Beitchman. New York: Semiotext(e).

Virilio, Paul (1991b) *Lost Dimension*, trans. Daniel Moshenberg. New York: Semiotext(e).

Virilio, Paul (1992) 'Big Optics', trans. Jörg von Stein, pp. 82–93 in Peter Weibel (ed.) *Zur Rechtfertigung der hypothetischen Natur de Kunst und der Nicht-Identität in der Objektwelt/ On Justifying the Hypothetical Nature of Art and the Non-Identicality within the Object World*. Köln: Galerie Tanja Grunert.

Virilio, Paul (1994) *The Vision Machine*, trans. Julie Rose. London: BFI.

Virilio, Paul (1995a) *The Art of the Motor*, trans. Julie Rose. Minneapolis: University of Minnesota Press.

Virilio, Paul (1995b) 'Speed and Information: Cyberspace Alarm!', trans. Patrice Riemens, in *CTheory* [http://www.ctheory.com/a30-cyberspace_alarm.html].

Virilio, Paul (1997) *Open Sky*, trans. Julie Rose. London: Verso.

Virilio, Paul and Sylvère Lotringer (1997 [1983]) *Pure War*, rev. edn, trans. Mark Polizotti, 'Postscript' trans. Brian O'Keefe. New York: Semiotext(e).

Sean Cubitt is Reader in Video and Media Studies at John Moores University, Liverpool. He has published widely on contemporary arts, media and culture, and his most recent book is *Digital Aesthetics* (*Theory, Culture & Society*/Sage, 1998). Forthcoming projects include an anthology on postcolonial science fictions co-edited with Ziauddin Sardar and special issues of *Screen* on special effects and of *Third Text* on global digital cultures.

Blinded by the (Speed of) Light

Scott McQuire

Speed; the coitus of the future.
(Saint-Pol Roux, in Virilio, 1997: 116)

[A]re we about to lose our status as *eyewitnesses* of tangible reality once and for all. . . afflicted with a kind of paradoxical blindness due to overexposure of the visible and to the development of *sightless* vision machines. . .? (Virilio, 1997: 91)

OVER THE LAST DECADE, the dissemination of Paul Virilio's writings outside France has generated a critical momentum which delineates a particular theoretical trajectory in contemporary thought. Framed by his long-standing interest in the social and political effects of technology, Virilio's major focus has been the twin 'revolutions' of transport and transmission.[1] In this article, I want to examine the close parallels between mechanical and media 'vehicles' that Virilio develops in his work, particularly regarding their capacity to transform the social relations of space and time. While I will express some reservations as to the adequacy of the phenomenological framework he mobilizes in order to understand the effects of telematics on the human body, perception and identity, I will argue that Virilio has clearly helped to pose the sort of fundamental questions which are vital when the parameters of the social and political world are themselves undergoing fundamental change.

The Last Vehicle?

At least since the publication of *Speed and Politics* (1986a) Virilio has sought to emphasize the role of different regimes of dynamic vehicles and the techno-political imposition of differential speeds of social interaction as

■ *Theory, Culture & Society* 1999 (SAGE, London, Thousand Oaks and New Delhi),
  Vol. 16(5–6): 143–159
  [0263-2764(199910/12)16:5–6;143–159;009963]

prime determinants of modern political economy. Yet, while acknowledging that the political revolution of modernity could itself be understood in terms of increasing mobilization, Virilio does not elevate unimpeded movement to an ideal as the path to absolute freedom.

> The events of 1789 claimed to be a revolt against *subjection*, that is, against the *constraint to immobility* symbolized by the ancient feudal serfdom (which furthermore persisted in certain regimes) – a revolt against arbitrary confinement and the obligation to reside in one place. But no one as yet suspected that the 'conquest of the freedom to come and go' so dear to Montaigne could, by sleight of hand, become an obligation to mobility. (Virilio, 1986a: 29–30)

For Virilio, it is this imposition of a state of 'permanent mobility' which places speed – and hence different types of engines or motors – at the heart of modern social and political life. The shift from what he dubs 'metabolic vehicles' (human bodies) to new generations of mechanical vehicles with superior velocity and acceleration has been integral to the development of industrial capitalism as a global phenomenon.[2]

Yet, despite constant acceleration throughout the 20th century, mechanical vehicles have found themselves increasingly outpaced by what Virilio (1989a: 106–19) has evocatively termed 'the last vehicle': the audio-visual one. Numerous landmarks could be cited in the consolidation of the new world information order in which geography has been increasingly subordinated to communications technology. Virilio (1995a: 49) highlights the first multiplex radio broadcast in 1938, when CBS correspondents were linked live from Rome, Berlin and Paris, noting:

> Subscribers were not so much buying daily news as they were buying instantaneity, ubiquity – in other words, their own participation in universal contemporaneity, in the movement of the future Planet City.[3]

Following the tracks of analysts such as Marshall McLuhan, Virilio has been consistently drawn to comparisons between the double impact of new vehicles of transportation and new media of communication on the human sensorium and human consciousness. However, where McLuhan's essentially optimistic vision of television in the 1960s enabled him to assume a position of influence in a corporate culture flattered by his image of heroic technocracy – a role readily assumed in the digital era by someone like Nicholas Negroponte – Virilio's analysis of global media has been far less celebratory.[4]

From Virilio's 'vehicular' perspective, automobiles are less 'riding' animals than *frames* (in the optical sense), and the self-propelled vehicle is not only a vector of change in physical location but also a new means of representation (Virilio, 1989a: 114). The profound unity of vehicular travel and the cinematic tracking shot established the modern subject as a voyager-voyeur (Virilio, 1991a: 58). But the effects of older vehicles and media pale before the impact of technologies such as broadcast television and networked computers which transmit information at the upper limit of the physical universe: light speed. Virilio (1995b) argues: 'To have reached the light barrier, to have reached the speed of light, is a historical event which throws history into disarray and jumbles up the relation of the living being towards the world.' One consequence of this threshold is the potential reversal of the migratory tendencies of the modern age of transportation.

> If in fact the end of the nineteenth century and the beginning of the twentieth experienced the advent of the automotive vehicle, the dynamic vehicle of the railroad, the street and then the air, then the end of this century seems to herald the next vehicle, the audio-visual one, a final mutation: static vehicle, substitute for the change of physical location, and extension of domestic inertia, a vehicle that ought at last to bring about the victory of sedentariness, this time an ultimate sedentariness. (Virilio, 1989a: 108)

Displacement of movement in space by the technological control of time, and the concomitant refiguring of the tradition of geopolitics by what Virilio calls chrono-politics, is predicated on the ubiquity of screen technologies. Once broadcast and distribution points are sufficiently generalized so that 'coverage' can assume the mantle of global completeness, and live events can be tele-distributed in 'real time' across geographically dispersed audiences occupying their own discrete 'private' spaces, the nature of the social contract becomes subject to new exigencies. Such a shift also implies a significant transformation in the constitution of contemporary subjectivity. Rather than the armoured body of the transport revolution eulogized earlier in the century by avant-gardists such as Marinetti and Ernst Jünger, Virilio posits the emergence of a human body which has ceded its motor functions to technology. The contemporary hype of computerized 'interactivity' would thus be the precursor to prolonged inactivity.

> The urbanization of real time is in fact first the urbanization of *one's own body* plugged into various interfaces (keyboard, cathode screen, DataGlove or DataSuit), prostheses that make the super-equipped able-bodied person almost the exact equivalent of the motorized and wired disabled person.... Doomed to inertia, the inactive being transfers his natural capacities for movement and displacement to probes and scanners which instantaneously inform him about a remote reality, to the detriment of his own faculties of apprehension of the real.... Having been first *mobile*, then *motorized*, man will thus become *motile*, deliberately limiting his body's area of influence to a few gestures, a few impulses like channel surfing. (Virilio, 1997: 11, 16)

While such a prognosis should not be blithely universalized – the global economy is still heavily reliant on manual factory labour even if the hyper-mobility of contemporary capital has seen certain forms of production flee the older 'developed' economies – the trajectory Virilio identified well before the take-off of the Internet in 1993 is of great significance. The generalization of 'audio-visual vehicles' which operate at 'light-speed' has the capacity to affect all aspects of social life, insofar as it involves the reconfiguration of borders of all kinds, from the physical boundaries of our houses, cities and nation-states, to the more immaterial architecture of our thought. In the telescoping of near and far which disturbs customary relationships of proximity and distance, and inscribes a new temporal regime privileging a 'permanent present', Virilio argues that the current 'crisis' of culture is born of a fundamental loss of orientation, and, ultimately, a loss of properly human measure.[5] What emerges is a new mode of being in the world in which the *extensive* revolution sustained by dynamic transport technologies which supported global trade and global migration is counterpointed by an *intensive* circulation of images and information, a virtual movement in which the human body is potentially reduced to a node within a network:

> The initially confined rise of the dynamic, at first mobile, then automotive, vehicle is suddenly followed by the generalised rise of pictures and sounds in the static vehicles of the audio-visual.... *From now on everything will happen without us moving, without us even having to set out.* (Virilio, 1989a: 112)

Transparency and Overexposure

What are the consequences of living in a world shrink-wrapped by global media in which 'events' increasingly enter our homes without knocking? In his influential essay 'The Overexposed City', Virilio (1986b) challenged the dominant currents of modern architectural theory, where the model home or office of the future was inevitably designed to be 'augmented' with every imaginable new communication device. For Virilio, the proliferation of screen technologies is less a simple enhancement of than a decisive interruption to traditional modes of inhabiting space. The ubiquity of the screen with its restless 'horizon' means:

> Urban form is no longer designated by a line of demarcation between here and there, but has become synonymous with the programming of a 'time schedule'. Its gateway is less a door which must be opened than an audio-visual protocol – a protocol which reorganizes the modes of public perception. (Virilio, 1986b: 19)

In contrast to popular images of broadcast television and the Internet offering the cosmopolitan viewer unfettered 'access' to the world at large, Virilio (1986b: 20) argues that the new electronic architecture promoted by telematics, while less apparent than the doors and windows of antiquity, is 'just as real, constraining and segregating'. But its full import is found in the promotion of new forms of social interchange: insofar as electronic media function to 'connect' people across previously discrete spaces, they also actively undermine the solidity of the ground on which both architecture and geography imagined themselves to stand.

> If in the nineteenth century the lure of the city emptied agrarian space of its substance (cultural, social), at the end of the twentieth century it is urban space which loses in its turn its geographical reality. (Virilio, 1986b: 20)

While this is a trajectory which dates at least from the profound de-composition of appearances set in train by the moving images of cinema, it is the active surface-boundary of the contemporary television screen or computer terminal which most radically accentuates the transmutation of physical space in the present.[6]

> We can now see more clearly the theoretical and practical importance of the notion of interface, that drastically new surface that annuls the classical separation of position, instant or object, as well as the traditional partitioning of space into physical dimensions, in favour of an almost instantaneous configuration in which the observer and the observed are roughly linked, confused and chained by an encoded language from which emerges the ambiguity of interpretation, an ambiguity which returns to that of the audio-visual media, especially that of live television... (Virilio, 1991b: 52)

According to Virilio, what emerges in the light-speed era of 'real time' media is a state of *atopia*, a condition defined by the exhaustion of natural relief (spatial perspective) and of temporal distance (chronology or suc-cession). Atopia is the spatial consequence of an insatiable screen culture which 'brings everything – absolutely everything – back to that place which has no place' (Virilio, 1986b: 21). For Virilio (1986a: 135), this raises the ominous prospect of what he has dubbed the omnipolis or 'world city', presaging a catastrophic levelling of culture through the 'geostrategic hom-ogenization of the globe'.[7]

The spanning of previously discrete sites of activity and the wholesale penetration of solid architectural surfaces by wired networks and immaterial information flows has fundamentally altered the division between public and private space. Such a transformation works along at least two axes simultaneously. On the one hand, the private home finds itself increasingly deterritorialized by transnational media vectors, while, on the other hand, the public realm is increasingly integrated with the politics of media spectacle. One way to approach this dual trajectory is via Virilio's evocative description of the electronic screen as 'the third window' (1988: 185–97), an appellation situating television and computer terminal as the historical successor to – but also the historical departure from – two prior 'windows'. The first is the door-window, the opening for the passage of bodies which is the minimum requisite for any dwelling, whether cave, frame house or smart office tower. The second window is the light-window, a specialized opening for illumination and ventilation of interior space. In comparison to its predecessors, the screen-window is constitutively different, insofar as the 'horizon' it reveals is both ephemeral and discontinuous, subject to the incessant mobility of perspective and the rapid oscillations of montage.

Despite this fundamental difference, it is instructive to compare the function of the contemporary screen-window with the aspirations that modern architects such as Le Corbusier held for the light-window. Writing and designing in the context of the 1920s avant-garde, Le Corbusier saw the horizontal strip window as the ideal means of opening interior space to the outside, thereby alleviating problems of design, health and morality alike. Not only does the horizontal window provide *more light*, thus aiding Le Corbusier's perennial quest to expose the domestic interior to the cleansing properties of universal transparency; significantly it is the 'objective' eye of the camera which finally legitimates the new design in his eyes.[8] As Beatriz Colomina (1996) has noted, the window-wall converts the house, which Corbusier famously described as a 'machine for living in', into something like a machine for making pictures. As an abstract frame which Corbusier intended to place in any landscape, the glass-walled house becomes a camera pointed at Nature. But today, as glass windows which admit solar light are juxtaposed with screen windows emitting their own luminescence, the modern affiliation between architecture and audio-visual media is taking another turn.

For Le Corbusier, the ideal of architectural transparency symbolized by the strip window was not only aesthetic and hygienic: above all, it signified the end of superstition and irrationality. The belief that rational housing would give birth to rational society courses through his work. This moral dimension, in which architectural transparency provides a compelling metaphor for a revolutionary transformation of consciousness, was also remarked on by Walter Benjamin in his 1929 essay on Surrealism:

> To live in a glass house is a revolutionary virtue *par excellence*. It is also an intoxication, a moral exhibitionism that we badly need. Discretion concerning one's own existence, once an aristocratic virtue, has become more and more an affair of petit bourgeois parvenus. (1985: 228)[9]

It is precisely this modernist faith in the revolutionary virtues of architectural and social transparency which is today being sorely tested in the crucible of the interactive screen-window. It has become increasingly evident that the spectacularization of public events and public space via the media doesn't simply make them 'available' to the domestic consumer; it also alters the nature of domestic space and unsettles the borders of the contemporary home. For Virilio (1994a: 64):

> Really, once public space yields to public image, surveillance and street lighting can be expected to shift too, from the street to the domestic display terminal. Since this is a substitute for the City terminal, the private sphere thus continues to lose its relative autonomy.

This 'loss of relative autonomy' today far exceeds the attack on bourgeois hypocrisy envisaged by Benjamin and his contemporaries, as the imagined virtues of 'moral exhibitionism' are counterpointed by the growing risks of *overexposure*. The blurring of divisions between public and private space entrained by electronic media has created a crisis of space which needs to be mapped simultaneously across a number of fronts or frontiers. In fact, a principal symptom of this condition is that where divisions between public and private space, or local, regional, national and international spheres once seemed relatively secure and stable, 'real-time' screen technologies ensure that all these sites are immediately implicated in each other: the deterritorialization of domestic space goes hand in hand with the increasing subjection of the public sphere, including the political realm, to the exigencies of media spectacle. As Virilio (1997: 18) notes: 'This crisis in the notion of physical dimensions thus hits politics and the administration of public services head on in attacking what was once geopolitics.'

Over the years since its inception, broadcast television has inspired numerous paeans to its capacity to sustain 'participatory democracy', an enthusiasm which was transferred almost seamlessly to the Internet with the utopic visions of 'cyberdemocracy' espoused across the mainstream political spectrum in the 1996 US presidential elections.[10] In contrast, Virilio's analysis here follows the pathway first laid out by Walter Benjamin in a remarkable footnote to his 'Artwork' essay, which signalled the emergence of an unholy alliance between 'the star' and 'the dictator' under the ubiquitous eye of the camera.[11] What Benjamin identified is the extraordinary latent power released by the 'personalization' of political image via the mass media, as politicians adopted the techniques and inhabited the terrain first staked out by Hollywood in the 1920s. While Nazi Germany was arguably more 'advanced' than its contemporaries in using radio, cinema and even a nascent television to orchestrate a new type of political constituency based on spatial ubiquity and temporal simultaneity, this mode of highly mediatized politics, in which spectacular rituals of national celebration are used to generate mass identification with a charismatic leader, has since become a staple across much of the world.[12]

While the ability of political leaders to project selected elements of their personalities into the public realm has enabled the creation of new mythologies, the underbelly of this modern 'cult of personality' can now be seen in the seemingly insatiable public appetite for 'intimate' details of leaders' private lives. In fact this appetite, originating in the highly controlled publicity machines which illuminated the movie stars of the 'classical' Hollywood era, has today spread out of control into the incessant exposure of the private lives of 'celebrities' of all kinds, whether painters, presidents or princesses. This situation is rapidly creating a new type of political crisis, particularly in the USA, as it proves increasingly difficult to find 'clean' candidates for high political office.

Similar appetites are also evident in the growing fascination with the private lives of 'ordinary people', manifested in the burgeoning circuit of television talk-show confessionals in the mode pioneered by *Donahue* and *Oprah*, and now spreading into a profusion of 'personal' Web pages and chatrooms on the Internet. Perhaps the most pointed case of 'overexposure' is the example set by Jennifer Ringley, a young Washington student, who generated enormous publicity when she began to live on-line several years ago, using a digital camera to upload images of her one room apartment to the Web every 2 minutes. Since its inception, the so-called 'Jennicam' has become a thriving business attracting sponsorships and subscriptions.[13]

While there is undoubtedly a pornographic element to the public interest in Ringley, the voyeurism involved goes well beyond the simple possibility of encountering nudity. Rather, it seems to be located in the fascination exercised by the fantasy of being able to observe the private life of a total stranger in all its minute details. This fantasy has been around for a long time, at least since the invention of the movie camera. Painter and filmmaker Fernand Léger long ago described his dream of a film which would record the life of a man and a woman over 24 hours. Nothing should be omitted or hidden; nor should they ever become aware of the presence of the camera (Kracauer, 1960: 63–4). Léger's ambition pales before the megalomania of the fictive 'director' in Peter Weir's *The Truman Show* (1998), a film which plays with the same fantasy of total surveillance over an unwitting individual's private life. But while *The Truman Show* provided a safety valve with the possibility that Truman can eventually escape his fishbowl exposure, 'real' television has never proved so easy to step outside. The contemporary popularity of 'real life' television scenarios of all kinds, from 'home video' and police and surveillance camera shows, to extended productions such as *Sylvania Waters* (1992), where a television crew lived with a Sydney family over several months, register the ambivalence of a desire which is difficult to master according to traditional categories of publicity and privacy.

The salient point concerns the role of television and on-line media in transforming the contemporary home into both a cell of surveillance and a scene of watching. Recalling Walter Benjamin's comment on the 'revolutionary virtue' of glass houses, today it needs to be recognized that electronic media have effectively placed us all in glass houses, where we are simultaneously watchers and watched.[14] The most intimate 'private' images are susceptible to instant display across transnational 'public' spaces, while 'public' events of all kinds penetrate what were once the most remote and secluded spaces of private life. While this erosion of private space is partly a function of the rise of sophisticated surveillance systems, it is also the result of the growing internalization of these mechanisms. When asked 'Why are you giving up your privacy like this?', Jennifer Ringley responded: 'Because I don't feel I'm giving up my privacy. Just because people can see me doesn't mean it affects me – I'm still alone in my room, no matter what.'

Such a comment also registers the seismic shift affecting notions of 'community' in the age of electronic media. Connecting media overexposure to the rise of 'single unit' families, Virilio (1991b: 126–7) comments:

> After the explosion of the ancient extended family that arose from rural living, the present disintegration of the urban nuclear family progressively relieves threatened populations of any prospect for organized resistance.

One need not subscribe wholly to his analysis of the family as 'a basic cell of resistance to oppression' – which leaves the question of patriarchy hanging – to acknowledge the profound changes in social bonding in cultures which implore their citizens to 'keep in touch' by telephone and computer.

Telepresence and the Accident of the Present

The overexposure of space which results in the effective collapse of geographical distance with relation to media events and the increasing annexation of public and private space by screen and terminal, is equally the overexposure of time. Virilio argues that the emergence of media vectors which operate at the speed of light (or time-light as he calls it) has led to a fundamental change in our mode of being in the world, putting at risk our sense of identity grounded in the experience of physical proximity and the primacy of face-to-face communication. From this perspective, live television, which is capable of distributing 'events' to a globally dispersed audience as an integral part of their everyday lives, does not so much 're-present' real events as undermine the very grounds for determining their reality.

> This is in the end what we could call a **temporal commutation**, a commutation also related to a sort of **commotion** in present duration, an accident of a so-called 'real' moment that suddenly detaches itself from the place where it happens, from its here and now, and opts for an electronic dazzlement.... (Virilio, 1997: 14; emphases in original)

Virilio contends that this situation has produced the possibility of a new type of 'accident'. Unlike the spatially localized accidents inaugurated with the invention of mechanical vehicles such as train and automobile, the emerging accident is primarily temporal: 'with the teletechnologies of general interactivity we are entering the age of the **accident of the present**...' (1997: 14; emphasis in original). A prominent example of this threshold is the so-called 'Y2K bug', an 'accident' situated less in geographical space than technological time. But, for Virilio, the 'accident of the present' arising from the increased privileging of global time over local time and the emerging dominance of 'telepresence' over 'presence', is the source of far deeper cultural convulsions. The Y2K bug is itself merely symptomatic of the radically truncated temporal horizons of contemporary political economy: even bearing in mind the fact that repairing the 'glitch' is an economic boon rather than a burden to the computer industry, it still beggars belief that the problem could not have been foreseen by computer programmers who created it as recently as the 1980s. The fact that it wasn't underlines John Berger's (1982: 109) point that contemporary capitalism lacks shared values which extend beyond a few years or even a few months. In similar vein, Virilio's analysis of the advent of technological time has consistently led him to identify history as the 'lost dimension', insofar as the extensive time of historical succession is being submerged by the immediacy of live action. From this perspective, telematics is less a passport to the ideal of 'world time' than the means of atomizing time by alienating us from both knowledge of the past and the capacity to imagine the future. What emerges instead is:

> ... the incredible possibility of a 'civilization of forgetting', a *live* (live-coverage) society that has no future and no past, since it has no extension and no duration, a society intensely present here and there at once – in other words, *telepresent to the whole world*. (Virilio, 1997: 25)

From this perspective, the 'problem' of the contemporary media no longer belongs to the traditional order of censorship and restricted flows of information, but concerns the overwhelming of the subject by the speed of information and the exhaustion of the world's spatio-temporal dimensions in a perennial state of overexposure. Far from satisfying human desire for knowledge and mastery, continued technological acceleration has produced a 'generalized delirium of interpretation' (Virilio, 1991b: 53) in which events seem to collide randomly with each other, producing a paradoxical state of 'blindness'.[15] Equally serious is the loss of critical points of reference arising from the emergent split between 'presence' and 'telepresence'. Virilio (1997: 37) argues that telematics induces a:

> ...split in time between the real time of our *immediate activities* – in which we act both here *and* now – and the real time of media interactivity that privileges the 'now' of the timeslot of the televised broadcast to the detriment of the 'here', that is to say, of the space of the meeting place.

However, despite his undoubted effectiveness in delineating this threshold, certain limitations in Virilio's analysis have become evident over the years since his work first appeared. At key moments, he continues to rely heavily on an unreconstructed phenomenological concept of presence:

> We might recall in passing that there is no true presence in the World – in one's own world of sense experience – other than through the intermediary of the egocentration of a *living present*; in other words, through the existence of one's own body living in the here and now. (Virilio, 1997: 38)

Curiously, Virilio has shown little interest in taking on board any elements of the critique of this definition of presence advanced in philosophy over this century from Heidegger to Derrida and beyond.[16] This leaves him with a conceptual armature barely adequate at crucial points to fully comprehend the shift he is describing, insofar as he inevitably drifts toward the same polarization of 'image' and 'reality' which has been a staple of Western thought since Feuerbach, if not Plato.[17] Adhering to this paradigm of representation, in which the image is positioned as both subordinate and subsequent to the real – as a matter of logic itself – is problematic, not least because the precedence of the real over the image is precisely what has been thrown into confusion by the era of live broadcasting in which the 'event' and its 'representation' frequently coincide.[18] A related problem is that, despite his interest in the effects of the spatial ubiquity and temporal simultaneity generated by media technologies, Virilio has been notably reluctant to extend his analysis to the metaphysics of presence and its uncritical implication in a humanist vision of the unified subject.

These problems are both strategic and conceptual. I would argue that attempting to develop a critical relation to the contemporary media in terms of the paradigm of representation, which inevitably gravitates towards a binary split between image and reality, is unlikely to have much purchase with those born into a post-television, post-Internet world. At a fundamental level, it is time to accept that the media *is* real – not in the totalizing sense asserted by the shadowy McLuhanesque figure of Dr Brian O'Blivion in Cronenberg's cautionary *Videodrome* (1982), who argued that the television screen had become 'the retina of the mind's eye' and hence a substitute for the real, but in the sense that the media is both a *constitutive* part of contemporary experience and a particular *frame* or context through which experience is filtered and understood. While Virilio is attentive to the importance of the media in shaping contemporary social and political life, his tendency to uncritically resort to the paradigm of representation frequently reduces 'the vision machine' to a distortion or veiling of the supposed purity of the phenomenological real. The emphasis on 'de-realization' tends to undermine the more original and productive elements of his analysis, namely the media's capacity to transform the social relations of time and space.

Virilio's reliance on a phenomenological notion of immediate presence is a more serious problem, insofar as it leads him to reproduce the ideal of the unified humanist subject as a theoretical norm. This emerges quite clearly in certain formulations:

> In days gone by, *being present meant being close*, being physically close to the other in face-to-face, vis-à-vis proximity.... If it is true that, from now on, we can not only act at a distance, but even teleact at a distance ... then the unheard of possibility arises of a sudden splitting of the subject's personality. (Virilio, 1995a: 106)

This reference to the 'unheard of possibility ... of a sudden splitting of the subject's personality' must be read in context of Virilio's almost total lack of engagement with poststructuralist theories of the 'decentred' subject.[19] Pointing this out is not to advocate the necessity of following theoretical fashion, but to question whether the theoretical resources he utilizes are capable of fully realizing the task he has set himself. To the extent that theories of decentred subjectivity are able to give expression to the heterogeneous temporality of consciousness, I would argue that they are more useful than Virilio's phenomenological humanism in challenging the vectors of universal linear time extended in global media. The problem with Virilio's de facto reliance on the traditional 'measure' of the unified subject is that his conclusions as to the effects of telematics tend to swing between extremes of nostalgia and apocalypse, rebounding between a 'once upon a time' of supposedly integrated identity and community and an emerging future defined by personal pathology and global 'desertification'.[20] This leaves his work bereft of any explicit political strategy as to how such a condition might be resisted or reversed beyond repeating Susan Sontag's (1979) earlier call for an 'ecology of images'.[21]

Virilio is clearly aware of his growing reputation as a doomsayer, asserting in a recent interview (1995c): 'I am not at all of an apocalyptic mind, I merely perform a critique of the technique', adding, 'I am conscious of all the positive aspects of technology, but at the same time I am also conscious of its negative aspects.' Such protestations seem somewhat disingenuous: the 'balance' in his work has always been heavily one-sided, which is undoubtedly part of its appeal. Where his descriptions of the 'positive' impact of telematics are brief and border on the banal ('it enables humanity to be brought together'), the bulk of his analytical effort and rhetorical power has been devoted to developing the idea that 'Totalitarianism is latent in technology' (Virilio, 1995c). From there it is a small step to the assertion that: 'The typical modern human is characterised by life under the dictatorship of the screen' (Virilio, 1995c).

The problem with such fundamentalist pronouncements is that they detract from the most interesting aspect of Virilio's work, which is his attention to the way in which the era of time-light media instantiates a society governed by an inordinate privilege granted to the present moment. Moreover, while his work describes the socio-political symptoms of this mode of temporality, what remains largely unexamined are the forces driving this trajectory. To understand this lacuna, it is vital to connect the contemporary desire for 'telepresence' to the paradox of the 'now' which is a founding presumption of humanist metaphysics.[22] Undoubtedly, this is a complex issue, inasmuch as it highlights the embeddedness of consciousness and identity in particular historic (and hence mutable) social relations of space and time.

One of the distinctive features of capitalism as a social form is that its dominant conception of identity as 'presence' is manifested in terms of the materiality of the here and now. This orientation meshes with a temporal order privileging the present moment or 'now' as the moment of plenitude and supports a heightened social investment in technologies of transport and communication as the means of mastering distance and absence. However, such an investment is inherently unstable, insofar as the impossibility of ever completely overcoming absence and living wholly in the present moment – at least this side of death – can only accentuate the quest for increasing acceleration and more speed. While ever increasing speed offers the subject the promise of technological transcendence – for example, the sense of mastery experienced by the voyager-voyeur in a cinema – satisfaction is only temporary. At the same time, the effect of the increasing saturation of the entire social fabric by telematics is to radically decentre and destabilize the cultural and perceptual framework which supported the ideal of the stable, centred, individual subject in the first place. In other words, pursuing subjective plenitude or identity as self-presence through the technological mastery of distance and absence imbricates the subject in a vicious circle. It is at this point that we can best situate the problems raised by Virilio's continuing recourse to a metaphysics of presence in order to critique the advance of telepresence: the two terms are mutually implicated. Pointing to the displacement of the 'here' by the 'now' is to recognize a significant transformation in the operation of the system, but it is also to remain within the same paradigm. As long as Virilio continues to deploy a concept of 'real presence' conceived on the basis of the 'here and now', his critique is ultimately grounded in the privilege of the present moment. This is precisely the same terrain that supports contemporary investment in 'telepresence' as a potential strategy of mastery.

Nevertheless, I would argue that Virilio's work provides important resources for constructing an effective critique of the social relations of the contemporary media in the face of the dominant political-economic currents eulogizing untrammelled media expansionism. The key move is to shift analysis away from the paradigm of representation and the problematic of 'de-realization' to one focusing on the temporal paradoxes that 'real-time' media accentuate. In the future, it seems increasingly likely that more of our social and political battles will be fought out in the dimension of time. In the same way that indigenous peoples were routinely stigmatized in the 19th century as 'backward', 'slow' and generally dwelling 'out of time' by European colonizers who proclaimed themselves as 'modern' and 'progressive', the emergence of the so-called 'information poor' at the end of the 20th century is symptomatic of the spread of a new temporal disjunction. As the nets of 'real-time' global media are stretched ever more tightly, attentiveness to the existence of differential regimes of temporality will assume heightened importance in articulating relations of cultural, racial and class difference.

Notes

1. In line with his marked proclivity for describing 'revolutions' in three phases, Virilio (1997: 51) has subsequently added a third stage: that of transplants.
2. Marx (1973: 539) clearly recognized rapid movement as critical to the development of the capitalist system: '[W]hile capital on the one side must strive to tear

down every spatial barrier to intercourse, i.e. to exchange, and conquer the whole earth for its market, it strives on the other side to annihilate this space with time, i.e. to reduce to a minimum the time spent in motion from one place to another. The more developed the capital, the more extensive the market over which it circulates, which forms the spatial orbit of its circulation, the more does it strive simultaneously for an even greater extension of the market and for greater annihilation of space with time.'

3. A similar landmark was the first satellite link-up of all five continents for a live television broadcast in 1964, following the possibilities indicated by Arthur C. Clarke's 1945 article 'Extra-Terrestrial Relays' which discussed the communications potential of satellites in geostationary orbit.

4. The relationship between Virilio and McLuhan deserves more space than I can give it here. As Arthur Kroker has pointed out, both developed their theories as practising Catholics, which perhaps goes some way to situating the marked theological tenor of many of their pronouncements. Contrary to McLuhan's vision of television functioning to restore the *gestalt* unity of human consciousness fragmented by centuries of print culture Virilio (1994b) has argued that: 'television is a media of crisis, which means that television is a media of accidents. Television can only destroy. In this respect, and even though he was a friend of mine, I believe that McLuhan was completely wrong. . .'.

5. Virilio (1991b: 24) has related this to the postmodern crisis of 'grand narratives', arguing: 'the crisis in the conceptualization of "narrative" appears as the other side of the crisis of the conceptualization of "dimension" as geometrical narrative, the discourse of measurement of a reality visibly offered to us all'. I will take up the issue of the residual humanism in some of his formulations below.

6. In relation to cinema, Virilio (1989b: 47) noted: 'When the offer of a trip "Around the World in Eighty Minutes" shone outside cinemas in the '30s, it was already clear that cinema was imposing itself on a geostrategy which for a century or more had inexorably been leading to the direct substitution, and thus sooner or later, the disintegration of things and places.'

7. Such pronouncements concerning the impact of global media in the formation of global culture are highly contentious. Here, I would merely note that Virilio gives little or no attention to theories which stress the role of the individual viewer/ consumer in actively 'making' their 'own' meanings from the media.

8. Corbusier writes: 'I have recently discovered in a photographer's chart these explicit graphics: I am no longer swimming in the approximations of personal observations. I am facing sensitive photographic film that reacts to light. The table says this: . . . *The photographic plate in a room illuminated with a horizontal window needs to be exposed four times less than in a room illuminated with two vertical windows . . .*' (cited in Colomina, 1996: 311).

9. Of course, Le Corbusier famously posed the equation slightly differently: architecture *or* revolution.

10. Josh Meyerowitz (1985: 323), for example, has argued that television has 'the potential of the closest thing the earth has witnessed to participatory democracy on an enormous scale'. Commenting on the public advocacy of 'virtual democracy' by leading political figures including Al Gore, Newt Gingrich and Ross Perot, Virilio (1995b) characterized their discourse as 'reminiscent of a fundamental mysticism'.

11. Benjamin (1973: 249) argued: 'Since the innovations of camera and recording equipment make it possible for the orator to become audible and visible to an unlimited number of persons, the presentation of the man of politics before camera and recording equipment has become paramount.... This results in a new selection, a selection before the equipment from which the star and the dictator emerge victorious.'

12. I have discussed this in more detail elsewhere (McQuire, 1998: 233–40). Virilio's analysis of modern media as an integral arm of politico-military strategy explores similar terrain. In relation to Hitler and Stalin, he observes: 'Perhaps it has not been properly understood that these miracle working dictators no longer ruled, but were themselves directors' (Virilio, 1989b: 53).

13. Ringley writes: 'Initially I bought the camera to update portions of my webpage with pictures of myself. A friend joked that it could be used to do a Fishbowl cam, but of a person. The idea fascinated me, and I took off with it. Initially the Jennicam had an audience of half a dozen of my close friends, and it spread like wildfire from there.' All quotes from Ringley taken from the FAQ page [http://www.jennicam.org/].

14. Elsewhere, I have discussed this condition of generalized overexposure in terms of 'the technological uncanny' (McQuire, 1997).

15. In a recent interview, Virilio (1995c) argued: 'Something other than history is now coming to the fore. In a sense, we are now standing at the foot of the wall of time. We have realised absolute speed on a global plane.... History is simply smashing into the wall of time. This is an extraordinary occurrence.'

16. Perhaps not all that surprising for one who has described the artists Malevich, Braque, Duchamp and Magritte as 'the last authentic philosophers' (Virilio, 1994a: 31).

17. For example, Virilio (1997: 19) argues that 'the current revolution in (interactive) transmission is in turn provoking a commutation in the urban environment whereby the image prevails over the thing it is an image of'. Numerous other examples employing this binary structure of a split between the real (as presence, face-to-face communication, etc.) and the image (virtual, telepresence, etc.) could be cited.

18. For an account of the way in which the subordinate and subsequent nature of the image is part of the temporal order of 'logic' itself, see Derrida (1981: 191).

19. In one of his few references to Lacan, Virilio (1994a: 24) describes the dominance of theories of language and linguistic being as 'forbidding any conceptual opening, and deploying to this end, massive reinforcement of Marxist-Freudian babble and semiological cant'. In fact, his position in this regard is neither entirely clear-cut or consistent. At certain points (1994a: 21), he argues that the spatio-temporal 'disorientation' caused by the spread of electronic media can be theorized in terms of Einsteinian relativity – a move which, extended to its fullest logic, implies a potentially critical attitude to the stability and centredness of the humanist subject. He has also disputed, in Bergsonian terms, the equation of retinal vision with unmediated perception, arguing in favour of a model which recognizes the irreducible implication of memory in any 'direct perception' (1994a: 1–19). While he doesn't acknowledge it, such a model has as much in common with psychoanalytical as phenomenological accounts of consciousness.

20. Virilio (1995c) has argued that the 'doubling' of reality caused by telematics is 'something that, to the best of my knowledge, results in clear pathological

consequences'. On the pollution of the world's dimensions, or 'desertification', see Virilio (1997: 125).

21. See Virilio (1997: 97) for his call for an 'ecology of images'.

22. Such a paradox, handed down from Aristotle to Kant, Hegel, Bergson and beyond, circles around the 'impossible' nature of the present moment conceived as 'now' – that it has no duration and therefore cannot properly 'exist'. I have discussed this at greater length elsewhere (McQuire, 1998: 248–53).

References

Benjamin, Walter (1973) *Illuminations,* trans. H. Żohn. London: Fontana.

Benjamin, Walter (1985) *One Way Street and Other Writings*, trans. E. Jephcott and K. Shorter. London: Verso.

Berger, John and Jean Mohr (1982) *Another Way of Telling*. New York: Pantheon Books.

Clarke, Arthur C. (1945) 'Extra-Terrestrial Relays', *Wireless World* 51(10): 305–8.

Colomina, Beatriz (1996) *Privacy and Publicity: Modern Architecture as Mass Media*. Cambridge, MA: MIT Press.

Derrida, Jacques (1981) *Dissemination*, trans. B. Johnson. Chicago, IL: University of Chicago Press.

Kracauer, Siegfried (1960) *Theory of Film: The Redemption of Physical Reality*. London: Oxford University Press.

McQuire, Scott (1997) 'The Uncanny Home: Or Living Online with Others', pp. 682–709 in P. Droege (ed.) *Intelligent Environments: Spatial Aspects of the Information Revolution*. Rotterdam: Elsevier Science.

McQuire, Scott (1998) *Visions of Modernity: Representation, Memory, Time and Space in the Age of the Camera*. London: Sage.

Marx, Karl (1973) *Grundrisse: Foundations of the Critique of Political Economy*, trans. M. Nicolaus. London: Allen Lane/NLR.

Meyerowitz, Josh (1985) *No Sense of Place: The Impact of Electronic Media on Social Behaviour*. New York: Oxford University Press.

Sontag, Susan (1979) *On Photography*. Harmondsworth: Penguin.

Virilio, Paul (1986a) *Speed & Politics: An Essay on Dromology*, trans. M. Polizzotti. New York: Semiotext(e).

Virilio, Paul (1986b) 'The Overexposed City', trans. A. Hustvedt, *Zone* 1(2): 14–31.

Virilio, Paul (1988) 'The Third Window', pp. 185–97 in C. Schneider and B. Wallis (eds) *Global Television*. New York and Cambridge, MA: Wedge Press and MIT Press.

Virilio, Paul (1989a) 'The Last Vehicle', pp. 106–19 in D. Kamper and C. Wulf (eds) *Looking Back on the End of the World*, trans. D. Antal. New York: Semiotext(e).

Virilio, Paul (1989b) *War and Cinema: The Logistics of Perception*, trans. P. Camiller. London and New York: Verso.

Virilio, Paul (1991a) *The Aesthetics of Disappearance*, trans. P. Beitchman. New York: Semiotext(e).

Virilio, Paul (1991b) *The Lost Dimension*, trans. D. Moshenberg. New York: Semiotext(e).

Virilio, Paul (1994a) *The Vision Machine*. Bloomington: Indiana University Press.

Virilio, Paul (1994b) 'Cyberwar, God and Television: Interview with Paul Virilio', in *CTheory* [http://www.ctheory.com/a-cyberwar_god.html].

Virilio, Paul (1995a) *The Art of the Motor*, trans. J. Rose. Minneapolis and London: University of Minnesota Press.

Virilio, Paul (1995b) 'Speed and Information: Cyberspace Alarm!', trans. P. Riemens, *CTheory* [http://www.ctheory.com/a30-cyberspace_alarm.html].

Virilio, Paul (1995c) 'The Silence of the Lambs: Paul Virilio in Conversation', trans. P. Riemens, *CTheory* [http://www.ctheory.com/ga1.7-silence.html].

Virilio, Paul (1997) *Open Sky*, trans. J. Rose. London and New York: Verso.

Scott McQuire lectures in Art and Architecture in the School of Social Inquiry at Deakin University, Australia. He is the author of *Crossing the Digital Threshold* (1997) and *Visions of Modernity: Representation, Memory, Time and Space in the Age of the Camera* (1998). He was recently awarded an Australian Postdoctoral Fellowship to research the relationship between architecture and mass media, and is currently completing a report on large format and special venue cinema entitled *Impact Aesthetics: Cinematic Subjectivity into the Next Millennium* (forthcoming).

The Tendency, the Accident and the Untimely

Paul Virilio's Engagement with the Future

Patrick Crogan

Introduction

'SPEED', SAYS VIRILIO in *Pure War* (Virilio and Lotringer, 1983: 30), 'is not considered important'. For him, however it is a crucial if neglected factor in all historical and political developments. He suggests that the ever increasing speeds of contemporary technologies of transportation, communication, destruction and representation threaten to overwhelm the capacity for conventional historical modes of interpretation to make sense of them. These speeds challenge the ability of historico-critical discourse to account adequately for their impacts on society, politics, culture and even the perception of reality. In exploring this challenge, Virilio has questioned the mainstream discourses of a 'future perfect' that accompany, promote and even generate techno-scientific advance. At a more profound level, Virilio's work addresses not only these technophilic discourses but also the humanist conception of history that allows both positivist and critical discourse to be articulated – including, necessarily, his own.

This article will examine Virilio's engagement with speed's challenge to criticality. In the first section I will characterize the widely perceived crisis in conventional critical discourse that Virilio has identified with the 'problem of speed'. This will involve reference to Gilbert Hottois's (1981) critique of futurology and Jacques Derrida's (1984) notion of the 'aporia of speed'. This last is, I will argue, a key formulation of the problem confronting criticism today. It will serve to orient our discussion of Virilio's work as

■ *Theory, Culture & Society* 1999 (SAGE, London, Thousand Oaks and New Delhi),
  Vol. 16(5–6): 161–176
  [0263-2764(199910/12)16:5–6;161–176;009964]

a response to this problem in the second and third sections of this article. In the second section, Virilio's interest in the accident and his stated aim of seeking the tendency in phenomena will be analysed as the crucial components of his response to the challenge of speed. How this response opens the possibility of a critical engagement with the 'untimely' future is the subject of the final section of this essay.

The Future of Futurology and the Aporia of Speed

In an article entitled 'The "Future Dimension" in Mythical, Historical and Techno-Scientific Temporality' (1981), Gilbert Hottois argues that the current interest in the future, evidenced by the rise of 'futurology' and the popularity of science fiction, is indicative of a shift in or even an overturning of the conventional concept of temporality that has held sway in the West since the 'Judeo-Christian vision' supplanted the mythical temporality which preceded it.[1] What he finds most revealing about futurological studies are the extraordinary reservations expressed in the prefaces of futurological books about the accuracy of their predictions concerning the state of humanity in the future. What becomes most apparent in these accounts of the future when these disclaimers are considered is that an account of the future cannot in fact be rendered; its unforeseeability is radical and not just of the order of a minor miscalculation of present tendencies. The source of this temporality of a completely 'open' and 'opaque' future is named by Hottois as contemporary techno-science (1981: 77).

Comparing the science of antiquity to techno-science, Hottois says that the former was:

> ... deductivist, conceptual, speculative – thought must in principle be capable of securing knowledge by deducing, without surprise, *a priori*, the body of science from premises. Logical and speculative, the former science was in some way *intemporal*. (1981: 77)

Contrasted to this is techno-science which is described as being entirely 'in time: the time of research and of construction' (1981: 77). It does not deduce from first principles but reacts to the most recent results of research and experimentation. The future is not the guarantee or end result predicted from the beginning but is always limited and contingent. Hottois writes: 'potentially, surprise, the unexpected are everywhere. Those in the know repeat it: "What is important in research is the unforeseeable". "All major discoveries are unforeseeable"' (1981: 77). It is for this reason that any attempt to envision the future quickly runs up against that which renders prediction logically unjustifiable. This situation is exacerbated by the fact that diverse scientific disciplines are more and more interlocked in research and that a particular discovery can have several different repercussions in different fields, leading to further interdisciplinary innovations and research projects.

In Hottois's view futurology, the projected history of the future, cannot be written because of this opaque, unforeseeable nature of techno-scientific change. The further implication of this is that neither can an adequate history of the present nor of the recent past be formulated, because of the pervasive influence of techno-science in the era of modernity. The reservations about predicting the future that Hottois focuses on are indicative, precisely, of the crisis in the interpretation of the present. The techno-scientific discovery and development of theories and technics in such fields as audio-visual media, motorized transportation and flight, atomic physics and nuclear weapons, bio-chemistry, birth control and genetic engineering – to name some of the areas which have had the most significant impacts over the last century – cannot be explained in a conventionally historical manner. In another text, *The Sign and the Technique* (1984), Hottois argues that what results from the effort to do so is a discourse of legitimation *after* the event which tries vainly to reinscribe the technical development in a meaningful anthropological narrative of progress:

> There exists a curious movement proper to technics: its causally autonomous growth tends to produce the illusion of progress toward ends which are only in reality justifications after the fact of a blind proliferation. (1984: 123)

Hottois goes on to say it is the technocratic and humanist socio-political discourses that provide the institutional and political framework for this illusion of technical 'progress'. Attendant on the 'benefit of humankind' and labouring under the illusion that technics exist as the neutral tool of humanity, these discourses produce this justification 'after the fact' (1984: 192). But these justifications appear more and more tenuous with each techno-scientific development. The intrinsically unforeseeable nature of these developments and their consequences undermines the effort of the discourses of progress and rationality to reinscribe them in a meaningful teleology. The impulse to effect a retroactive legitimation of techno-science is the desperate measure of the predictive Enlightenment discourses of progress in the face of their increasing irrelevance today. Their enabling assumption of discernible continuities and coherencies in the linear, onward march of time is grievously shaken by what Hottois calls the 'blind proliferation' of technics.

In 'No Apocalypse, Not Now' (1984), Jacques Derrida addresses this challenge that modern techno-science poses to historico-critical interpretation in a different, but not unrelated context. He is discussing speed's effects on society and politics – both the speeds of modern technological communication, transportation, etc. and the speed of advance in these fields. Like Hottois, Derrida calls into question the viability of traditional historical modes of interpretation in accounting for techno-scientific developments and the radical changes in the speeds of cultural and political existence they bring. But this does not lead Derrida to a total rejection of historical interpretation. As we will see shortly, this questioning leads him to propose an 'aporia of speed' that confronts critical work today.

First, I want to follow Derrida's interrogation of what he calls the 'speed race in search of speed' that has dominated social and political life globally since the end of the Second World War. This will help us better understand the problematic concerning speed that leads Derrida to formulate the notion of the 'aporia of speed'. Writing in the early 1980s Cold War revival under the then American President Ronald Reagan, Derrida is initially referring here to the arms and space races, but he goes on assert – in a move characteristic of Virilio's discourse on 'pure war' (to be examined in the next section) – that all techno-scientific developments must be considered in the light of this speed race (1984: 23). Indeed, he says that 'no single instant, no atom of our life (our relation to the world and to being) is not marked today, directly or indirectly, by that speed race' (1984: 20).[2]

Derrida first poses the question about how to understand this 'speed race' of (military) techno-science and the effect it is having on human existence thus: 'Is it new? Is it the first time "in history"?' (1984: 20). The quotation marks around ' "in history" ' are then immediately foregrounded as the sign of a questioning of the validity of this question: 'Is it [the speed race] an invention, and can we still say "in history" to speak about it?' (1984: 20). This questioning of the question is elaborated as an uncertainty about the adequacy of history to the experience of this 'speed race', to the contemporary experience of speed:

> Are we having today, *another*, a different experience of speed? Is our relation to time and to motion qualitatively different? Or must we speak prudently of an extraordinary – although qualitatively homogeneous – acceleration of the same experience? (1984: 20)

Conventional historical discourse would want to maintain the concept of speed as a characteristic of things – objectively measurable because of its constant quality across quantifiable changes (accelerations, decelerations, changes in direction). Modern physics has shown this to be only a conventional understanding of speed with a limited validity. Heisenberg's principle and the general theory of relativity before it have undermined the 'objectivity' of speed in undermining belief in the absolute character of space and time.[3] The question, 'Is it the first time "in history"?' was 'simplistic' because it opposed quantity and quality:

> ... *as if* the concept of speed, linked to some quantification of objective velocity, remained within a homogeneous relation to every experience of time – for the human subject or for a mode of temporalisation that the human subject – as such – would have himself covered up. (1984: 20)

Derrida suggests that speed has to be rethought beyond the simple opposition of quality and quantity in view of its all-encompassing influence today. Such a rethinking would be more than a consideration of how modern technology has increased the speed and efficiency of modern work, warfare, construction, etc. In addition, it would need to theorize the impact of these technologies on the experience of these phenomena, and on how these new experiences of speed have affected the nature of the world they constitute.

But this theoretical project would not be immune from the problems facing critical interpretation that both Hottois and Derrida discuss, for it would also depend on a conventional critical assumpton of the possibility of articulating present phenomena with historical developments, *even* in the effort to theorize the novelty of contemporary cultural and political realities. This critical assumption is challenged by the unforeseeable nature of techno-scientific development (Hottois) and the possibility of the alteration of the human experience of time under the speeds of contemporary social, political and individual existence (Derrida). While the attempt to 'locate' the current state of affairs 'in history' would appear to be problematical, Derrida will go on to state his 'belief' that 'the historian's critical vigilance' does have an important role to play in analysing what he calls the 'nuclear age', even if this analysis carries the risk of not seeing what is radically new about this age (1984: 21).

This is the challenge facing critical work today, one which is unavoidable: how to think the new, the unforeseeable in terms of the old, the conventional – and this at a time when the new developments of techno-science appear to be rendering the conventional modes of critical thought untenable. Derrida proposes that it is the present situation which has thrown up this challenge and hence allowed us the opportunity to confront what he calls the 'aporia of speed'.

According to Derrida, the aporia of speed concerns an obligation to move quickly over against the need for potentially infinite consideration. The criticism of the nuclear age must proceed from a decision about whether this age represents an entirely unforeseen development of the human *socius* or whether it must be theorized historically in terms of earlier forms of the nexus of the social and the technical. While Derrida's text oscillates from one alternative to another on this initial question, the text is nevertheless traversed by the urgency of the situation, a situation requiring a decisive departure for the inquiry into the nuclear age. Recognizing the dilemma that what he calls the 'the critical slowdown may thus be as critical as the critical acceleration', Derrida goes on to ask:

What is the *right* speed, then? Given our inability to provide a good answer for that question, we at least have to recognise gratefully that the nuclear age allows us to think through this aporia of speed (i.e., the need to move both slowly and quickly); it allows us to confront our predicament starting from the limit constituted by the absolute acceleration in which the uniqueness of an ultimate event, of a final collision or collusion, the temporalities called subjective and objective, phenomenological and intra-worldly, authentic and inauthentic, etc., would end up being merged into one another. (1984: 21)

The 'limit' of 'absolute acceleration ... of a final collision or collusion' in which 'the temporalities called subjective and objective would end up being merged into one another' refers explicitly to nuclear holocaust in this 1980s text. But it also figures implicitly the end of criticism in the speed of technological advance (the 'final collusion'). This limit point is, Derrida argues here, both the 'ultimate threat' and the best starting point for the necessary confrontation with 'our predicament'. These pairs of opposed 'temporalities' are highly allusive to Western thought's most influential attempts to confront its situation, its object(s), its 'self'. The pairs 'subjective and objective, phenomenological and intra-worldly, authentic and inauthentic, etc.' function as a shorthand description of the various major attempts to construe and interpret events in time, including the Hegelian dialectic of subject and object and all its progeny, and the Heideggerian rethinking of history in terms of authentic and inauthentic apprehensions of temporality, 'etc.'.

Without exploring all the ramifications of this shorthand reference to the major 'philosophemes' of modernity, we can perceive that the threat of the end of criticism lies in the dissolution – under the tranformative press-ure of acceleration – of the distinctions upon which these modes of inter-pretation depend for their significance. This threat posed by the nuclear age, namely, that critical interrogation of it will no longer be possible, is also, paradoxically or aporetically, the opportunity it affords us. For if the urgent decision on the question of how to approach the age (quickly or slowly, historically or as a totally novel phenomenon) cannot be made and the path of questioning leads only to the aporia of speed, this is not necessarily the end for criticism. If criticality is in crisis because it faces its end, this crisis always carries with it the opportunity for a renewed confrontation, for renewed interpretations.

The task, concludes Derrida, for those in 'the humanities', that is, those who practise critical work in the disciplines experiencing this aporia of speed, is to 'reinvent [critical] invention' by rethinking the relations 'between the invention that finds what was already there and the one that produces new mechanisms or new spaces' (1984: 21). It cannot be a ques-tion of simply abandoning as outmoded historical interpretation that 'finds what was already there'. That move would relinquish all possibility of articulating the present with earlier modes of the cultural-technological formation, resulting in a critical belief tantamount to holding that the present sprang fully formed in an instant without precedent. But nor can it be a case of ignoring what is unlooked for in the present and unforeseeable in the future, for this would lead – and indeed has led – to the increasing irrelevance of conventional critical work. Critical invention must also attempt to produce 'new mechanisms or new spaces'. The task Derrida describes is one of rethinking the relations between the two critical efforts required.

The future, one might say, depends on this attempt being made. As I will discuss in the following sections, Virilio's work represents just such a task of thinking between conventional criticality and its undoing in the invention of 'new mechanisms'. His project encounters the aporia of speed through its form of encounter with both historical and contemporary techno-scientific and cultural phenomena. The teleological model of history and of the future is the terrain in which this encounter takes place. I will argue that Virilio's work can be understood as a form of anti-futurology that faces up to the unforeseeable nature of today's techno-scientific future in a way that attempts the aporetic task of moving both slowly and quickly in the face of the transformative speeds of contemporary existence.

The Tendency and the Accident

Virilio's work is best thought of as an ongoing series of 'tendential analyses' that privilege the accident over the substance of any given techno-scientific development. The tendency and the accident are crucial concepts in Virilio's discourse and it will be necessary to examine each in detail. Above all, understanding how they function together in Virilio's work is essential to comprehending his response to the aporia of speed.

The form of Virilio's writing immediately bears witness to his effort to meet the challenge that speed has posed to criticality. The speed of his own discourse is the most apparent and widely recognized feature of his critical engagement. Virilio's work is rapid. It executes fast-moving analyses of contemporary phenomena and historical developments so as to outline what he sees as the major tendencies inherent in them. His writing privileges a sketching-out of these tendencies over the detailed historico-critical analysis and interpretation of the various phenomena which in combination constitute those tendencies. For the most part, his books are collections of essays, many of which are published individually prior to their appearance together in book form. While they maintain a thematic consistency, the essays in a book by Virilio do not come together to build a homogeneous, linear argument as so many chapters of a unified study. Each essay moves quickly from one idea to the next, from consideration of one phenomenon to another, without extensive analysis or interpretation. In addition, the thematic linkage between two ideas or phenomena is often evoked in such a way as to challenge traditional modes of interpreting such linkages.

Immediately one can see the risk involved in Virilio's project. His emphasis on writing 'rapid books' leaves him open to criticism on the grounds that he fails to substantiate, via careful and rigorous analysis and discussion, the claims he makes. This is undoubtedly correct in many instances – Virilio often relies on brief evocations of well-established interpretative models such as Marxism, positivism and the discourses of military history and theory which he summarily subverts, diverts or inverts.

But this weakness is, I will argue, also paradoxically what constitutes the strength of Virilio's engagement with the aporia of speed.

What is the tendency, then, for Virilio, and why does he prefer the rapid sketching out of the tendency over the more measured steps of historico-critical analysis? In the light of our discussion in the first section of this article we can hypothesize that Virilio is responding to the crisis in historical modes of interpretation by attempting to bring critical discourse 'up to speed' as it were with contemporary developments. Virilio would seem to confirm this when he talks about his preference for the tendency over the 'episode' in the long interview with Sylvère Lotringer published as *Pure War*:

> I work in staircases – some people have realized this. I begin a sentence, I work out an idea and when I consider it suggestive enough I jump a step to another idea without bothering with the development. Developments are the episodes. I try to reach the tendency. Tendency is the change of level. (1983: 39)

The tendency is the elusive element, the faintly perceived movement of an event, something which will have future consequences not immediately apparent when the event appears in its conventional form as one part of a development that has led to the present. To posit the presence of an unnoticed tendency in past events is to recast the historical interpretation of those events, challenging the established sequence of the salient and substantial elements of a particular historical development. As Hottois has argued, this established sequence is increasingly problematical today as the rationalist discourse of progress attempts to legitimate techno-scientific advances that bear less and less relation to the humanist model of scientific and social progress. The jump from one step in 'the staircase' of ideas that Virilio ascends to another attempts a refiguring of the historical chain of cause and effect, undoing its apparent continuity and reinventing it in a parallel but heterogeneous enchainment.

Virilio's jumps are suggestive; they work with absences, with the gaps between the levels of different ideas, different developments. His project – with its leaps from one state of affairs to a qualitatively different state of affairs – relies on these absences, these gaps in the tracks of historico-critical interpretation and the accidents that make interpretation jump tracks across these gaps. We will examine the nature of these accidents shortly.

The opposition between tendency and episode that Virilio uses to describe his project derives from a statement by Winston Churchill (cited earlier in *Pure War*) that 'in ancient warfare, the episodes were more important than the tendencies; in modern warfare, the tendencies are more important than the episodes' (1983: 11). Virilio's effort to reach the tendency reveals, therefore, that his is not only a discourse on war – more specifically, what he calls 'pure war', and the speeds of its techno-scientific proliferation – but also a discourse at war with pure war, one which is trying to match the speed of its tendential changes of level and their widespread impacts on cultural and political reality.

Pure war, probably Virilio's most well known concept, is his term for the overarching tendency discernible in the post-Second World War era. As such it makes an excellent example for our consideration of Virilio's tendential mode of critical analysis. The pure war tendency is one in which war has mutated: war is overflowing the bounds of its traditional dwelling place in actual hostilities and seeping into the 'pure' form of its preparation. The arrangement and maintenance of a permanent state of preparation for war, an arrangement which increasingly dominates social and political formations in the post-war period, has tended toward a radical alteration of those formations. This alteration is not adequately theorized by the standard accounts of the Cold War and the rise of the military-industrial complexes of the Superpowers, for they rely on conventional assumptions about the relations between economics, politics, the military and the social. Pure war tends to indetermine the distinction between war and peace and along with it traditional models of the state–individual relationship and of the military and non-military ('domestic') spheres.

The rapid passage of the Second World War from the politico-strategic level to the extremes of total and nuclear war is a key factor, according to Virilio, in the post-war acceleration of the tendency toward pure war. The tendential element that Virilio perceives in the formation of the strategy of nuclear deterrence is the deterrence not only of nuclear war, but of previous forms of political and cultural relationships at individual, local, national and international levels. This was an unforeseen, transformative element of nuclear deterrence that has had profound consequences beyond the field of military strategy and geopolitics. It has amounted to a speeding up of what Virilio has characterized as the 'logistical' reordering of the state and the social that is pure war.[4]

Logistics is a key term in Virilio's characterization of the pure war tendency. It is generally associated with the economic, supply and transport considerations taken into account by military planning staff in their preparations for war or for maintaining standing armed forces. Manuel de Landa defines logistics as 'the art of assembling war and the agricultural, economic and industrial resources that make it possible' (1991: 105). It has also gained a wider usage in describing economic resource management and deployment more generally.[5] Virilio, for his part, has taken this term and pushed its implication – that war and the military cannot be considered as separate from the socio-economic and cultural spheres – to the forefront in his characterization of pure war. In this 'avant-garde' position, the term 'logistics' always announces a question for Virilio about the overflowing of the military into every domain of life: the economic, the social, the political and the cultural. Broadly speaking, his earlier texts dealt with the social and political dimensions of this tendency. Later texts such as *War and Cinema: The Logistics of Perception* (1989 [1984]), *The Vision Machine* (1994 [1988]),

L'Inertie polaire (1999 [1990]) and *The Art of the Motor* (1995 [1993]) have examined the wider impacts of the influence of logistics in such areas as architecture, design, communications, vision and visual culture.

As mentioned above, for Virilio the tendency towards pure war gains momentum dramatically in the Second World War. It is during this long conflict that logistical considerations begin to dominate traditional strategic and political modes of organization under the impetus of the policies of total mobilization. This dominance extends beyond the end of open hostilities into the Cold War period. Virilio sees in General Eisenhower's management of the Allies' D-Day invasion of occupied France the culmination of an 'a-national logistical revolution', subsequently instantiated in an early post-war definition of logistics that issued from the Pentagon: 'Logistics is the procedure following which a nation's potential is transferred to its armed forces, *in times of peace as in times of war*' (Virilio and Lotringer, 1983: 16; emphasis added).

It is an accident, however, that occurs during the First World War which plays a major role in the formation of the logistical tendency. Virilio describes this accident and its immediate consequence in *Pure War*:

> After several months of trench warfare – that is, of position warfare, since the armies could no longer move – they realized that their current war production, the traditional production foreseen during peacetime, could no longer meet the demands of military consumption (in the number of shells fired, of bombs, of planes, etc.).... This was the 'technical surprise', as it was called, of World War One. They could no longer say that on one side there was the arsenal which produced a few shells, and on the other civilian consumption and the budget. No, they noticed that they needed a special economy, a wartime economy. This wartime economy was a formidable discovery, which in reality announced and inaugurated the military-industrial complex. (1983: 16)

The 'technical surprise' of the Great War is an excellent example of Virilio's notion of the accident. It was the unforeseen result of technological 'progress' in a range of areas, from industrial modes of production in general and weapons manufacture in particular to logistical systems of transport and communication. Instead of producing the anticipated short and decisive conflict befitting the modern machine age, this technological 'progress' led to the protracted, immobilized bloodbath of trench warfare – a bloodbath which was also a black hole for the economic resources of the warring nations. It is this accident that induced the 'discovery' of the wartime economy, the origin of the military-industrial complex of pure war.

The 'technical surprise', then, is just the type of accident Virilio is concerned with in his work. Virilio's interest in the accident is central to his critique of the positivist, technophilic discourses of progress, those discourses that Hottois characterized as legitimating technological developments after their (unforeseen and often violent) advent. His interest is succinctly elaborated in *Pure War*:

The riddle of technology ... is also the riddle of the accident. I'll explain. In classic Aristotelian philosophy, substance is necessary and the accident is relative and contingent. At the moment, there's an inversion: the accident is becoming necessary and substance relative and contingent. Every technology produces, provokes, programs a specific accident. For example: when they invented the railroad, what did they invent? An object that allowed you to go fast, which allowed you to progress – a vision *à la* Jules Verne, positivism, evolutionism. But at the same time they invented the railway catastrophe.... I believe that from now on, if we wish to continue with technology (and I don't think there will be a neolithic regression), we must think about both the substance and its accident – substance being both the object and its accident. The negative side of technology and speed was censored. (1983: 32)

Virilio recasts the relation between what is considered essential and what peripheral to technological 'advance' by punning on the buried relationship between the classical, philosophical notion of accident as an 'inessential' attribute or quality of a thing and the everyday sense of the term accident as an unexpected mishap. In doing so Virilio proposes not just to remove the censorship of positivism by acknowledging the 'specific accident' of a given technology. Instead he calls for a rethinking of technological development so as to address the substance/accident 'inversion' through which the accident is not only a regretable contingency but becomes something 'every technology produces, provokes, programs'.

This is why war and military developments are so crucial for Virilio. 'What are war machines?', Virilio asks in an interview with Chris Dercon: 'They are machines in reverse – they produce accidents' (Dercon, 1986: 36). This explains to a significant extent Virilio's focus on theorizing war as a central aspect of modernity. War not only provides a major impetus for the development of new technologies of speed – it is, he says in the same text, the 'laboratory of modernity' (1986: 36). The war machine, in its reversal of the commonsense notion that machinery is essentially productive, promotes this 'negative side of technology' which Virilio argues is a central aspect of all technologies. This negative side, he says in another interview (with Florian Rötzer), is always there, doubling the side of 'productive reason' (Rötzer, 1995: 100). In privileging the accident over the substance Virilio sees himself as a theorist of this hidden negativity, correcting, he says, the Western metaphysical tradition's denial of 'military intelligence': 'When Aristotle says there is no science of the accidental, he puts into motion the process of denying the negative' (1995: 100).[6]

Virilio provides further insight into his privileging of the accident in 'La Musée de l'accident' (in Virilio, 1996).[7] Taking the occasion of the opening of a museum of technology at the Parc de la Villette in Paris, he repeats his assertion of the 'symmetry between the substance and the accident' and speculates on the need for and the possible design of a 'museum of accidents' to counter the positivism of conventional museological practices (1996: 110). Describing the approach of such a museum as 'postpositivist', he argues that its goal – to 'expose the accident' – would be to 'expose the unlikely, the unusual yet inevitable' (1996: 112). This would serve to expose to 'us' 'that to which we are habitually exposed' as a form of protection from it. To achieve this 'preventive perspective' the museum would need to comprehend the accident as:

> ... no longer identifiable simply with its deadly consequences, its actual results: ruins and scattered debris, but also with a dynamic and energetic process, *a kinetic and cinematic sequence* not bound to the relics of all kinds of destroyed objects and rubble. (1996: 114)

This *'kinetic and cinematic sequence'* is the inverse of the positivist conception of the dynamic process of historical progress. It is the double of progress in that it borrows the 'progressive' assumptions of linear temporality and teleological inevitability, as well as the notion that a visible image of the movement of progress is discernible across the passage of time. The revealing of this sequence that Virilio identifies with the accident would challenge the habitual understanding of the connection between historical and technical developments by 'showing the advent of something in what seems to happen unexpectedly' (1996: 115).[8]

What Virilio's 'meta-museography' of the imaginary museum of accidents amounts to is a characterization, in a typically rapid, evocative form, of his theoretical project. The kinetic sequence of the unexpected that doubles the narrative of historical/technological progress is another description, I would suggest, of the tendency. As seen in the relation between the 'technical surprise' of the First World War and the logistical tendency toward pure war, the accident plays a central role in the 'vectorization' of the tendential sequence.[9] Indeed, it is the 'substance' of the tendency's change of level, the motor of its unexpected detouring of the rational course of progress. Virilio's writing attempts to sketch out the tendency through a description of the accidents of technological (post)modernity. These descriptions are in effect critical reinscriptions of these adventitious yet somehow constitutive mishaps of techno-science.

The tendency is, therefore, accidental – it arises and gains momentum in and through these unforeseen detours of techno-scientific 'advances' in civilization. But these unexpected events are, paradoxically, 'substantial'; they link up to form the dynamic sequence that perturbs the march of forward progress by doubling and disfiguring its teleology. The tendency is made up of these enigmatic accidents that Virilio says 'every technology produces, provokes, programs'.

The Untimely

We are now in a position to articulate Virilio's project in terms of the aporia of speed confronting critical work discussed in the first section of this article. It was stated there that the aporia of speed concerned the contradictory necessities for criticism in the era of techno-science to move quickly, in order to account for the rapidly transforming present, over against the need for careful consideration of the continuities between past and present. Finding the 'right speed' for critical interpretation is an aporetic task which must nevertheless be attempted, for it is the opportunity that presents itself to criticism even as the critical discourses of the humanities find themselves in crisis in the face of the techno-scientific transformation of culture. To recall, this task involves rethinking the relations between what Derrida calls 'the invention that finds what was already there and the one that produces new mechanisms or new spaces' (1984: 21).

This is what Virilio's tendential analyses attempt. They represent a profound meditation on the relation between traditional historical modes of interpretation and the new event that challenges the coherence of such historical interpretation. As we have seen, the tendency appears as a double of the discourse of progress in its mirroring of the structure of linear temporal development toward a future endpoint. For instance, the pure war tendency would culminate in the total merging of the military and non-military spheres and the complete dominance of logistics over all other considerations (economic, social, political, ethical) in the ordering of the social. In such a situation there would be no possibility of a criticality outside of logistical imperatives. In doubling the discourse of progress, his rapid analyses retain a link to the historical form of criticality. Virilio reaffirms the traditional mode of historical analysis even as he attempts to counter the more or less explicit positivism that pervades conventional accounts of techno-science. His efforts to bring the negative side of technological advance into focus by exposing the accidents that have contributed to the generally unnoticed, dynamic tendencies that shadow and transform 'progress' are, in this sense, efforts toward a corrective form of anti-futurology. This anti-futurology avoids the retroactive legitimation of techno-scientific developments and the increasingly tenuous prediction of the inevitable advance of (Western) world civilization. It raises crucial questions about the nature of techno-scientific development by proposing a perverted version of the dominant teleological narratives told about it.

But this corrective anti-futurology is not the only dimension of Virilio's response to the aporia of speed. In his focus on the accident, Virilio does more than reverse the positivist censorship of the negative in standard discourses on technology. By treating the accident as somehow both unforeseen and integral to a dynamic process of transformation, his project addresses the aporetic task of thinking 'between the invention that finds what was already there and the one that produces new mechanisms or new spaces' (Derrida, 1984: 21). The accident becomes a paradoxical object of Virilio's analysis that mediates between these two forms of critical invention. As integral to the tendency, the accident is described as contributing/ having contributed to an established and future-directed chain of events. As what is unforeseen, however, the accident in its very nature eludes all critical 'pre-destining' or explanation in terms of a foreseeable outcome.

When Virilio says that studying the accident allows one 'to see the advent of something in what seems to happen unexpectedly' (1996: 115), he evokes the aporetic nature of his critical enterprise.

The accident is unforeseen; when it happens it changes everything suddenly, like a vehicular accident that violently and unexpectedly breaks a journey. It postpones the arrival at the destination or perhaps even eradicates the original destination by necessitating a new journey(s). The accident threatens the possibility of achieving a rational, homogeneous, linear development. While the accident will come to be incorporated in a narrative which will assimilate it after the fact to a sequence of events (the 'original' journey started, the accident happened, new journeys/a delayed journey resulted), the accident will always have been experienced as the irruption of another temporality, other to the anticipated continuity of the journey. In the accident, time is, momentarily at least, 'out of joint'.[10]

The accident is this spatio-temporal/conceptual disjunction. It is 'untimely' in that it is inassimilable to the temporality of historico-criticality. It can never be questioned as such even if it allows – and indeed necessitates – the commencement of (historico-critical) questioning. This questioning may discover a certain substantial development in and through which the accident is explained, and this is so also for Virilio's own refigurings of technological developments as tendencies leading to and from certain accidental events. But in its untimeliness the accident will always be outside the temporality of these interpretations. It will have been that which interrupts their journey and promises others. Virilio's work tries to think the relation between those well-known paths and those that are unforeseeable yet which will have been necessary. It engages the future in the aporia between its radical unforeseeability and its potential as alternative endpoint to the end of progress.

Notes

1. All translations of Hottois are my own.

2. As mentioned above the paper was first presented in 1984 in the renewed Cold War climate of the Reagan administration at a colloquium on 'Nuclear Criticism'. For an account of the intellectual and political context of this colloquium see the first chapter of Ken Ruthven's *Nuclear Criticism* (1993). Hence the question may be asked of its relevance to the contemporary state of affairs after the end of the Cold War and the mutation of nuclear deterrence. But Derrida's text is investigating precisely the issue of whether conventional historical modes of understanding socio-political and cultural changes are valid in the era of the ongoing speed race of techno-science. As such, his meditations on this issue would bear on the question of the relevance of Derrida's analysis in view of the recent progress of history, that is, the question of whether his analysis is 'dated'.

3. See Stephen Hawking, *A Brief History of Time*, on 'the situation' in the general theory of relativity: 'when a body moves or a force acts, it affects the curvature of space and time – and in turn the structure of space-time affects the way in which bodies move and forces act. Space and time not only affect but are affected by everything that happens in the universe' (1988: 36).

4. For Virilio, this process of logistical reordering has continued after the end of the Cold War and the collapse of the former Soviet Union. Nuclear deterrence has transformed into a different form of dissuasion, evidenced in such events as the Gulf War. See Virilio's *L'Écran du désert: chroniques de guerre* (1991: 168–9).

5. This more general usage of the term is already an indication of the diffusion of a military model into the 'domestic' sphere. And according to Manuel de Landa, the interrelation between military logistical considerations and the development of modern mass production has a long history. See his discussion of the interplay between the US Department of Ordnance and private enterprise munitions producers from the 1830s onwards and the influence it had on the development of the 'American system' of manufacture and on the later formulation of the 'scientific principles of management' (1991: 30–1).

6. For a corroborating perspective on the hidden but essential side of the tradition of Western metaphysics see John Onians' fascinating discussion of the centrality of military concerns in the development of Greek art and thought in 'War, Mathematics, and Art in Ancient Greece' (1989).

7. Translations from this text are mine.

8. Virilio's description of this 'dynamic and energetic process' associated with the accident as 'cinematographic' links up with his concluding claim in this essay that the television screen, with its constant projection of catastrophes and disasters, is the museum of accidents. This is a characteristically polemical move by Virilio that attempts to provoke a 'postpositivist' review of television – specifically in regard to the conventional understandings of television as a (more or less flawed) medium of mass and global communication and information dissemination. Moreover, it is an attempt to figure the kind of rapid, mobile regard the theorist requires in order to perceive the elusive sequence that inheres in a given accident. This is why, for Virilio, a 'museum of accidents' could not be merely a collection of damaged or destroyed objects but would need to embrace an 'aesthetic of disappearance' in order to portray a 'landscape of events' in time (1996: 115).

9. The notion of the vector is used in a number of places in Virilio's text to describe the directed movement of a certain technological or tendential development. For instance, in *Pure War* he describes the inauguration of logistics in the coordination of ordnance transportation and delivery systems that amounts to 'a system of vectors, of production, transportation, execution' (Virilio and Lotringer, 1983: 16). The media theorist, McKenzie Wark, has elaborated Virilio's concept of the vector as a major aspect of his project. See his *Virtual Geography: Living with Global Media Events* (1994: 11–13).

10. See Jacques Derrida's 'The Time is Out of Joint' (1995). My allusion to this piece is by way of a suggestion of the relatedness of Virilio's work – especially in its figuring of the accident – to what Derrida has to say there on the aporetic 'experience' of time, space, the real, life and death that 'is' deconstruction. Deconstruction, we might say – all too precipitously and without the careful and detailed consideration required of such a comparison of disparate theoretical projects – takes place in the 'accidental' temporality Virilio evokes.

References

Dercon, Chris (1986) 'An Interview with Paul Virilio', trans. Daphne Miller, *Impulse* 4(12): 35–7.

Derrida, Jacques (1984) 'No Apocalypse, Not Now (Full Speed Ahead, Seven Missiles, Seven Missives)', trans. Catherine Porter and Philip Lewis, *Diacritics* 14 (summer): 20–31.

Derrida, Jacques (1995) 'The Time is Out of Joint', in Anselm Haverkamp (ed.) *Deconstruction is/in America: A New Sense of the Political.* New York: New York University Press.

Hawking, Stephen (1988) *A Brief History of Time: From the Big Bang to Black Holes.* London: Bantan.

Hottois, Gilbert (1981) 'La "Dimension du futur" à travers la temporalité mythique, historique et techno-scientifique', *Cahiers Internationaux du Symbolisme* 42–4: 69–84.

Hottois, Gilbert (1984) *Le Signe et la technique: la philosophie à l'épreuve de la technique.* Paris: Aubier.

de Landa, Manuel (1991) *War in the Age of Intelligent Machines.* New York: Zone Books.

Onians, John (1989) 'War, Mathematics, and Art in Ancient Greece', *History of the Human Sciences* 2(1): 39–62.

Rötzer, Florian (1995) *Conversations with French Philosophers*, trans. Gary E. Aylesworth. New Jersey: Humanities Press.

Ruthven, Ken (1993) *Nuclear Criticism.* Melbourne: Melbourne University Press.

Virilio, Paul (1989 [1984]) *War and Cinema: The Logistics of Perception*, trans. P. Camiller. London: Verso.

Virilio, Paul (1991) *L'Écran du désert: chroniques de guerre.* Paris: Éditions Galilée.

Virilio, Paul (1994 [1988]) *The Vision Machine*, trans. J. Rose. Bloomington and Indianpolis: Indiana University Press and British Film Institute, London.

Virilio, Paul (1995 [1993]) *The Art of the Motor*, trans. J. Rose. Minnesota: University of Minnesota Press.

Virilio, Paul (1996) *Un Paysage d'événements.* Paris: Éditions Galilée.

Virilio, Paul (1999 [1990]) *Polar Inertia*, trans. P. Camiller. London: Sage.

Virilio, Paul and Sylvère Lotringer (1983) *Pure War*, trans. Mark Polizotti. New York: Semiotex(e).

Wark, McKenzie (1994) *Virtual Geography: Living with Global Media Events.* Bloomington: Indiana University Press.

Patrick Crogan teaches film, television and new media theory in the Screen Studies Department of the Australian Film, Television and Radio School in Sydney. His doctoral thesis explored critical theories of technology, concentrating on the work of Paul Virilio.

Virilio, Stelarc and 'Terminal' Technoculture

Nicholas Zurbrugg

A CCORDING TO THE AMERICAN poet John Giorno, 'All great art is a mistake – it's like falling down the stairs and seeing stars – and then you realize what the mistake is, and you continue doing it. You realize what you've done good' (1994: 101). Viewed from this perspective, the milestones of 20th-century culture offer a series of happy accidents or mistakes, as different creative spirits make successive lucky breaks from this or that status quo.

From Paul Virilio's point of view, the most significant 'accidents' of 20th-century technoculture require confrontation rather than celebration. Remarking that his generation is 'obliged to acknowledge breakdowns and examine accidents' (1998a), and questioning whether technocultural accidents have ever really 'done good', Virilio aligns himself with those children of 'total war and post-war totalitarianism' – such as the East German writer Heiner Müller – who share his conviction that 'all the misery of the world arises from man's feeling that he can be improved by machines invented to take his place' (1997b: 7–8).

Explaining, 'I'm not afraid of fire! I'm not afraid of being burned' (1998b), Virilio might well define himself as a man caught within late 20th-century cultural crossfire or as Müller puts it, 'The man between the ages who knows that the old age is obsolete', but who feels that 'the new age has barbarian features he simply cannot stomach' (Müller, 1980: 137). Or, more accurately, Virilio is perhaps the man between the ages who knows that the most superficial aspects of the 'old age' are obsolete, but who shores past fragments against contemporary ruin, finding it almost impossible to look beyond the most barbaric aspects of the 'new age'.

By contrast, Virilio's principal technological *bête noire*, the Australian

- *Theory, Culture & Society* 1999 (SAGE, London, Thousand Oaks and New Delhi),
  Vol. 16(5–6): 177–199
  [0263-2764(199910/12)16:5–6;177–199;009965]

cybernetic performance artist Stelarc, seems to be the man beyond the 'old age', unable to stomach what he thinks of 'those old metaphysical distinctions between the soul and the body, or the mind and the brain', and alarmed that contemporaries should still attempt to justify or condemn new technologies in terms of 'obsolete desires' (1998).

Fervently resisting conceptual closure, but at the same time remaining firmly enclosed within their respective logics, Virilio's and Stelarc's conflicting priorities find eventual resolution in the work of what one might think of as 'new age' multimedia visionaries such as Stelarc's American contemporary, the video-artist Bill Viola. Confident that both past and present 'desires' await articulation in the 'new alphabet, new words, new semantics' and 'new grammar' (1996) identified by the mid-century technological avant-garde, and remarking, 'new technologies of image-making are by necessity bringing us back to fundamental questions, whether we want to face them or not' (1995: 257), Viola stirringly concludes:

> Media art, in its possession of new technologies of time and image, maintains a special possibility of speaking directly in the language of our time, but in its deeper capacity as art, it has an even greater potential to address the deeper questions and mysteries of the human condition. (1995: 257)

In much the same way, the American digital composer Steven R. Holtzman argues that 'as we approach the twenty-first century, we can return to an integrated view of art, science, and the mystical' (1995: 292).

Virilio comes closest to Viola's and Holtzman's conclusions in the more spontaneous speculations of his interviews, rather than in the cautiously argued hypotheses of his books. For example, finding present cultural transitions 'in many ways comparable to the Renaissance' (1988: 57), and remarking that few 'explorers' are 'ready and able to analyze' the 'great opaque block' of contemporary imaging, he calls for interdisciplinary collaboration between 'Scientists, artists, philosophers', in 'a kind of "new alliance" for the exploration of the nebular galaxy of the image'.

> Everybody has a piece of it. Nobody understands that he has to put his piece in a common pot, and that he has to try to enter that sphere of reciprocity and intelligence that made for the phenomenon of the Renaissance, in which everyone could participate. Even before being a question of the organization and geometrical perfecting of the city, the Renaissance was first of all a question of organizing a way of seeing. (1988: 61)

While Virilio clearly hesitates before notions of 'tele-reality at a distance', protesting that 'That's an unheard-of phenomenon like the splitting of the atom, but here what's being split is reality', he concludes this interview by acknowledging that 'this isn't to say that one won't be capable of reconstructing a reality through the new images of tomorrow' (1988: 61).

Reassessing the viability of this kind of 'alliance' between science, art and philosophy, Virilio's most intransigent recent writings and interviews envisage increasing antagonism between those faithful to 'the god of transcendence' and those converted to 'techoscience' and 'the machine-god' (1996b: 81). Indeed, while Virilio insists that he 'is not opposed to technology or technological performance' (1996a: 122), and argues that 'it's quite evident that my writings on art are all clearly in favour of technology' (1996a: 117), his single-minded discussion of things he 'cannot stomach' in *L'Inertie polaire* (1994) and *Open Sky* (1997a) consistently obscures the subtlety of his other recent accounts of those pre-technological, partially technological or wholly technological 'resistant' practices that he most passionately champions or condemns.

As becomes apparent, the full complexity of Virilio's vision is most clearly evinced by the tension between his blistering attacks upon what he takes to be the neo-fascist or neo-eugenicist artistic 'resistance' of the modernist and postmodern technological avant-gardes, in *The Art of the Motor* (1995), and his equally fervent advocacy of the kinds of positive artistic 'resistance' that he outlines in his interviews with Philippe Petit in *Cybermonde, la politique du pire* (1996b) and with Marianne Brausch in *Voyage d'hiver* (1997b).

Generally speaking, Virilio's ambiguous responses to the postmodern avant-garde coalesce most obviously in his responses to Stelarc, whom *The Art of the Motor* both counts among postmodern culture's foremost 'fallen angels' (1995: 111), and discounts as little more than a human 'laboratory rat' (1995: 113). Subsequently offering Stelarc's agenda more moderate consideration, Virilio explains:

> I think of Stelarc as being the Antonin Artaud of technology – that's what I find so interesting in his work... He's an artist whose work has religious dimensions without really being aware of it! He thinks that technological forces will allow him to transfigure himself – to become something other than what he is. An angel, an archangel, a mutant, a cyborg or whatever. There's a sort of devotion in his work to the machine god – to a *deus ex machina* – and Stelarc is its prophet.... But for me, man is the last of God's miracles. Hence my rejection of all eugenic theories based upon the argument that man is only a prototype awaiting improvement. And Stelarc's research is quintessentially eugenicist in the sense that he's trying to improve his condition. His is a kind of body-building, a kind of body-art! And I'm fundamentally opposed to eugenics! I believe that man is finished! (1998a)

As Virilio indicates, his technological and existential priorities hover mid-way between those of Stelarc and Viola. For Stelarc, the future can best be improved by 'cyber-systems' redressing the 'technophobic streak and Frankensteinian fear' generated by 'platonic metaphysics envisioning a soul driving a zombie-like body', and enabling the body 'to function more precisely and more powerfully' (1995: 46–8). For Viola, media art should 'address the deeper questions and mysteries of the human condition' in order to restore 'balance between the emotions and the intellect' and reintegrate 'the emotions, along with the very human qualities of compassion and empathy, into the science of knowledge' (1995: 257).

But for Virilio, individual and planetary survival depend upon humanity's dual capacity to curb its compulsion to engineer eugenic calamities rivalling the worst nightmares of 'total war and post-war totalitarianism' (1997b: 7), and to cultivate its capacity for tangible, real space, face-to-face relationships. Anticipating both the increasing mediatization and 'Sicilianization' (1996c: 69) of a society fraught by local civil wars, Virilio concludes that 'Salvation lies in writing and speaking' (1996b: 85) rather than in the 'alternate interfaces' that Stelarc associates with 'extended fields of operation' (1998). Concluding that humanity's presently 'finished' – or completed – condition already provides the best conditions for survival in a world stabilized by a sense of 'here' and 'now', and calling for more 'vigilance regarding the ethics of immediate perception' (1997a: 102), *Open Sky* urgently warns:

> How can we really live if there is no more *here* and if everything is now? How can we survive the instantaneous telescoping of a reality that has now become ubiquitous, breaking up into two orders of time, each as real as the other: that of presence here and now, and that of a telepresence at a distance, beyond the horizon of tangible appearances?
>
> How can we rationally manage the split, not only between virtual and actual realities but, more to the point, between the *apparent* horizon and the *transapparent* horizon of a screen that suddenly opens up a kind of temporal window for us to interact elsewhere, often a long way away?' (1997a: 37)

In much the same way, *The Art of the Motor* insists that the 'question of freedom' is 'central to the problematic of technoscience and of neuroscience', anxiously asking to what extent the individual can 'avoid sensory confusion', 'keep his distance when faced with the sudden hyperstimulation of his senses' and generally resist technological 'dependency or addiction' (1995: 118–19). Briefly, if Stelarc is 'the Antonin Artaud of technology' (1998a), Virilio seems to be the Hamlet, Prince of Cyberculture, not so much pondering 'to be or not to be', as wondering whether it will even prove possible 'to be' on a planet 'not only polluted but also shrunk, reduced to nothing, by the teletechnologies of generalized interactivity' (1998a: 21). Generally envisaging technologically enslaved rather than technologically enhanced existence, *Open Sky* concludes: 'Service or servitude, that is the question' (1997a: 20).

Somewhat as his 'bloodbrother' (1997a: 8), Heiner Müller explains that he stood 'with one leg on each side' of the Berlin wall because 'no other position' seemed 'real enough', Virilio seems to find – or place – himself in a similarly 'schizophrenic position' (Müller, 1990: 32–3). On the one hand, he celebrates real space: a realm in which the material and the metaphysical comfortably coexist, where 'True distances' and 'the true measure of the earth, lie in my heart' (1997a: 64), and where 'The Old Testament ... seems something that I've personally experienced' (1997b: 54). On the other hand, particularly in *Open Sky*, Virilio struggles against the currents of real time and 'the speed of liberation from gravity' (1997a: 2), contemplating a limbo offering '*no space worthy of the name*' (1997a: 3), and no 'action worthy of the name' (1997a: 131), where he feels we may well become 'at once exiled from the exterior world' and 'the interior world' (1994: 165).

As Virilio explains in *Voyage d'hiver*, he associates 'action worthy of the name' with the responsibility of those 'men of good will' (1997b: 88) working to improve society, and waging a war of resistance against what *The Art of the Motor* thinks of as 'the *quiet legalization of disinformation*, in total mediatization' (1997b: 96). Both sharing Félix Guattari's sense that 'It is in underground art that we find some of the most important cells of resistance against the steam-roller of capitalistic subjectivity' (1995: 90–1), and shunning such mediatized 'underground' art as Stelarc's research, Virilio repeatedly seeks inspiration from the past, somewhat as Joyce's Stephen Dedalus seeks strength from his 'Old father' (1972: 253).

The Art of the Motor, for example, commends the example of 'the ancient stoic', likening technoculture to what Petrarch damns as 'that *plague of phantoms* who dissipate our thoughts and whose pernicious variety bars the way to luminous contemplation' (1995: 61), while *Voyage d'hiver* defends the function of the artist by invoking romantic revelation:

'The artist is surely the most authentic observer: he intuits the meanings of things, and has the ability to identify and understand the most important aspects of fugitive and unfamiliar reality', writes Novalis. Here we have the perfect definition of perceptive energy, iconic energy or more precisely, informational energy. (1997b: 102)

Nothing could be less accurate, in other words, than *Cybermonde*'s modest suggestion that Virilio merely conducts 'statistical research' in order to 'avert disaster' (1996b: 64). Far from simply stacking statistics, Virilio attempts to decode such omens as the 'signs in the sky', 'in the clouds' and 'in the water' that he associates with 'the year of signs, 1986, rich in major accidents' (1996c: 129), seeking out calamities that 'exceed ... statistical approximation' (1996c: 179), asking questions that 'nobody else asks' (1996c: 140), and working as it were against the clock and beyond the clock, in order to 'analyze' and 'overtake' terminal symptoms of 'accident' and 'negativity' (1996b: 87). Confronted by what he thinks of as a 'super-human' (1996b: 92) task, Virilio's prophetic writings evaluate 'unfamiliar reality' as best they may, reading between and beyond the lines – across disciplines, continents, cultures and centuries – in terms of an immense array of multicultural paradigms drawn from Old and New Testament writings, ancient and modern philosophy, urban and sociological research, folkloric and romantic wisdom, and modernist and postmodern aesthetics.

I'm a painter who writes, you know! Surely you feel that my books are very visual – they're very, very visual books! They're not words, they're visions! I'm painting, you know! If I can't see it I can't write about it. (1998a)

Yet despite his sense of being a theoretical artist – or an artistic theorist – orchestrating a 'logic of extremes', Virilio stubbornly predicts 'the end of contemporary art' (1998a), and in consequence systematically overlooks many of the most 'luminous' contemporary technocultural practices, at best explaining: 'I always consider the worst. I'm forced to consider the worst!' (1998a). Arguably, Virilio's method is far more subtle than this. Censuring 'the worst' of the present in terms of exemplary precursors, he never allows the reader to forget 'the best' of the past. And censuring 'the best' of the present, by employing a logic of 'negative extremes', according to which things can only go from bad to worse, he never allows the reader to forget 'the worst' of the present. Heads, the past wins; tails the present loses.

However much Virilio generally claims to address the 'global dimensions' of contemporary culture, his principal examples in *L'inertie polaire* are self-consciously restricted to realms of general social mediocrity 'without any relation to "artistic" representation' (1994: 10). But why should analysis purporting to address the 'global' ignore positive artistic practices? Again, Virilio's explanation is deceptively simple. 'That wasn't my concern here. My main concern here was the general impact of technologies' (1998a). Significantly, wherever Marshall McLuhan's earlier study of global technoculture – *Understanding Media* (1964) – finds potential light, Virilio finds potential darkness, generally deploring almost everything that left 'McLuhan drooling' (1995: 10).

Yet at first sight, McLuhan and Virilio seem to share identical values. Both address what McLuhan calls 'the transition from mechanical to electric technology' and both agree that 'the peculiar drama of the twentieth century' derives from the difficulty of living with old and new technologies 'at the same time' (1964: 297). Likewise, both endorse Novalis's dictum that artists 'understand the most important aspects of fugitive and unfamiliar reality' (Virilio, 1997b: 102), and both generally conclude that 'The artist picks up the message of cultural and technological challenge decades before its transforming impact occurs' and builds 'models ... for facing the change that is at hand' (McLuhan, 1964: 70).

In turn, just as McLuhan notes that the artist's ability 'to sidestep the bully blow of new technology' and 'parry such violence with full awareness' is often fatally frustrated by 'the inability of the percussed victims, who cannot sidestep the new violence, to recognize their need of the artist' (1964: 71), Virilio regrets that his most visionary writings seem fated to fall upon permanently percussed Parisian ears. 'Neither Baudrillard nor I are accepted here – we're not good Cartesians. There's no sensitivity here to irony, to wordplay, to argument that takes things to the limit and to excess. This kind of thought is virtually forbidden' (1998a).

At its most sensitive, Virilio's research memorably champions the ways in which the most illuminating kinds of multimedia creativity evince exemplary 'excess', remarking for example, how 'a masterpiece of video- installation' such as the Canadian artist Michael Snow's *La Région centrale* (1969) is clearly comparable to 'the work of Beckett or Kafka' (1998a), and acknowledging that 'There's a quality of truth in the work of the best of these artists that clearly corresponds to that of the great writers, the great painters – and the great architects' (1996a: 120).

Likewise, at its most flexible, *Cybermonde* emphasizes the swings and roundabouts quality of a world in which 'there is no gain without loss' (1996b: 49), and perhaps no loss without gain. Or perhaps not. Sensing that even implicit optimism edges too close to 'the superficially positive discourses of publicity, as opposed to the more rigorous discourse of critical theory' (1996a: 118), Virilio promptly nips hope in the bud. 'The world being a finite place', he reasons, 'a day will come when its losses will become intolerable and its gains will no longer appear.' And 'The 21st century will probably make this discovery: the discovery that our losses outweigh our gains' (1996a: 49).

Predictably, *Understanding Media* ends on a more upbeat note. Dismissing 'Panic about automation'; reasoning that 'Persons grouped around ... a candle' are 'less able to pursue independent ... tasks, than people supplied with electric light'; and anticipating more rather than less 'artistic autonomy' (1964: 311); McLuhan seems to conclude 'Candle bad, electricity good'. 'Electricity bad, candle quite good', Virilio virtually ripostes.

But need one reduce debate to the kind of 'either–or proposition' that William Burroughs deplores as 'one of the great errors of Western thought' (1965: 27)? As American multimedia performance artists such as Laurie Anderson and Meredith Monk remind us, neither candle-power nor cyber-power necessarily cause sensorial or existential deprivation. In Anderson's terms, 'fire's magic, and so is technology' (1991: 12), and when all is technologically said and done, electronic media are merely 'a way of amplifying or changing things'.

> It's just a different way of doing it. No better or no worse. It is really just a tool. And a lot of people focus on it as if it were something important. It's the least important thing about what I do. . . . The latest thing that I did was extremely intimate, and at the same time had this huge amount of high-tech stuff. It was a solo thing. Seventeen people came on tour for this so-called solo thing. But I felt myself that it was by far the most intimate thing that I've ever done. (1991: 13)

Arguing in turn that both technological and pre-technological practices can counter mass-cultural 'numbing', Monk similarly concludes:

> You use technology when you use it for what it can do. I certainly sing in front of a microphone and I use lights, although I also feel that I'd be very comfortable singing with one candle – and that's it! Basically I think that

> what we need to do now, all of us – as human beings and as artists – is just to learn how to be incredibly flexible. I think that's why the hard times in a sense are kind of interesting. They're calling us to be very fluid and very flexible with what comes up. (1992)

Passionately diagnosing global techno-disaster rather than dispassionately weighing the merits of particular techno-practices, Virilio frequently sacrifices conceptual and empirical flexibility, and even when outlining the rationale for his 'logic of excess', tends to slip out of line into self-caricature as a lone resistance-fighter, struggling against a culture of collaborators.

> If I make my case somewhat forcefully it's because few others bother to do this.... I am not at all opposed to progress, but I feel that it would be unforgivable ... after the ecological and ethical catastrophes that we've been through ... to allow ourselves to be duped by the kind of utopian thought claiming that technology will restore greater happiness and humanity to the world. My generation cannot just sit back and let that sort of thing happen.... New technologies and media are a kind of Occupation. And I'm working in the 'resistance' because there are too many enemy 'collaborators' championing the ways in which progress will allegedly save, emancipate and free mankind from all constraint, etc. (1996b: 77–8)

Elsewhere in *Cybermonde* Virilio distinguishes himself from the kind of '*thaumaturge*' who 'acclaims the miraculous quality of every kind of technology', and defines himself as a '*dramaturge*' who, while not opposed to progress, 'wishes to reveal its drama, and the losses that it entails' (1996b: 54). As the most startling descriptions in *Open Sky* indicate, Virilio's '*dramaturgian*' skills frequently rival those of Cronenberg and Ballard. Tracing the probable decline of the individual 'super-equipped able-bodied person' (1997a: 11), for example, to the figure of the '*citizen-terminal*', decked out to the eyeballs with interactive prostheses based on 'the pathological model of the "spastic"', Virilio envisages the 'catastrophic' prospect of:

> ... an individual who has lost the capacity for immediate intervention along with the natural motricity and who abandons himself, for want of anything better, to the capabilities of captors, sensors and other remote control scanners that turn him into a being controlled by the machine with which, they say, he talks. (1997a: 20)

Likewise, predicting that 'terminal' humanity will bifurcate into either the terrestrial 'sedentary type of the great metropolis' (1997a: 33), or the astronautic sedentary type, 'not so much *on the moon* as in the gravitational inertia of a *fixed point*, without *spatial* reference' (1997a: 121), Virilio conjures Dantesque images of permanently lost bodies and souls, washed up on and off the planet as it were, with all the 'exhaustion and helplessness' of the drowned giant in J.G. Ballard's *The Terminal Beach* (1966: 47), and with all the pathos that he associates elsewhere with:

> *Tourists of desolation*, like the Albanians who landed half-naked and lugga-geless on the hostile coasts of Mezzogiorno, the most poverty-stricken region of the European community, only to realize that they had been had and that the land of milk and honey shown on Western TV never existed. (1995: 97)

L'Inertie polaire introduces its genealogy of domestic, cybernetic and astronautic inertia by describing how the automated currents in Tokyo swimming pools hold swimmers 'on the spot' (1994: 39), just as currents of Internet information similarly immobilize cybernauts before their screens. In such circumstances, 'Polar inertia begins' (1994: 46). Real-time inter-activity subsequently aggravates early 'clinical' symptoms of 'domestic electronic incarceration' (1994: 70) to levels of 'pathological fixity' (1994: 136) and to the *'technical equivalent of the coma'* (1994: 133). And worse follows:

> As we prioritize the 'real time' of interactivity, as opposed to the real space of everyday activity, are we going to see more and more inter-residential activity, analogous here on earth to those of astronauts orbiting on high? Regrettably this is all too likely, since the *generalized transmission* of facts and images finally places us in ... domestic inertia which will radically modify our relations with the world, our relations with the REAL environment, be these terrestrial or extra-terrestrial. (1994: 135–6, my translations)

Looping the apocalyptic loop, *L'Inertie polaire*'s final pages bow out with the extraordinary conjecture that those defying terrestrial and conceptual grav-ity may well become petrified in outer space – 'the perfect equivalent of a star, or an asteroid' – having reached 'that point of inertia at which the weight of the human body becomes identical to that of a planet' (1994: 166). In turn, just as *L'Inertie polaire*'s ecological subtext warns that the 'advanced extermination' (1994: 165) and 'the premature ageing of this world' (1994: 146) is rapidly approaching 'organic senility' (1994: 144), *Open Sky* predicts that the speed of telematic *'interactivity'* will induce corporeal disintegration 'analogous to the disintegration of the elementary particles of matter caused by *radioactivity*' (1997a: 115).

Worse still, *Open Sky* advises, 'home automation' will sell us the televisual 'straitjacket' (1997a: 97) or lure 'Telesexual' initiates into states of 'precocious dementia' (1997a: 112); the 'transplantation revolution' will incarcerate us within the 'biotechnical ... straitjacket' (1997a: 53); retreat from 'mundane space-time' will deliver us to the 'cybernetic strait-jacket of the virtual-reality environment control programme' (1997a: 131); and mis-sions beyond our 'native world' will maroon us in 'gravitationless space' (1997a: 131–2). Put very simply, 'Things aren't looking very good, Houston.' The crew of *Apollo 11* thus become 'the prophets of doom of humanity's unhappy future' (1997a: 139). Neil Armstrong was only belatedly 'aware of what he had done "up here" ', and arguably *'did not really live it'* (1997a: 139); Buzz Aldrin's disorienting experience of 'moving directly from total shadow into sunlight, without any transition' (1997a: 138), seems to have prompted 'two nervous breakdowns' and eventual confinement 'in a psychiatric ward' and Mike Collins's 'strange feeling *of having been both present and absent at the same time, on the earth as on the moon*', portends the collective 'loss of the *hic* and the *nunc*' that Virilio likens to 'precocious senility' (1997a: 139–40).

Perhaps *Open Sky* should have been titled *Closed Sky*. For while initially hinting that we may 'soon need to change our bearings' towards a 'secret perspective . . . on high' if 'we really want to reorient our daily lives' (1997a: 2–3), *Open Sky* rapidly reverses gear, and by the end of its introduction ominously equates vertical take-off with the worst possible kind of 'Philosophical let-down', warning that 'the speed of light' may well eradicate all *'idea of the real'* (1997a: 6).

Indeed, envisaging a Beckettian future where 'Nothing happens, nobody comes, nobody goes' (1977: 41), *Open Sky* predicts an 'endless perpetuation of the present' in which *'contemporary man no longer arrives at, achieves, anything'*. Anticipated, it seems, by 'Kafka's sense of inertia', and exemplified by 'our astronauts on their return from their extraterrestrial cruise' (1997a: 143), this crisis offers the Miltonian prospect of lost 'angelic attributes' as we more or less 'shed our "wings", in a fall from – a forfeiting of – grace into a corpse-like fixedness' (1997a: 68). In such circumstances, Virilio advises, we should lower our sights, follow old maxims such as 'if you stop running around the playground it will appear much bigger' (1997a: 57), and generally heed scriptural or folkloric wisdom.

> 'What doth it profit a man if he gain the whole world, but lose his only soul', his *anima*, that which moves him and allows him to be both animated and loving, allows him to draw towards himself not only the other, *otherness*, but the environment, *proximity*, by moving from place to place.
>
> An Armenian proverb puts it well: 'If my heart is narrow, what is the good of the world being so wide?' (1997a: 64)

Reasoning that all attempts to explore space and extend experience with technology lead us away from the essential insights of the heart, and that attention to the illuminations of the heart must in turn prohibit technological and astronautical aspirations, Virilio's *Cybermonde* argues that 'We must stop speculating' about 'realms beyond the world, beyond Earth or beyond mankind'. So far as Virilio is concerned, 'There's nothing beyond mankind', because 'man is terminal, and represents the completion of God's miracles'. 'One cannot improve mankind' because 'The human species does not lend itself to eugenics' (1996b: 86).

As becomes evident, Virilio's objections to technological research arise not so much from urban, socio-political or ecological considerations, as from ethical, theological and historical convictions prompting his fear that 'the future transplantation revolution and the ingurgitation of micromachines, *the technological fuelling of the living body*' (1997a: 53) will almost inevitably injure the general 'miracle' of humanity.

While sharing Virilio's general sense that 'techno-scientific power, like political power, or like religious power' can be 'at once both a blessing and a calamity' (1998a), Stelarc reverses Virilio's priorities, warning that dogmatic use of notions of the 'soul' may well obstruct interactive technological research seeking 'multiple possibilities rather than coercive solutions' beyond the 'old metaphysical distinctions between the soul and the body' (1998). Once again, then, we confront examples of deadlocked 'Either-or thinking' (Burroughs, 1965: 27), and of what Beckett, contemplating the vicissitudes in Proust's writing, calls the 'great mind in the throes' (1934: 975), as both Virilio and Stelarc defend or condemn what we might think of as 'grand' values which – as both 'a blessing and a calamity' – seem neither wholly defendable nor wholly condemnable.

Intuitive visionaries, instinctively reaffirming their species' finest qualities, Virilio and Stelarc unanimously reject the petty orthodoxies of institutional and industrial logic, and the totalitarian claims that Lyotard defines as 'the legitimating power of the grand narratives of speculation and emancipation' (1994: 38). Just as Virilio dismisses the way in which the 'publicity mentality' (1996a: 123) indiscriminately celebrates 'the miraculous quality of every kind of technology' (1996b: 54), Stelarc condemns the complacency with which 'corporate' approaches to technology 'simply affirm the status quo of everything' (1998), and generally argues that the technologically enhanced body should function 'more as an artist than as a bureaucrat' (1995: 49).

Likewise, just as Virilio remarks: 'My father was a Marxist and I was more of an anarchist, but we believed that the grand narratives offered salvation. But all of that is finished!' (1998a), Stelarc still more insistently disputes the claims of ideological master narratives.

> I don't want to participate in political ploys. Political rhetoric is often simplistic, dogmatic and vindictive. What's interesting is alternative aesthetics and speculative ideas. I guess that's why gender issues irritate me because they represent social and political agendas that I've intentionally never been a part of. (1994: 381)

Clearly then, despite their considerable suspicion of repressive master narratives, neither Virilio nor Stelarc ever wholly abandon 'master' values or master 'questions'. Acknowledging 'communism's death', and reflecting that 'there's no point in pretending that its corpse is still alive', Virilio, for example, concludes: 'Let's work instead at something else, in terms of the relationship between the individual, which is always at the heart of history' (1998a). Likewise, in the very process of distancing himself from gender debates, Stelarc identifies further 'fundamental questions' (1994: 381):

I see things from a human stand-point, not so much from a gendered stand-point. That might sound contradictory and certainly if this person is a male, what this person says is going to be highly charged by the culture of patriarchal society. That's a fair comment. But the point in time when gender issues become an issue is the very moment when more fundamental questions should be asked. Can the issue of what it means to be human be situated in cyber systems rather than in the biological status quo? (1994: 392)

At their most interesting, both Virilio and Stelarc consciously 'diverge' from the status quo, provocatively pursue logics of excess and metaphorically invoke their 'visions' rather than statistically imposing 'closure'. Yet for all their shared virtues and mutual respect, they seem fated to remain closed to one another's 'master values', propelled beyond reconciliation by their respective convictions, intuitions and beliefs. For his part, Stelarc regretfully concludes:

Virilio's one of my favourite writers, but I think that his critique in this instance is one that is in a sense obsessed with an ethical and a very human-based concern – he sees technology as a kind of threat to the body.... Technology outside the body might be OK, but he seems to see technology as more of a threat when it invades the body's tissues – as if it betrays a body operating with a capital 'I' – a body with a possessed mind, a body that is a possessed individual. This is just a query, but is it possible to consider a body without an 'I', without a self, in the traditional metaphysical way? ... these are central questions, I think. (1998)

As Virilio emphasizes in *Cybermonde*, he is extremely unwilling to countenance such questions, and as 'a limited man forced to address a limitless situation', he finds can 'only say "no"' (1996b: 51); a strategy that he endorses in terms of his sense that 'The essential characteristic of man is his capacity for resistance' (1996b: 25). But living in the 'terminal' 1990s, how can one best say 'no', and to what should one say 'no'?

At his most censorious, Virilio considers the possibility of extending the 'speed limit' imposed upon the arms race (1996c: 184) to 'legal sanctions' generally restraining the ways in which acceleration exhausts 'temporal distances' (1997a: 25). But as *Cybermonde* concedes, 'Withdrawing oneself from the problem is no solution', given that 'It's no more possible to disinvent genetic engineering or the atomic bomb than it is possible to disinvent nuclear energy.' Accordingly, 'Our work consists not so much in disinventing, as in overtaking. One can only fight one invention with another invention. One can only fight one idea with another idea, or with another concept' (1996b: 35).

At this point Virilio's and Stelarc's arguments once again converge. Like Virilio, Stelarc concludes that artists 'can't suppress surveillance and military technologies', and like Stelarc, Virilio insists that the 'real' artist or 'real' critic' has to 'try to generate new uses, new aesthetics ... alternative possibilities for those technologies' (Stelarc, 1994: 391).

In Virilio's terms, 'A real artist never sleeps in front of new technologies but deforms them and transforms them', and 'If one is a critic one doesn't ever accept things at face value and one doesn't ever sleep in front of new technologies' (1998a). For Stelarc, new technologies are most significant as catalysts empowering the artist to work 'beyond spaces of certainty', 'between biology and silicon-chip circuitry', in projects exploring 'those thresholds, those zones of slippage, those areas of interface, with anxiety, with hope and desire, but without romantic nostalgia' (1995: 49).

But once again, Virilio parts company from Stelarc in terms of his sense that the key questions posed by late 20th-century technoculture are not so much whether humanity can maintain hopeful exploration of new 'zones of slippage', as the question of whether humanity can simply survive its battle for self-preservation 'against technoscience, against cloning, robotics and so on' (1998a). Doubting whether humanity can long remain 'free in the face of science and technology', and yet at the same time insisting that things can only go forwards, Virilio cautiously concludes:

> Personally, I think that the next political struggle ... will be the struggle against technoscience, against the reign of technoscience, against cloning, robotics and so on. But this ... doesn't imply a return to a previous situation. It means the attempt to fight against technology itself – not in order to destroy it, but in order to transfigure it.... I've never been an 'ecologist' as it were, proposing a return to a lost paradise. Not at all. (1998a)

As *Cybermonde* indicates, Virilio models his tactics for resisting the 21st-century 'tyranny of technoscience' (1996b: 34) upon the 'extraordinary quality of divergence ... in the work of the 19th-century painters' (1996b: 25).

> Quite simply, we have to invent divergence. And this time it's the turn of science to a kind of impressionism or cubism ... commensurate with our culture's problems.... It's this kind of invention which allows us to reattain equilibrium and a common culture, not to speak of the possibility of democracy. The work of the poets, painters and film-makers has always diverged in this way. We now need to know whether or not contemporary scientists are capable of doing the same. (1996b: 37)

Predictably, Virilio answers this question negatively. The very concept of there being a kind of technocultural resistance to technoculture seems to strike Virilio as both an alarming and an unacceptable paradox, and however much a technological artist such as Stelarc may emphasize that their work explores 'the divergent rather than the convergent' (1998), such 'divergence' from Virilio's metaphysical 'master' values seems doomed to disapproval. Thus, whereas Roland Barthes's essay 'The Third Meaning' distinguishes the way in which innovative multimediated practices may well be 'born technically' or 'aesthetically' long before they are finally 'born theoretically' (1977 [1970]: 67), Virilio's implacable conceptual 'closure' before what he thinks of as the eugenicist impulse within technological performance renders it more or less axiomatically 'still-born'. Live arts such as dance and theatre win Virilio's loyalty, and partially architectural technological practices such as video-installation win his interest, but thereafter Virilio, like Beckett's Estragon in *Waiting for Godot*, seems persuaded that there is 'Nothing to be done' (1977 [1956]: 9).

> I can't see many signs of this divergence or struggle in contemporary art save in dance – which I adore! and theatre – which I adore! – Heiner Müller, for example! Apart from dance, from theatre and one or two video-installation artists, I can't see any real traces of critical divergence or any attempt to do something else, in some other way.... Like Baudrillard I'm conscious of a crisis in contemporary art and even of something like the end of contemporary art. But not an end in the sense of there no longer being any art, but in the sense of witnessing the end of a certain kind of art, or what Beckett would call the 'endgame' of art – in every sense of the word. (1998a)

Finally then, despite its acknowledgment that 'Technological culture is just as necessary as artistic culture', *Cybermonde* argues that technological art is most conspicuous in terms of its absence, that 'Only critical responses can help technological culture to develop', and that 'Unless we see an increasing number of art critics over the next few years, we will lose all freedom before new multimedia technologies' (1996b: 33–4).

At this point, Virilio turns to 'the wonderful biblical image of Jacob wrestling with the angel' (1998a), in order to introduce the salutary potential of the kind of rigorously resistant critical discourse towards which he feels an almost existential or religious obligation.

> Jacob met his God in the person of an angel and he wrestled with this angel for a whole night and at the end of this night he said to the angel, 'Bless me, because I have fought all night'. What does this symbolize? It means that Jacob did not want to sleep before God. He wanted to respect him as a man. He wanted to remain a man before God ... he fought, rather than sleeping as though he were before an idol. Technology places us in the same situation. We have to fight against it rather than sleeping before it. And me, I don't sleep at all before technology! I adore it! I adore technology! (1998a)

Virilio's 'adoration' for technology is obviously strictly rhetorical. As *Cybermonde* indicates, he envisages the late 20th century as a battlefield where those faithful to 'the god of transcendence' must confront converts to the 'machine god', and where nobody can 'behave like unbelievers'.

> Henceforth, we all have to choose our faith. Either one believes in technoscience ... or one believes in the god of transcendence. It's an illusion to

claim to be an atheist. In reality, all atheists today are followers of the machine-god. (1996b: 81)

Clearly then, Virilio's 'closure' before technological culture derives from two principal complaints; his sense that virtual culture negates transcendent values, and his sense that it eradicates the more mundane values of 'near and far' that make up 'the necessary conditions for sensory experience' (1997a: 45). In turn, as his discussions of the technological avant-garde in *The Art of the Motor* indicate, Virilio's systematic rejection of technoculture pivots upon his fear that the futurist impulse in 20th-century creativity is inseparable from eugenicist and fascist ideologies.

As we have already remarked, Virilio's *Voyage d'hiver* unequivocally argues that 'all the misery of the world arises from man's feeling that he can be improved by machines invented to take his place', and summarily dismisses any art form tainted by 'the fatal illusion of eugenics' (1997b: 7–8). Observing in turn that he still 'has a score to settle with Italian Futurism', Virilio still more explicitly explains:

> Like them my approach is futurist, but whereas their work is positive, mine is negative. And I completely reject the fascist impulse that I perceive in their work. For me it's quite clear. Those who are optimistic about technology are very closely allied to fascism. He who is critical of technology is not fascist. (1998a)

Ironically then, Virilio's sympathy for ways in which the painterly avant-gardes (such as Impressionism, Pointillism and Cubism) 'resist' realist photographic culture seems counterbalanced by his antipathy towards the ways in which subsequent partially technological avant-gardes (such as Futurism and Surrealism) offer still more radical resistance to 19th-century cultural conventions. Consistently discrediting the technological aspirations of the modern and postmodern avant-gardes according to a 'closed' logic determining: 'Pre-technological art, good. Technological art, bad', *The Art of the Motor* typecasts the technological avant-garde into obscurity, clearing the way for *Open Sky*'s worst-possible-scenario surveys of a doomed techno-planet unredeemed by any trace of aesthetic invention.

Vigorously refuting rather than rigorously researching 20th-century technoculture, *The Art of the Motor* reflects the same lack of aesthetic faith in the integrity of the modernist avant-garde that one finds in Jürgen Habermas's still more conservative claim that 'the failure of the surrealist rebellion' (1981: 6) affronts 'the standards of . . . communicative rationality' (1981: 8). In Habermas's terms, Surrealism fails because it addresses only 'a single cultural sphere – art', and therefore cannot influence 'all spheres – cognitive, moral-practical and expressive' (1981: 11), and because its 'non-sense experiments' merely induce 'destructured form' rather than any 'emancipatory effect' (1981: 10).

In turn, Virilio dismisses Surrealist art because he too finds it without emancipatory value, and because its technological aspirations seem to anticipate contemporary calamity. Thus, while *Voyage d'hiver* hails Marcel Duchamp as 'a real philosopher', acknowledging that 'philosophy can paint and can film' and 'doesn't have to end up in books' (1997b: 80), it is as an artist working with constructions such as his doubled *Door: 11 rue Larery, Paris* (1927) – rather than as a kinetic and filmic artist – that he wins Virilio's approval.

More specifically, *The Art of the Motor* condemns Surrealism for the same reason that it condemns mainstream digital art; because its mediocrity affronts what one might think of as 'communicative poetry' and 'communicative philosophy', exhausting what Virilio calls 'the fragile sphere of our dreams' (1995: 70–1). In Virilio's terms,

> The works of the Surrealists ... showed us the poverty of the trivial dream, which is so curiously lacking in variety and imagination that the representation of our desires becomes a load of drivel, with endless repetition of a few limited themes. The same thing can be said of digital imagery, which merely imitates the special effects and tricks of the old 3D cinema or animated cartoon. (1995: 71)

Subsequently endorsing Artaud's charge that '*Surrealism was an elusive virtual hope and probably as much of a con as anything else*' (1995: 146), *The Art of the Motor* dismisses the 'virtual hope' of virtual reality as a chimera concealing imminent collective incarceration. In such 'an artificial world peopled by imperative signals, the man of tomorrow will not for long be able to escape an environmental control', and will 'no longer be at liberty to construct some kind of mental imagery' (1995: 146).

Such prospects, *The Art of the Motor* concludes, make a mockery of the Surrealist boast that 'science will kill travel by bringing the country we want to visit to us' (1995: 151). Indeed, so far as Virilio is concerned, mass-mediated humanity is already a '*Victim of the set*' (1995: 152), hoodwinked by high-tech counterparts to 'the famous mobile sets Prince Potemkin had ranged along the horizon, the entire length of his sovereign's itinerary, to give her a false impression of how civilized and prosperous her immense empire was' (1995: 78–9).

In much the same way, Virilio suggests that the exultant Futurist vision of 'Man multiplied by the machine' (1973: 97) introduced in Marinetti's 'Destruction of Syntax – Imagination – without – Strings – Words – in – Freedom' Manifesto (1973 [1913]: 97), and the equally assured Surrealist ideal of 'Pure psychic automatism' in 'the absence of all control exerted by reason' outlined in André Breton's 'First Surrealist Manifesto' (1965 [1924]: 72), decline into the automated and disoriented thought of those 'shattered' – or, we might say, 'shuttered' – by present technologies.

So far as *The Art of the Motor* is concerned, if 'the cutting loose initiated by Futurism' has any recognizable consequences, these culminate in the wholly negative spectacle of the 'new man-machine'; a being

'Controlled to an unimaginable degree' (rather than enjoying 'Imagination – without – Strings' or 'Pure psychic automatism'), and traumatized by forces 'shattering man's unity of perception and ... producing, this time AUTOMATICALLY, the persistence of a disturbance in self-perception that will have lasting effects on man's rapport with the real' (1995: 146–7).

Finally, anticipating *Open Sky*'s claim that 'terminal' culture eradicates one's 'only soul', one's '*anima*' and the 'very being of movement' (1997a: 25), *The Art of the Motor* concludes with the suggestion that 'cybernetic ideography' merely brings us 'belated conformation of Antonin Artaud's desperate observation about the immediate postwar period: "What defines the obscene life we are living is that all our perceptions, all our impressions have been distilled for us" ' (1995: 147).

Ironically, the more one reads Virilio's accounts of postmodern escalations of the imperfection implicit within the modernist technological avant-garde, the more obvious it becomes that his own arguments similarly leave 'all impressions' of technoculture unfavourably 'distilled for us'. Like the revisionist historians that *Voyage d'hiver* condemns as 'Negationists, perversely camouflaging historical reality' (1997b: 33), Virilio's *The Art of the Motor* offers a surprisingly 'camouflaged' account of the Futurist and Surrealist traditions.

Briefly, while Virilio defines his general approach to contemporary culture as the attempt to resuscitate 'ill-perceived or voluntarily neglected incidents and details' from the public pool of 'great events' (1996c: 11), his choice of 'neglected' incident and detail is telling selective. Or put another way, if 'the real problem of the press and television' derives from 'what they manage to obliterate, to hide' rather than from 'what they are able to show' (1995: 3), the 'real problem' in Virilio's writings similarly derives from their tendency to hide – and virtually obliterate – all traces of positive technological practices.

From Virilo's viewpoint this kind of 'distillation' of the facts is perhaps a necessary evil. Resisting deceptive reassurance, *Voyage d'hiver* insists that 'those who say ...."things will finally work themselves out", are not only liars but ... negationists ... counteracting the difficult work of social workers, sociologists, doctors and all men of good will' (1997b: 88). But in much the same way, Virilio's worst scenarios similarly hinder recognition of those creative 'men of good will' whose techno-compositions still await theoretical explanation. As case-histories suggest, the positive lineage between the modernist and postmodern avant-gardes frequently receives more lucid recognition from the veterans of the modernist avant-garde than from the luminaries of postmodern critical theory.

Writing in his 'Open Letter to André Breton' of 2 June 1971, for example, the veteran Surrealist Louis Aragon observes how the American director Robert Wilson's Paris production of *Deafman Glance* (1971) projects the Surrealist project into a realm which he defines as being 'not surrealism at all', but 'what we others, who fathered surrealism, what we dreamed it might become after us, beyond us' (1987). While sympathizing with those 'who think that science may come to take the place of art, who fear the "robotization" of humanity', Aragon insists that when technology is used with the finesse of a multimedia artist like Wilson, 'A play like DEAFMAN GLANCE is an extraordinary freedom machine', generating 'Freedom, radiant freedom of the soul and the body' (1987).

Likewise, writing in a letter of 1 August 1979, the veteran Dadaist Marcel Janco similarly acknowledges the ways in which the tape-recorded *poésie sonore* of postmodern poets such as Henri Chopin project Dada's 'new expression of life' into the still more forceful realms of compositions incorporating 'the fantastic mechanical and technological progress of today ... radio waves, stereo, the tape-recorder' (1982: 75), and in turn, recounting the reaction of Virilio's most respected modernist master to his first public presentation of the *audio-poème* '*Espace et Gestes*' at the Galerie Mesure in Paris in 1961, Chopin tellingly recounts:

> An artist who had been listening to the tape gave me his address and said, 'Come to my studio and I'll give you a painting, because you've achieved with sound something which we could never have done'. So I went to visit him. It was Marcel Duchamp! (1995: 23)

By contrast, *The Art of the Motor*'s accounts of the ways in which 'the Italian Futurists' dream actually come true' (1995: 103), merely offer further parables of escalating degradation. If 'Marinetti trumpeted ..."Let's make way for the imminent and inevitable identification of man with the motor"' (1995: 129), postmodern technoculture – it seems – ends up 'treating the living being like a motor, *a machine that needs to be constantly revved up*' (1995: 123), as humanity lurches towards what Virilio describes as 'a new type of FUNDAMENTALISM ... one no longer associated with trust in God of traditional beliefs, but with ... the "technocult", of a perverted science' (1995: 120).

Left to its own devices, *The Art of the Motor* concludes, such a 'perverted science' will transform humanity into the kind of technological untouchable that Virilio associates with the 'profane body', or into the kind of technological unsavable that he thinks of as the 'body-without-a-soul' (1995: 113). But as Viola suggests, there is no reason to suppose that technoculture is necessarily any more perverse than its precursors. 'The video camera is well suited to looking closely at things, elevating the commonplace to higher levels of awareness' (1995: 78), and 'One of the most interesting aspects of recording media' is the way in which they can offer 'surrogate sensory perceptual systems, in some ways similar, in some ways different, from our own, but nonetheless with a specific set of characteristics that we can hold up and compare against ourselves' (1995: 65).

Far from identifying the advantages of such surrogate awareness and insight, *The Art of the Motor* argues that the body of 'the wholly hyperactivated man' (1995: 120) may well quite literally lose all its senses when exposed to the kind of informational overload 'whose advent Pascal evoked, when he wrote, '"Our senses cannot perceive extremes ... Extreme qualities are our enemies. We no longer feel anything; we suffer"' (1995: 132). Yet again Virilio projects his writings into Beckett country, where one can 'only suffer' events resisting all attempts 'to saddle them with meaning' (1963: 75–6).

But for Virilio, such extreme prospects seem far from fictional. Once we 'not only act at a distance, but even teleact at a distance – see, hear, speak, touch, and even smell at a distance', he observes, we may well witness 'the unheard-of possibility ... of a sudden splitting of the subject's personality', as 'the classic distinction between "inside" and "outside" ' flies 'out the window' (1995: 106–7). But since when did any self-respecting 20th-century writer or artist lose sleep over the co-presence of 'inside' and 'outside' experience? Reconsidering his claim that he wishes 'to see more of what's out there, to look outside', whereas 'Beckett wants to go inward' (1965: 23), Burroughs, for example, effortlessly concludes, 'Well of course ... there's no dichotomy there. At some point inward becomes outward, and outward becomes inward. It's just a part of the spectrum' (1987: 33).

Likewise, as Virilio himself remarks in *The Aesthetics of Disappearance* Proustian evocations of the mind's 'entry into another logic' (1991 [1980]: 35) – such as the following sentence from *Swann's Way* – typify the assurance with which the modernist text evokes dissolving distinctions between such 'classic' distinctions as here and now, solid and liquid, inside and outside, and 'container' and 'contained'.

> I enjoyed watching the glass jars which the village boys used to lower into the Vivonne to catch minnows, and which, filled by the stream, in which they in their turn were enclosed, at once 'containers' whose transparent sides were like solidified water and 'contents' plunged into a still larger container of liquid, flowing crystal, conjured up an image of coolness more delicious and more provoking than they would have done standing upon a table laid for dinner, by showing it as perpetually in flight between the impalpable water in which my hands could not grasp it and the insoluble glass in which my palate could not enjoy it. (1989 [1917]: 183–4)

In turn, *The Aesthetic of Disappearance* notes how Magritte similarly evokes the co-presence of 'familiar things' and 'something else of an unfamiliar nature' (1991: 36), and describes the ways in which Bernadette de Soubirous's mystical revelations reflect 'the passage from the familiar to the unfamiliar', slipping out of focus like 'those surprising moments that precede epileptic absence', before 'perceiving the kind of infra-ordinary reality' for which 'you'd give a whole lifetime' (1991: 37–8). Briefly, while associating Proust's, Magritte's and de Soubirous's visions of 'infra-ordinary reality' with positive kinds of temporal and spatial travel, Virilio suggests that the technological blurring of 'inside' and 'outside' reality only leads to a kind of permanent 'epileptic absence'.

Anticipating such negative responses to his long-distance cybernetic collaborations; admitting that these could be unfavourably caricatured as 'electronic voodoo where you're prompting the body to move'; and generally discounting the hyperbole of 'infra-ordinary' categorization; Stelarc remarks that his work still frequently awaits more pragmatic discussion according to its artistic and conceptual merits, 'as a kind of true interactive situation where I can borrow a part of your body and make it perform a task in another space' (1995: 48).

> These performances aren't about shamanistic displays of human prowess. They're not pseudo-medical scientific research. They're not yogic feats of fine-tuning to attain higher spiritual states. They're none of these things. They're simply works of art, exploring intuitively new realms of aesthetics and images. (1995: 49)

In turn, patiently reassessing – rather than precipitately dismissing – 'the unheard-of possibility' of 'splitting ... the subject's personality' (Virilio, 1995: 106), and the still more unheard-of condition of the 'split body', Stelarc speculates that variants of both conditions may well offer significant advantages to those still championing the hypothesis that the technological artist may well be 'capable of reconstructing a reality through the new images of tomorrow' (Virilio, 1988: 61).

> I'm intrigued by the way in which our psycho-social and historical and cultural development has always tended to perceive the notion of the split personality as pathological. We query whether it's possible to function with multiple personalities. But in our cyber-real of existence, it'll be an advantage to have a split personality – where one body might function in multiple and unconnected ways. You see limbs move as alien arms remotely actuated by agents elsewhere. You have a split body – your right side collaborating with local awareness with the alien left side of your body.... In our Platonic, Christian, Cartesian and Freudian pasts this might have been considered pathological. But in this terrain of cyber-complexity that we now inhabit the inadequacy and the obsolescence of the ego-agent driven biological body cannot be more apparent. A transition from the psycho-body to cybersystem becomes necessary to function effectively and intuitively in remote spaces, speeded-up situations and alien information beyond sensory experience. (1998)

As Stelarc observes, his research follows the assumption that 'To be human is to be augmented, extended and enhanced by technology', actively and critically attempting to explore the potential of unexpected kinds of performative interaction in situations where 'you have the choice' to define the performance situation, and where 'because you are aware of what's going on, this loop of consciousness creates the possibility of response and interaction' (1998).

In other words, his performances in works such as such as *Ping Body* (1996) are neither those of a 'willing victim' (Virilio, 1995: 114) wholly sacrificed to the 'CYBERNETIC programming of vital rhythms' (1995: 128), nor those of a 'total automaton', but the reactions of a willing collaborator, intentionally physically and mentally exploring what he thinks of as 'alternate and possibly augmented experiences' in a kind of partially voluntary and partially involuntary dance with – and within – 'the structural, spatial and temporal parameters of the internet'. Here, Stelarc explains, 'you're using the structural parameters of the net to activate the body, but then, in turn, to upload it' in a 'very intriguing' kind of 'looping, uploading/downloading' operation, as 'movements initiated by the internet activity were then in turn uploaded to a website on the net' (1998).

Here too, perhaps, we witness something very like a contemporary counterpart to Virilio's favourite image of critical resistance – the spectacle of Jacob wrestling with the angel, *'measuring himself* against *some incommensurable being*, without either one letting go', 'forced to acknowledge the limits of his own body' (1995: 84) and as Stelarc puts it, 'querying the limits' of 'knowledge and experience' (1994: 381).

Like Virilio, Stelarc is a global traveller, an irresistible *agent provocateur*, and as 'real' a philosopher as Duchamp, if one accepts *Voyage d'hiver*'s general dictum that philosophy 'doesn't have to end up in books', but can also 'paint' and 'film' (1997b: 80) – and one might add, 'explore cybernetic interactive performance'. Revising this dictum, we can also surely posit that 'art can philosophize and write' and 'doesn't have to end up in galleries', and can surely conclude – hopefully for the better rather than for the worse – that Virilio himself is quite as 'real' an artist as Duchamp or Stelarc.

Unrepentantly offering the warnings of a 'child of total war and post-war totalitarianism' (1997b: 7), and in many respects sharing Heiner Müller's sense of being a writer more interested in 'conflict' than in 'answers and solutions' (1990: 34), Virilio commands respect as one of the most compelling cultural theorists of the last decades. Stelarc is surely not alone when he remarks that 'Virilio's one my favourite writers.'

Note

1. The translations from Virilio's *L'Inertie polaire* (1994), *Cybermonde* (1996b), *Un Paysage d'événements* (1996c) and *Voyage d'hiver* (1997b) are my own.

References

Anderson, Laurie (1991) 'Interview with Nicholas Zurbrugg', *Eyeline* 17: 12–14.

Aragon, Louis (1987) 'Open Letter to André Breton (2 June 1971)', in Programme for Heiner Müller, *Hamletmachine*, trans. Linda Moses. London: Almeida Theatre, unpaginated.

Ballard, J.G. (1996) *The Terminal Beach*. Harmondsworth: Penguin.

Barthes, Roland (1977 [1970]) 'The Third Meaning, Research Notes on Some Eisenstein Stills', in *Image-Music-Text*, ed. and trans. Stephen Heath. Glasgow: Fontana.

Beckett, Samuel (1934) 'Proust in Pieces', *The Spectator* 22 June: 975–6.

Beckett, Samuel (1963 [1953]) *Watt*. London: Jupiter.

Beckett, Samuel (1977 [1956]) *Waiting for Godot*. London: Faber and Faber.

Breton, André (1965 [1924]) 'First Surrealist Manifesto', in *Surrealism* ed. and trans. Patrick Waldberg. London: Thames and Hudson.

Burroughs, William S. (1965) 'The Art of Fiction XXXVI', Interview with Conrad Knickerbocker, *The Paris Review* 35: 13–49.

Burroughs, William S. (1987) 'A Footnote to William Burroughs's Article "Beckett and Proust" ', Interview with Nicholas Zurbrugg, *The Review of Contemporary Fiction* 7(2): 32–3.

Chopin, Henri (1995) Interview with and trans. Nicholas Zurbrugg, *Art and Design* 10(11/12): 21–31.

Giorno, John (1994) 'Poetry, Entertainment, and the Mass Media', Interview with Nicholas Zurbrugg, *Chicago Review* 40(2/3): 83–101.

Guattari, Félix (1995 [1992]) *Chaosmosis: An Ethico-Aesthetic Paradigm*, trans. Paul Bains and Julian Pefanis. Sydney: Power Publications.

Habermas, Jürgen (1981) 'Modernity versus Postmodernity', trans. Seyla Ben-Habib, *New German Critique* 22: 3–14.

Holtzman, Steven R. (1995) *Digital Mantras: The Languages of Abstract and Virtual Worlds*. Cambridge, MA: MIT Press.

Janco, Marcel (1982) Letter of 1 August 1979, trans. Nicholas Zurbrugg, in *Stereo Headphones* (Brisbane) 8–10: 75.

Joyce, James (1972 [1916]) *A Portrait of the Artist as a Young Man*. Harmondsworth: Penguin.

Lyotard, Jean-François (1994 [1979]) *The Postmodern Condition: A Report on Knowledge*, trans. Geoff Bennington and Brian Massumi. Manchester: Manchester University Press.

McLuhan, Marshall (1964) *Understanding Media: The Extensions of Man*. New York: Signet.

Marinetti, F.T. (1973 [1913]) 'Destruction of Syntax – Imagination without Strings – Word – in – Freedom', in *Futurist Manifestos*, edited by Umbro Apollonio, trans. R.W. Flint. London: Thames and Hudson.

Monk, Meredith (1992) Unpublished interview with Nicholas Zurbrugg.

Müller, Heiner (1980) 'Heiner Müller: The Despair and the Hope', Interview with and trans. Carl Weber, *Performing Arts Journal* 12: 135–40.

Müller, Heiner (1990) 'Walls', Interview with Sylvère Lotringer, in *Germania*, edited by Sylvère Lotringer, trans. Bernard and Caroline Schütze. New York: Semiotext(e).

Proust, Marcel (1989 [1917]) *Swann's Way*, in *Remembrance of Things Past*, vol. 1, trans. C.K. Scott Moncrieff and Terence Kilmartin. London: Penguin.

Stelarc (1994) 'Just Beaut to Have Three Hands', Interview with Martin Thomas, *Continuum* (Perth) 8(1): 377–93.

Stelarc (1995) 'Electronic Voodoo', Interview with Nicholas Zurbrugg, *21.C* (Melbourne) 2: 44–9.

Stelarc (1998) 'Telematic Tremors: Telematic Pleasures – Stelarc and "Fractal Flesh" ', Interview with Nicholas Zurbrugg in *Carnal Pleasures: Spaces of Public Desire*. Seattle: Bay Press (forthcoming).

Viola, Bill (1995) *Reasons for Knocking at an Empty House: Writings 1973-1994*. Cambridge, MA: MIT Press.

Viola, Bill (1996) Unpublished interview with Nicholas Zurbrugg.

Virilio, Paul (1988) Interview with Jérôme Sans, trans. Henry Martin, *Flash Art*, 138: 57–61.

Virilio, Paul (1991 [1980]) *The Aesthetics of Disappearance*, trans. Philip Beitchman. New York: Semiotext(e).

Virilio, Paul (1994) *L'Inertie polaire*. Paris: Christian Bourgois.

Virilio, Paul (1995 [1993]) *The Art of the Motor*, trans. Julie Rose. Minneapolis: University of Minnesota Press.

Virilio Paul (1996a) 'A Century of Hyper-Violence', Interview with and trans. Nicholas Zurbrugg, *Economy and Society* 1: 111–26.

Virilio, Paul (1996b) *Cybermonde, la politique du pire*, Interviews with Philippe Petit. Paris: Les Editions Textuel.

Virilio, Paul (1996c) *Un Paysage d'événements*. Paris: Galilée.

Virilio, Paul (1997a [1995]) *Open Sky*, trans. Julie Rose. London: Verso.

Virilio, Paul (1997b) *Voyage d'hiver*, Interviews with Marianne Brausch. Paris: Editions Parenthèses.

Virilio, Paul (1998a) Unpublished Interview with and trans. Nicholas Zurbrugg.

Virilio Paul (1998b) Conversation with and trans. Nicholas Zurbrugg.

Nicholas Zurbrugg is Professor of English and Cultural Studies, and Director of The Centre for Contemporary Arts at De Montfort University, Leicester.

The Passenger
Paul Virilio and Feminism

Verena Andermatt Conley

W HEN RECENTLY ASKED if he'd rather be a cyborg or a goddess, Paul Virilio, with an air of malice, responded: 'Neither'. Indeed, the chronicler of teletopia, the present-day archivist of the future, does have a sense of humor. True, at first, his pronouncements have little if anything to do with feminism. He is a *vir*, man + *leo*, or lion. A masculine man. Though puns and anagrams have, much to the delight of serious American scholars, all but disappeared from the horizon of cultural theory, it is still acceptable to think that one is prisoner of one's name. How could such a masculine man be interested in gender? And in the French republican universalist tradition, isn't there only one? The question does not even pose itself! To corroborate our findings further, we can add that Virilio was trained as an urban architect. And architecture does not have much space for gender questions – yet. Planning cities, designing the future, deal with concrete and pragmatic issues that presumably leave architects with little space, let alone time, to make such frivolous distinctions! How is it possible then, we may ask, to open a space for feminism in Paul Virilio? Or, to put it yet another way, how is it possible to bring the architect turned culture critic into the space(s) of feminism(s)?

A fascination for bunkers, airplanes, air raids and general war paraphernalia, witnessed possibly first-hand during his teens and later through a slew of American war films and posters unloaded onto France from the 'Liberty Ships', sailing under the Marshall Plan, may have caught Virilio's youthful imagination. His fascination with technology never prevented him from reflecting on the horrors of war. Under his account of technological dazzle, there is a strong will to denounce violence, the enslavement of humans, especially of ordinary people – men, women and children included

- *Theory, Culture & Society* 1999 (SAGE, London, Thousand Oaks and New Delhi),
  Vol. 16(5–6): 201–214
  [0263-2764(199910/12)16:5–6;201–214;009966]

– carried out by successive groups in power who wield ever more perfected technologies.

Using a Heideggerian blueprint but politicizing the German philosopher's ideas, Virilio argues that the history of the West reads according to the development of technologies – from war machines to teletechnologies that include the media. It is one of increasing enframing, dispropriating and domesticating from those he calls 'soldier-proletarians' to entire civilian populations. Technologies in the service of war and speed lead to a progressive loss of habitable space. He singles out two recent events that marked turning points in the history of the logistics of the West: first that of the real and symbolic crumbling of the Atlantic Wall when Allied planes flew over and penetrated into civilian territory behind. Suddenly, lines criss-crossed inside a territory and introduced war into everyday life. Citizens are no longer protected by city walls and battles lose their status as spectacles. This shift already prefigured the second event, the conquest of outer space and the advent of cyberspace that, for Virilio, dispenses with social interaction entirely by coupling man to machine. Both the historical and technological implications of these two moments determine radical changes in humans' relations to time, space and habitat.

Let us see if, and where, in these rather universalist declarations, we can disengage some gender lines and how the latter might criss-cross or weave themselves through Virilio's *oeuvre*. Though not immediately noticeable because they are often taken up in arguments concerning the general population, the question of women in Virilio's work also follows that of the general history of technologies whose acceleration is inversely proportionate to the loss of animal and social territories, that is of bodily, human ways of interacting and dwelling. It cannot be separated from ecological and economic questions. This general argument that includes women is accompanied by myriad provocative, if not systematically developed remarks concerning sexual relations and gender that may infuriate some women readers, make others laugh, but that will also prompt them to inflect their investigations in new directions.

Throughout his work, Virilio's main argument focuses on the loss of a fleshy body and of a fixed, habitable space. His line of reasoning is based on a rather classic notion of space – Virilio reasserts the latter throughout his work by means of analyses that, at the same time, trace its progressive disappearance. The argument is punctuated by another that deals more specifically with sexual difference. Repeatedly, Virilio claims that woman is man's first vehicle in a series of relays that leads from the prehistoric *pugilat* (fight) to present-day teletopia and that goes along with the progressive loss of 'Mother Earth'. She is the vehicle; he is the passenger. This argument is often brought in to eroticize the evolution of the technological object from that of the prehistoric *femme-objet* to the *objet-femme* in cyberspace. While mainly subtending the long history of enslavement and displacement of humans by machine, the example of woman-vehicle and male-passenger also serves to theorize space along the lines of sexual difference no longer in static but dynamic – and erotic – terms.

Tracing the evolution of war and speed from a certain *pugilat*, with the early metempsychoses or transmigrations of the soul of the hunter in the days that would have existed before the invention of fortifications, Virilio ascertains that hunt and war, predicated upon the demarcation of a space, of a field, begin with woman as the carrier of man. He is literally and figuratively brought into the world by her. A mediator, but also an initiator, woman is the first in a series of relays that helps launch man progressively further into space and away from animal and social territories in his pursuit of total control. In this reverie of origins, the hunter's subsequent metempsychoses led from the domestication of women to animals – horses – to that of other people, such as the soldier-proletarian and, ultimately, to the machine (Virilio, 1977a).

A variant of this episode, less historic than mythic, deals with the Fall and the expulsion from Paradise of the original couple in the Judeo-Christian tradition. While the allusion to the woman-vehicle recurs time and again in Virilio's work, the biblical episode is introduced only in *The Aesthetics of Disappearance* (Virilio, 1991: 78). Linking science fiction narratives to Genesis, Virilio writes that

> Satan, appearing in the Bible as seducer of woman who in turn seduces man, commences then the cycle of humanity sworn less to death than to disappearance, that is to expulsion from the world in which it has lived, this being accomplished, initially, as a phenomenon of consciousness. (Virilio, 1991: 78)

Seduction, linked to a succession of visual phenomena and a change in perception, is a rite of passage from one world to another that implies

> ... the beginning of a navigation of body and sense from something immovable toward another category of Time, a space–time essentially different because it is sensed as unstable, mobile, conductive, transformable, like the creation of a second universe depending entirely on this initial rite of passage. (Virilio, 1991: 77)

Here, the loss of space is more complicated. Suspending a more general, phenomenological approach to his objects of interest, Virilio introduces the possibility of an ungrounding through eros that facilitates the emergence of a new world. Woman becomes a force of attraction, her body as communicational body – and not simply flesh – the ideal vector between man and the new world in which the attraction of bodies is linked to gravity. Movement henceforth is primary and the trajectory is forever to be invented. The coupling is seen as a 'yoking' that implies the territorial body as third partner. More even than in the first episode of woman-vehicle, where Virilio hovers between fixed and dynamic space, in the biblical tale, instead of

204 Theory, Culture & Society

mourning the loss of being, he hints at a possibility of ungrounding and becoming. Yet, again, Virilio is ambiguous. He closes the parenthesis by asserting that the story of Genesis was prompted by a threat, that of the disappearance of human intermediaries and the emergence of a sexuality directly connected to the technical object. In the Bible, woman as seductress is leading man astray on his search for the perfect technological object.

Apart from these two variants on a similar theme – woman as carrying off man and as seductress – that dynamizes space through eros, Virilio is concerned primarily with domestication and enslavement of humans and the progressive loss of habitable space that is complete today with the impact of electronics technology that functions in real time. Women's oppression is part of a larger domestication of entire populations. Writing out of the Cold War period, Virilio is concerned with a type of everyday war that, in the late 1970s, he sees as extending all over the world. This war aims not only at the destruction of enemy armies but also of social and territorial bodies as well as of the identity and the honor of civilian populations. Industrial war in the 20th century ruptures the social status quo between civilians and military; it replaces the millenary pact of semi-colonization with one of total colonization because it now reaches all spheres of life (Virilio, 1978: 48).[1] Henceforth, the notion of 'popular defense', in use since the construction of the first fortifications, loses its military significance and becomes part of a strategy of survival in a devastated habitat. Nietzsche's aphorism, 'the desert grows', is to be taken both literally *and* metaphorically. Defense becomes physiological *and* psychological.[2] More and more, an invisible system in power tries to eliminate popular resistance by undoing social solidarity and by extending the destruction of political and unionized networks to that of the family. By emancipating women, by lowering the voting age and granting the right to abortion, divorce and euthanasia, a false liberalism opens the way to the self-destruction of families by themselves (Virilio, 1978: 77–8).

Such pronouncements will not bring Virilio any prizes for feminist scholarship but add an interesting twist in the familiar tale of heroic feminist resistance and agency. Indeed, by inserting women's cause in a wider social and political framework, Virilio's arguments show how, in a complex system, the fluctuations of, and tensions between, many terms render possible the emergence of a new order. Change hinges less on the resistance of one term alone or on individual agency, where humans are said to be engaged in flows or tendencies.

The new society Virilio outlines in the late 1970s – a decade that witnessed the withering of the hopes of '68, the renewal of the Cold War with the beginnings of Reaganomics and the continuing military oppression in much of South America – is no longer that of the great 'enclosure', the disciplinary society that Foucault emblematized with the panopticon. Progressively, because of advances in technologies, surveillance and control can be located everywhere and nowhere. With the advent of 'pure war', populations are physically and mentally deterritorialized. Resistance is made difficult if not impossible.[3] The territorial body has disappeared under myriad networks and different media that dictate their strategies and do away with 'Mother Earth' (Virilio, 1986).

In developing his argument about loss of habitable space and bodily interaction, Virilio provides a provocative analysis of the restructuring of urban centers under the influence of rapid transportation and now electronic communication. Curiously, it is his understanding of what he denounces – such as the radical transformation of life and urban centers under the impact of teletechnologies – that becomes the compelling part of his argument more than the critique itself. For Virilio, the restructuring of the French territory, of cities such as Paris, leads to an emptying out of its people. Communication networks are superimposed over the map of the city that has long lost its function of *polis* with its active citizens. International jet sets and tourists roam the inner parts of the cities at the expense of its inhabitants, displaced to the peripheries. The people are made to move to the *grands ensembles*, described in the American press as 'these large, ugly, concrete buildings' in the distant suburbs. They lose their freedom of movement *and* of dwelling (Augé, 1996; Evenson, 1979; Godard, 1969).[4] Virilio joins here with the findings of feminists for whom a kind of agitated and enforced movement has little to do with an existential force necessary to break both visible and invisible walls. From Hélène Cixous to Luce Irigaray, French feminists in the 1970s equally insisted on the right to movement and on that of simply being there, on a *Dasein* or *être-là*.

Along similar lines, Virilio links present-day eviction strategies by the French government in many cities to those of British colonialists who weakened tribal structures the better to conquer indigenous people. In the West, an invisible military and industrial power set out to divide and conquer the family. No longer working where they live, family members are dispersed, isolated. They spend much of their time being shuttled around. The single status of many women cannot be seen only as emancipation, it is also part of a process that weakens a cell of potential resistance.[5] Again, Virilio argues here for a grounded space, a territory, that is taken away from humans. The family unit is seen as a social unit of communication and interaction rather than as a locus of oppression.

Some of the latter hypotheses, while not without critical punch, are bound to be unpopular with feminists who refuse to consider familial structures (be they nuclear or extended) as carriers of great solidarity and support but who see in them the cold fact of oppression. Yet, Virilio's razor-edged remarks provide a fresh look at social, political *and* economic transformations that women cannot simply ignore. From de Beauvoir to Badinter, French feminists asked for changes in production and reproduction, in familial *and* economic structures. They declared that women could not simply try to integrate themselves into a system that had made possible their repressions in the first place. A general change in politics and ecopolitics, they felt, was needed. Many of these changes never came about. Emancipation came along with the destruction or withering away, rather than the transformation of certain key institutions.

Deploring a general erosion of animal and social territories in the ongoing War of Speed, Virilio gives much praise to those who resist, to producers of existence, mainly women. *Défense populaire et lutte écologique* (1978), weighing the possibility of Revolutionary Resistance in the era of Pure War, is dedicated to 'The People without land, The Disappeared Ones (*Los Desparecidos*), The Madwomen of the Plaza de Mayo (*Las Locas de la Plaza de Mayo*).' Virilio here refers specifically to the Dirty War in Argentina during the 1970s when the military, often in collusion with church and government, murdered thousands. Some women, called the Madwomen, took up resistance. They took to the streets and protested in silent marches against the dispossession of the people under a military dictatorship. They fought for their right to existence often at the expense of their own lives. Below the dedication, in an epigraph borrowed from Caspar David Friedrich, Virilio underscores the fact that ordinary people – *le peuple* – have no voice, no conscience and are not permitted to honor themselves. Paying double homage to these last 'existential heroines', the *Folles de la Place de Mai*, the revolutionary women who risked their lives while defending their rights to social, animal and territorial bodies, Virilio makes it clear that, in an era of progressive loss of habitat, the only struggle worth fighting for is a truly ecological struggle. In this perspective, ecology is not that slightly archaic, folkloristic activity of people who wish to put 'Paris in the country'. Rather, it is a struggle for the right to move, but also to be, a struggle for which women become the true representatives.

Next to 'pure war' in the aftermath of the Second World War, the second moment Virilio singles out in this race for speed is that of the move into cyberspace. It perfects the coupling of humans and machine and completely alters all our notions of space, geography, politics of the last 2000 years. The Cold War atmosphere tied to the military-industrial complex still perceptible in the late 1970s has given way in the final years of this century, to a market 'dromocracy' that reigns supreme. The year 1989 marked not only the 'fall of communism', it also coincided with the generalization of electronic or speed space.

From his earliest publications, Virilio, flamboyantly and with rhetorical bravura, chronicles the technological developments in the West and the implicit transformation of humans' positions in time and space. Two constants prevail in his archeology of the future: (1) acceleration goes hand in hand with an increasing loss of territory, with a doing away of 'Mother Earth', with the animal and social body; (2) objectification through technology does away with soul or conscience and enslaves all those who are not in power. Underscoring present 'dangers' and praising those who resist, Virilio denounces the contemporary myth of global salvation through technological progress. His vision could be dubbed pessimistic. 'With the realization of a dromocratic-type progress', he writes, 'humanity will stop being diverse' (Virilio, 1986: 47). It will tend to divide only into hopeful populations (who are allowed the hope that they will reach, in the future, some day, the speed that they are accumulating, which will give them access to the possible – that is, to the project, the decision, the infinite: speed is the hope of the West) and despairing populations, blocked by the inferiority of their technological vehicles, living and subsisting in a finite world. Thus, 'the related logic of knowing-power, or power-knowledge, is eliminated to the benefit of moving-power – in other words, to the study of tendencies, of flows' (Virilio, 1986: 47). To make his point, he has recourse to the same quotation by Caspar David Friedrich already used as epigraph in *Défenses populaires et luttes idéologiques* (1978). Yet over time, he will replace *le peuple*, the people in the sense of class, and class struggles, with *les peuples* as peoples or nations, when he writes: 'Peoples will have no more voice. They will not be permitted to have a conscience and to honor themselves' (Virilio, 1998: 84–5).

The world, for Virilio, is henceforth divided into haves and have-nots, into those who do have speed and those who do not; those who operate in speed-space and those who are in anthropological – or finite – space. Rarely does Virilio broach these issues of what he calls 'technological and economic imperialism' exclusively along gendered lines. When he does, he mainly deals, as we have seen, with ordinary women and 'the people', not with the elite of either sex that – because it has moving power – is always suspect to him.

One of the main questions now – at least among the hopeful women – is whether, with the shift from territorial grounding often identified with a nationalistic and patriarchal subject to teletopic simultaneity, mobile geographies and virtual subjects – electronic transmission dooms women's animal and social bodies and their territories or whether, by disconnecting them from space and place, it enables them to reconnect in entirely different and novel ways. A second question might be whether the poor living in a more anthropological space have no control or whether their lives too are altered in other than purely negative ways.

Virilio leaves no room for doubt. He refuses to see teletechnologies as enabling humans to rethink and transform their more traditional spaces such as body, city, territory. In *Vitesse de libération* (1995c) and even more in *Cybermonde, la politique du pire* (1996) and *La Bombe informatique* (1998), he broaches the politics of speed less in ecological terms of habitat than in relation to a quality of life and its negative urbanization under the influence of machines. Even more than for 'Mother Earth', he sees the necessity to opt for 'real space and one's own world, that is one's own body since one cannot separate the body from one's own world' (Virilio, 1996: 51). He refuses to follow those lines of flight that would lead to a positive ungrounding. Again, in spite of Virilio's gloom, his incisive analyses of the transformation of a 'real' space like that of the neighborhood or the city in a teletopic era can be of interest to women few of whom – with the exception of observers, such as Saskia Sassen (1991) – deal with new 'urban facts' in other than romantic and antiquated ways.

Next to the loss of 'real space', Virilio examines the implications of the passing of a new frontier, that of the screen in cyberspace that disconnects humans in his view and connects them entirely with the machine. The threat of the biblical prophecy has been fulfilled: man has become one with the machine. After having deplored the death of the family, seen as the basic operative unit in an climate of increasing fear of the bodily other, Virilio now condemns cybersex in no uncertain terms:

> In fact, if industrial technologies have progressively brought about the decline of the *extended* family of the rural world, in favor of the *bourgeois* family, then the *nuclear* family (so well designated), during the era of urban expansion in the last century, the end of the supremacy of physical proximity in the megalopolis of the postindustrial era will no longer simply promote the expansion of the *single parent* household, it will provoke an even more radical break between man and woman that will threaten directly the future of sexed reproduction ... the 'Parmenidean' cut betweeen masculine and feminine principles will intensify as a result of lovemaking at a distance. (Virilio, 1995c: 130)

One could counter-argue that cybersex, somewhat like earlier phone-sex, has not yet replaced the coupling of bodies. Electronic machines may have changed bodies' *relations* to the world in such a way that information now circulates instead of people. In the process, the increasing irrelevance of muscular strength at the basis of much sexual division of labor, may have benefitted many skilled women.

Nonetheless, Virilio answers feminist critics who celebrate movements in speed space as 'authorless digital interactions' or as 'bodies moving and gliding over surfaces' quite decisively. Most bodies in cyberspace are neither the nomadic bodies of Deleuze and Guattari's 12th plateau nor are they simply moving through smooth spaces. The spaces most women inhabit are heavily striated so that the agitation called 'movement' is often empty repetition rather than change. In *Cybermonde, la politique du pire*, in his exchange with Philippe Petit, Virilio praises Gilles Deleuze for his insistence on an existential depth (*épaisseur*) that he sees as threatened with extinction in today's world under the sway of speed and the media:

> I have a nostalgia for an inscription in a spatial and temporal depth, in a depth of the relation to the other and of meaning. Gilles Deleuze worked a lot at that level. I am sure that my interest for him is linked to this. (1996: 104)

The focus on the loss of lived space gives way here to a stringent critique of live time in the age of media. With the increasing privileging of speed, information and advertisement, the depth that comes with words, stories and communication are lost. Paradoxically, this loss is equated with a progressive mental and physical slowing down to the point of immobilization.

Virilio sees little or no convergence between dromological progress and human or social progress. The philosopher of speed enumerates five stages in the development of Western societies:

1. A society without vehicle where the woman plays the part of the logistic wife.
2. The domestication of bodies without soul as vehicles.
3. The empire and the speed of technological vehicles.
4. Rivalry between the metabolic and the technological vehicle. Victory of technology.
5. End of the proletariat and end of History in the war of Time. (Virilio, 1986: 96).

Exploitation is complete and all class war but an illusion. Members of the military gave the proletariat for a short while the illusion of being able to dominate the bourgeoisie, a class that came up with the city, already ruined by highways, media, radio, telephone and soon, television and computers. The crisis of liberal democracies is the end of a type of mobilization (mobility) of its male *and* female citizens. Mobility, synonymous with the concept of freedom since the Age of Enlightenment has been lost. Any attempt at 'reclaiming the streets' cannot be but artificial. Yet this state of things is kept secret. People in power try to keep the masses in strategic and social convictions that are largely superannuated. They keep them occupied with dead thought. Not just sports, as in Roman times, but many cultural and leisure activities, many topics of research and investigation, are there to keep people from exploring real political issues. Quoting James Baldwin saying that, 'tomorrow you will all be negroes', Virilio reminds his readers how the black book of French colonialism equated Africans with 'furniture'. They could be moved or set in place. The French discouraged Africans from building a civilization. Similarly today, despite all the hype to the contrary, people – especially women – as long as they are controlled by the media, are prevented from freely constructing animal or social territories.

Throughout his work, Virilio decries a progressive loss of animal and social territory and points to the difficulty of inventing new cultural practices in the current climate that eliminates diversity and strives toward monoculture.[6] He denounces the political use of superannuated mental frameworks out of which even women sometimes operate when they construct subjectivities that do not account for consequences of scientific or technological innovation, or when they speak of 'agency' without problematizing the latter accordingly. Their actions will thus be tolerated, even encouraged, because the consequences will be considered quite limited.[7] Virilio's argument forces women to rethink the terms in which they speak and launch their calls to action.

Globalization seen through this lens is no longer the realization of a dream of universal connectedness. Quite the contrary. It means the end of an entire world, the world of the particular and the localized (Virilio, 1995c). The emergence of the information (super)highways has transformed the world of history that humans knew for centuries, with its traditions, conventional space, geographical territories, physical journeys and the like.[8] Humans – men and women alike – are at the foot of a new wall, that of time. On the one hand, Virilio recognizes the positive aspects of this new situation that could bring humanity together because of a free flow of information.[9] On the other, he denounces it as an unprecedented, totalitarian situation.[10]

More than ever, an ecological struggle – Virilio calls it 'grey' or 'urban' ecology, that is, an ecology that deals with the transformations of habitat under the impact of electronics technologies – seems necessary to obviate the absolute power of information with its totalitarian features. The past two decades have witnessed the progressive disappearance of reality. First, 'reality was a matter of mass; then it became mass + force; today it is mass + force + information.' Virilio cautions that the totalitarianism of the information-medium might be even more powerful than the traditional political totalitarianism of the old national-socialist or communist hues. The dangers are greater and the stakes are higher. Where are these danger zones? Virilio seems a bit reluctant to elaborate. He continues to caution against the immobilization of the valid invalid and, as I have shown elsewhere (Conley, 1997: 76–90), he joins many feminists who argue for the freedom of writing over the castrating effects of the image (Virilio, 1995b). Images threaten to destroy the possibility of conjuring up mental pictures and productive phantasms. Humans no longer write, they call. Soon, he adds, they will no longer speak.[11] This will be 'the silence of the lambs!' (Virilio, 1995a) that goes with an atrophy of the limbs. Speech, words are producers of existence. Humans no longer construct habitable spaces in a closed world dominated by the machine.

In a recent interview with Catherine David, Virilio softens his position by declaring that he is not advocating the end of *THE* world, but the end of *A* world, as we knew it, that is, the material and anthropological world with its bodily contact and human exchange (Virilio, 1997). Today's world, Virilio warns his readers, is not simply one in which we move along surfaces or communicate and celebrate in cyberspace but one in which virtual universes of fascism loom large. Some women may decide to accompany Paul Virilio and explore the unlimited possibilities of celebration opened by teletechnologies to his dissident tune of caution. For cyberphiles like Donna Haraway, Sherry Turkle, Allucquère Rosanne Stone, Christine Boyer, Sadie Plant and others, Virilio's racy visions may appear like those of an unwelcome passenger accompanying males and females who roam through cyberspace.

Virilio discusses transformations of the world in ways rarely adressed by women who are more focused on the dilemmas of subjectivity. He bemoans the loss of physical space by humans and praises those women who resist this tendency and who, thereby, 'accede to existence', in a quasi-Sartrian way. The space lost is a phenomenological, grounded space with echos of Heidegger whose name is quoted repeatedly in *Vitesse de libération* (1995c). Gendered questions are developed in relation to the loss of ground, existence and the disappearance of a fleshy body with the advent of real time first through acceleration in transportation and then through electronic transmission.

Yet, there are moments, or glimpses, when space in relation to gender functions differently. Disrupting Virilio's more general, phenomenological approach to, and critique of, space and the body, I earlier mentioned the passages of biblical seduction and of the woman-vehicle carrying off the male as passenger. To these, I would now like to return. In the biblical scene, the most explicit of them all, seduction of the man by the woman leads to the fall, is accompanied by a sudden change in perception and the emergence of a new world where movement is 'originary'. Similarly, though a bit less radical, in the instance when woman-as-vehicle carries off man-as-passenger, time is dynamic and space becomes a moving trajectory. This episode that mediates between a more conventional sense of space and a more radical one brought about by woman, is first mentioned in 'Métempsychose du passager' (1977a: 11–18), quoted again in footnote 1, on page 94 of *Vitesse et politique* (1977b) and in footnote 5 of Chapter 3 of *L'Esthétique de la disparition* (1980: 137). Not content with this, Virilio decides to reprint the article under the same title in *L'Horizon négatif* (1984: 35–52) and briefly alludes to it in *Vitesse de libération* (1995c: 135). Virilio has a point to make. His position, though ambiguous, gives us a fleeting glimpse of another time–space when he argues that woman is man's first 'vehicle'; he is her first 'passenger' not only at birth but also in sexual relations! Paraphrasing Samuel Butler, he writes:

> One could say that the female [*femelle* in the French text] is the means that the male found to reproduce himself, that is, to *come* into the world. In that sense, woman is the first means of transport of the species, its first vehicle, the second would be the coupling of dissimilar bodies, geared up for migration, for the common trip. (Virilio, 1984: 38)

Here, time is dynamic and space becomes a moving trajectory. As in the Bible, movement is initiated by women and is linked to eros and affect. This opening on to another time and space is quickly closed when Virilio adds:

> In a sense, woman was at the origin of the first continuation of battle, the first 'revolution' of transportation, she enabled the hunter to specialize in the obscenity of the narcissistic, male duel.... Through domestication, the weak sex [sic] made possible the invention of the enemy beyond the prey ... the invention of the road, the revolution of technological and not only of metabolic transportation. (Virilio, 1984: 39–40)[12]

The dynamic space opened through trajectory and movement in connection with eros opens to an affective diagram quite different from that of calculation that elsewhere, in Virilio, is said to lead to eradication of space. It is perhaps from these moments that deal with affect and the sexes, with changes in perception, that we could develop notions of space, body and gender with the help of Virilio's incisive analyses of contemporary transformations of cities, geography and geopolitics that would open to possibilities of transformations.

Despite the delphic style of a Gallic orator, despite his seeming posture of gloom, the French philosopher of speed may help women recompose notions of agency, resistance, ecological struggle and myriad other concepts whose anachronistic use is favored by the media (urban, city, heterosexual, family, single parent...). He cautions women against simply and non-critically buying into a controlling system while thinking they are emancipating themselves. As a lone voice of caution in the midst of all the glitz and hype about communities and liberation in cyberspace, Virilio resists the teletopic trendiness and stylish bashing of social causes. Somewhat ironically, he himself seems to be one of these immobile subjects – or smart travellers – who gather information by scanning the screen and the printed page rather than by spanning the globe. At the same time, he surges ahead, chronicling the future with its object-women, while regretting the *woman-vehicle*, or her recent avatars, such as the Madwomen of the *Plaza de Mayo*. The insistent repetitions in Virilio's work make it clear that, for him, women are more immanent. They are also more mobile. Hence, they are more capable not only of mediating between animal or social territories and speed-space but also of constructing an elsewhere to Virilio's anticipated, totalitarian closure, that is, of reinventing space and territory.

Notes

1. In a provocative remark, Virilio adds that when the Allies invaded [sic] France and Germany in 1944–5, they brought with themselves a rich experience in economic and physical violence, a memory of ethnocides, human deportation, slavery and colonialism.

2. Baudrillard (1983) claims that all war is to liquidate resistance of autochtonous people against the military-industrial complexes.

3. Virilio is also close to the hypotheses of Michel de Certeau (1986), to those of Gilles Deleuze and Félix Guattari (1988) and to Guattari (1989).

4. Jean-Luc Godard underscores Virilio's hypotheses against Giscard d'Estaing's restructuring of Paris and weakening of familial ties by showing the link between consumption and prostitution in the Parisian 'grands ensembles'.

5. Here we can remind the reader once again that McDonald's was founded by Ray Kroc in 1960 to cater to single mothers who had no time for life at home. Kroc foresaw, and indeed fostered, the shift in family structures and with a keen sense of business took advantage of it.

6. This results in a banality that is different from Michel de Certeau's 'art of everyday life' (1986) and from Jean Baudrillard's hypotheses (1991).

7. In connection with these hypotheses we could see a noticeable increase in the number of 'people's stories' in the newspapers not as a progressive personalization but as a form of anachronism.

8. The end of history in the sense of Virilio has nothing to do with that of Francis Fukuyama.

9. A case in point is the recent closing down of free email exchange by the Chinese government, that views it as a political threat. Roger Cohen in his article on Brazil (*New York Times*, 5 Feb. 1998) notes that peasants can organize their resistance faster because of access to electronic devices.

10. Much has been said about the abolition of the boundaries between private and public, etc. But also, technologies allow the speedy transfer of money and exchange of currencies for unprecedented profits and at the expense of many ordinary people.

11. For many French theorists, language is equated with freedom. The eradication of language is seen as the loss of diversity and the advent of monoculture. Virilio here echoes the pronouncements of feminists as diverse as Hélène Cixous, Luce Irigaray and Assia Djebar.

12. On the question of narcissistic homosexual male duel, Luce Irigaray and Hélène Cixous reached similar conclusions. In addition, the feminists differentiated this type of homosexuality from another, less 'fraternal' type. Going against much contemporary theory, Virilio in a passing remark mentions how heterosexual relations in the French legal codes were devised by a homosexual count, Jean-Jacques de Cambacérès, who favored the relations of men and made women miserable. Virilio's provocative remarks add an interesting twist to the by now cliched expression, 'compulsory heterosexuality' (Virilio, 1995c: 80).

References

Augé, Marc (1996) 'Paris and the Ethnography of the Contemporary World', pp. 175–9 in M. Sheringham (ed.) *Parisian Fields*. London: Reaktion Books.

Baudrillard, Jean (1983) *Simulations*. New York: Semiotext(e).

Baudrillard, Jean (1991) 'L'Amérique ou la pensée de l'espace', in J. Baudrillard et al. *Citoyenneté et urbanité*. Paris: Seuil.

de Certeau, Michel (1986) *The Practice of Everyday Life*, trans. Michael Rendall. Berkeley: University of California Press.

Conley, Verena A. (1997) *Ecopolitics*. New York: Routledge.

Deleuze, Gilles and Felix Guattari (1988) *A Thousand Plateaus*, trans. Brian Massumi. Minneapolis: University of Minnesota Press.

Evenson, Norma (1979) *Paris: A Century of Change*. New Haven, CT: Yale University Press.

Guattari, Félix (1989) *Les trois écologies*. Paris: Galilée.

Godard, Jean-Luc (1969) *Two or Three Things I Know About Her*.

Sassen, Saskia (1991) *The Global City: New York, London, Tokyo*. Princeton, NJ: Princeton University Press.

Virilio, Paul (1977a) 'Métempsychose du passager', *Traverses* 8: 11–18.

Virilio, Paul (1977b) *Vitesse et politique*. Paris: Galilée.

Virilio, Paul (1978) *Défenses populaires et luttes écologiques*. Paris: Galilée.

Virilio, Paul (1980) *L'Esthétique de la disparition*. Paris: Balland.

Virilio, Paul (1984) *L'Horizon négatif*. Paris: Galilée.

Virilio, Paul (1986) *Speed & Politics*, trans. Mark Polizotti. New York: Semiotext(e).

Virilio, Paul (1991) *The Aesthetics of Disappearance*, trans. Philip Beitchman. New York: Semiotext(e).

Virilio, Paul (1995a) 'Global Algorithm 1.7: The Silence of the Lambs: Conversation with Carlos Oliveira', trans. P. Riemens. *CTheory* [http://www.ctheory.com/gal1.7-silence.html]

Virilio, Paul (1995b) *The Art of the Motor*, trans. Julie Rose. Minneapolis: University of Minnesota Press.

Virilio, Paul (1995c) *La Vitesse de libération*. Paris: Galilée.

Virilio, Paul (1996) *Cybermonde, la politique du pire*, Entretien avec Philippe Petit. Paris: Editions Textuel.

Virilio, Paul (1997) 'The Dark Spot of Art', Interview with Catherine David. *documenta documents* 1: 47–67.

Virilio, Paul (1998) *La Bombe informatique*. Paris: Galilée.

Verena Andermatt Conley teaches in the Literature Program at Harvard University. Recent publications include an edited volume, *Rethinking Technologies* (University of Minnesota Press, 1993) and *Ecopolitics: The Environment in Poststructuralist Thought* (Routledge, 1997). She is currently working on problems of transformation of space in contemporary culture.

The Conceptual Cosmology of Paul Virilio

James Der Derian

P AUL VIRILIO, like the truth, is out there. From his 1976 exhibition
on bunker archeology to his recent millennial project on the integral
accident, Virilio's relentless inquiry into the interdependent relationships of speed and politics, technology and ecology, and war and cinema has
left many a reader breathless, befuddled and sometimes in the dust. A not
atypical Virilio chapter begins with a comparison of the phenomenologist
Edmund Husserl to the astrophysicist Stephen Hawkings, and ends with
account of the billionaire recluse, Howard Hughes. A single Virilio sentence, full of concatenated clauses and asyndetic phrases, can collapse a
century of political thought, dismantle a foundation of scientific absolutes.
His take on a deterritorialized, accelerated, hyper-mediated world redefines
outlandish. Nonetheless, when shit happens – events that defy conventional
language, fit no familiar pattern, follow no conception of causality – I reach
for Virilio's conceptual cosmology.

And I did so again, when Monicamania, Iraq redux and a live-feed
frenzy took the USA once more to the brink of what Virilio identified several
years ago in *The Art of the Motor* as a '*data coup d'état*' (Virilio, 1995a
[1993]: 23–34). Virilio's study of a virtually mediated reality provided a
template for the domestic scandal and foreign crisis which befell the Clinton
White House and spread, as Virilio would have it, like radioactivity through
the infosphere. Indeed, the chapter titles alone of *Art of the Motor* read like a
chronology of the events and actors of Zippergate, from the first salacious
rumours to the final impeachment melodrama: 'The Media Complex', 'The
Data Coup d'Etat, 'The Shrinking Effect', 'A Terminal Art', 'Victims of the
Set', 'From Superman to Hyperactive Man'. Virilio's melding of the military-
industrial-media complex anticipates the deliberations of the pundits who

■ *Theory, Culture & Society* 1999 (SAGE, London, Thousand Oaks and New Delhi),
Vol. 16(5–6): 215–227
[0263-2764(199910/12)16:5–6;215–227;009967]

began, usually in a single sentence, to collapse topics like the ambiguity of defining a 'sexual relationship' with the efficacy of Cruise missiles in eradicating terrorist threats. Unlike the academic 'specialist' who has little time for the everyday, Virilio immerses himself in the minutial of mass culture. Moving from Plato to Nato, finding high theory in daily headlines, matching intellectual alacrity with rhetorical superficiality, Virilio's pronouncements cannot help but be – by reflection and evaluation – at once hyperbolic and prescient: 'movement creates the event'; 'information explodes like a bomb'; 'the televised poll is now a mere pale simulation of the ancient rallying of citizens' (1995a: 23–34). Virilio illuminates the current shift of representation into what he calls the 'virtual theatricalization of the real world': it has taken us from statistical management to electoral polls to video wars, until politics becomes a form of *'cathodic democracy'* (1995a: 23–34).

He seeks to reclaim the medium with a serious message: obsessive media vigilance over behavior combined with political correctness transforms democracy from an open participatory form of government into a software program for the entertainment and control of all spectators. Speed enhances this phenomenon through a global 'shrinking effect': 'With acceleration there is no more here and there, only the mental confusion of near and far, present and future, real and unreal – a mix of history, stories, and the hallucinatory utopia of communication technologies' (1995a: 35). The coeval emergence of a mass media and an industrial army was the signifying moment of modernity, of a capability to war without war, producing 'a parallel information market' of propaganda, illusion, dissimulation. However, technological accelerants like satellite link-ups, real-time feeds and high-resolution video augment the power of television to dissimulate in time as well as space. Now the danger lies in the media's power to 'substitute' realities. With the appearance of a global view comes the disappearance of the viewer-subject: in the immediacy of perception, our eyes become indistinguishable from the camera's optics, and critical consciousness goes missing.

In the abstract, Virilio's attribution of such powers to media technology might seem to be overstated, even border on reification. Yet consider again the mediated event called Monica, from the first Linda Tripp-wire, when data was accumulated, manipulated and substituted through multiple media, to the Starr Report, which at one moment appeared likely to topple a US President and at the next propels him to his highest approval ratings. At moments, it seemed as if Virilio was writing the script himself. The day after the news broke of Tripp's tape-recordings, PBS's Jim Lehrer assembled his team of pundits; movement of information, that is, speed, quickly became the primary discussion point. Presidential scholar Doris Kearns Goodwin contrasted the slow deliberative process of Watergate to the accelerated news cycle of today; journalist Haynes Johnson responded that 'Speed has conditioned us to daily scandal'; and revolving-door David Gergen, evoking the film in which the White House brings in Hollywood to produce an imaginary war in Albania, warns of a 'Wag the Dog Syndrome' that would make it impossible for the President to send Iraq an unequivocal signal. Soon after, James Carville, Clinton's hound-dog loyalist, bayed on *Meet the Press* that 'there's going to be a war.'

And war we got. A deadly abstraction of conflict like Virilio's 'pure war', so-named not to suggest out propriety but the immaculate conception of a war without 'real' warring, a war based on the mediated ideology of deterrence.

The weeks that followed were full of transgressive events transformed by sensational reportage into trivial moments – and sometimes the other way around. Major newspapers used the p-word; networks debated whether oral sex constituted a 'sexual relationship'; and Camille Paglia appeared on talk radio – much too often. Then, predictably, like Red Guards just before the defenestration of a bourgeois intellectual, the media broke out into a rash of auto-critique. In one of the first of many self-flagellating, self-righteous essays, *New York Times* media critic, Janny Scott, put the spotlight of blame on the new media, especially the Internet, for being just too damn *fast*:

> The episode provides another cautionary tale in the reporting of a story as fast-paced as the one that broke two weeks ago centering on accusation that the President has sex with an intern in the White House and encouraged her to lie about it under oath. The speed with which news travels has been accelerated in recent years by the rise of the Internet and 24-hour cable television news. (1998: B10)

At the height of the scandal, the Blairs, the Clintons, and just about every significant player from Disney, Dreamworks and the whole media-entertainment complex took time out for a State Dinner, and got down to an overly symbolic pairing of Stevie Wonder and Elton John for the Beatles-Motown hit, 'Money (that's what I want)'. But the very next day, President Clinton went to the Pentagon to address the brass. After gilding the microchip – 'bit by bit the information age is chipping away at the barriers – economic, political and social – that once kept people locked in and freedom and prosperity locked out' – he warned of the data-abusers hanging out in the shadows :

> But for all our promise, all our opportunity, people in this room know very well that this is not a time free from peril, especially as a result of reckless acts of outlaw nations and an unholy axis of terrorists, drug traffickers and organized international criminals. We have to defend our future from these predators of the 21st century. They feed on the free flow of information technology.[1]

Soon thereafter, center court in the basketball arena of Ohio State University, Messengers Albright, Cohen and Berger, intent on sending – with a little help from CNN – a signal of resolution to Saddam Hussein, were undone by the power of the live feed and a group of noisy protesters ('One, two, three, four, we don't want your racist war'). In Baghdad, an agitated pharmacist told a reporter, 'I think this may be the first time a lot of people may die because your President has turned the White House into a brothel' (Ibrahim, 1998: A9). Rahm Emmanuel, one of Clinton's senior advisers, made duration the significant factor, declaring that the 'only common thread' between Whitewater and Lewinsky is that 'they're both twenty-four years old' (Anderson, 1998: 34). In one *New York Times* op-ed article, Maureen Dowd wrote: 'Slick Willie has morphed into Tricky Dicky. Kenneth Starr has morphed into the *X-Files* Cigarette Man' (Dowd, 1998: A29). In another, Thomas Friedman claimed, 'It is only when you combine the medieval with the postmodern that you can fully grasp this Iraq story' (1998: A27).

But it got much worse. After US embassies were truck-bombed on the same day in Sudan and Kenya, the dog of war wagged again as Cruise missiles hunted down former freedom-fighter turned terrorist-bomber, Omasa Bin Laden. The semen-stained dress from the GAP required the President to provide a DNA sample. An apology race to the abject bottom took over the air-waves. Finally, the Starr Report was put on the Web by the Congress (yes, the same guys who passed the Communications Decency Act), and over four million hits were registered (with access denied to any users who had porn-screening programs on their computers). French Minister of Culture Jack Lang and British actor/activist Vanessa Redgrave organized a global petition campaign against the sexual McCarthyism of the 'Starr Tribunal'. Asked about the impending release of the President Clinton's four-and-a-half hour video testimony, Germany's Chancellor Helmut Kohl says, 'It makes me vomit.' And the private sphere contracted ever smaller, until it imploded under the concentric pressure of a prurient public voyeurism.

Such is the dark power which Virilio discerned within the 'hallucinatory utopia of communication technologies'.[2] We might just be witnessing the first of the 'integral accidents' predicted by Virilio, where global interconnectedness destroys the firewalls of civil society, information flows outstrip the powers of deliberation, truth is further relativized by velocity, and crises spread like a contagion.[3] The Military-Industrial-Media-Entertainment Network (MIME-NET) becomes the infrastructure for Pure War.

Against this backdrop of the everyday bizarre, the apocalyptic hype and rhetorical hyperbole of Virilio seems almost normal. His remarkable cosmology of concepts continues to provide an inexhaustible array of *dispositifs*, those investigatory instruments and prescriptive strategies which produce mental images to disturb commonsensical views of the world, to capture the highly mutable and often peculiar forms of the truth *out there*. Virilio is best-known for his use of *speed* as a variable, *chronopolitics* as a concept and *dromology* as a method to produce new understandings of an ever-accelerating global politics. However, in practically every book he coins new concepts which take on new heuristic as well as political value as they are reinterpreted and re-circulated by others.

Like Deleuze, Virilio construes concepts as mental images for disturbing conventional, commonsensical views of world events – but with the added visual warp of a life lived at the speed of cinema, video, light itself (Patton, 1996: 1–17). It is not, then, a criticism (nor, for that matter, an unqualified recommendation) to say that reading Virilio will probably leave one feeling mentally disturbed, usually compounded by a bad case of vertigo, since speed is not only the subject but the style of Virilio (helping to account for a dozen books in as many years). In a typical Virilio sentence, which often elongates into a full paragraph, the concepts can spew out like the detritus of a *Mir* supply-ship. Many get recycled in later books. Some, benefiting from refinement and new empirical settings, stand out like polished gems. But almost all of them provide radically different takes on the social implications of new technological forces, liberating their analysis from the customary academic dullness and expert narrowness.

Some of the concepts, often the most neologistic ones, burn brightly but briefly, flaming-out once they are lifted from Virilio's seductive rhetorical flow and subjected to the atmosphere of contemporary politics. Such might be an interpretation of one of the opening paragraphs from the last chapter of *L'espace critique*:

> In effect, the geopolitics of nations that yesterday still presupposed the hierarchical privilege of the center over its peripheries, of the summit over the base, the 'radioconcentrism' of exchanges and horizontal communications, loses its value in the same way as does the extreme vertical densification to the benefit of an inapparent morphological configuration. The NODAL succeeds the CENTRAL in a preponderantly electronic environment, 'tele-localization' favoring the deployment of a generalized eccentricity, endless periphery, forerunner of the overtaking of the industrial urban form, but especially of the decline of the sedentary character of the metropolis to the advantage of an obligatory *interactive confinement*, a sort of inertia of human populations for which the name of *teleconcentrism* may be proposed, while waiting for that of 'homeland' to replace that of the large suburb. The secular opposition city/country is being lost while the geomorphological uniqueness of the state is dissipating. (Virilio, 1984: 156)

Now it is all too easy – and all too often a gambit of the hack critic – to take a complex sentence or paragraph out of context and to assert its incomprehensible character. In this paragraph Virilio is actually leading up to a very important and central claim of the book, that the *exo-colonialism* of the industrial, imperial period has become introverted – internally by the de-industrialization and pauperization of the urban center, and externally by the rise of an intensive transnational capital and transpolitical megalopoles – into a post-industrial *endo-colonization*: Mexico City, Shanghai, São Paulo, and the South African Homelands are presented as pointed examples. Perhaps there are simpler ways to introduce or to translate this idea. But it would probably take at least three more paragraphs and a lot of loose translation to do it.

Because I have found it to vary by the reader whether Virilio's concepts offer a supernova flash of illumination or a black-hole obscuring of complex subjects, I will not pretend to have a sure measure of the heuristic value of his concepts. However, not least because Virilio has such a yen for astrophysics (he once remarked that a lack of formal training in the sciences was one of Baudrillard's shortcomings), I will risk belaboring the astral metaphors to make one supernal *caveat lector*: there are in Virilio some conceptual wormholes which can take the reader to very strange and not always rewarding places. They often appear just as a rhetorical dead-end looms, and imaginative or empirical exhaustion is setting in, as Virilio tries to bolster an extravagant claim or weak concept by piling on superficial evidence, like the moment in 'The Suicidal State', where he goes from a very long, deeply political account of the persecution of *nomadism* under the German Third Reich, marked by the rounding up and killing of gypsies and bohemians, to the trivial, modern-day right of a Frenchman to park his camper anywhere he damn well pleases (Virilio, 1993: 41).

At other times and different places, Virilio's wormholes can open doors of perception (think of Blake rather than Huxley) that make the trip well worth the effort. For instance, take *Polar Inertia* (1999 [1990]), one of his most difficult and most philosophically dense works. Virilio returns to Germany in the 1930s, to posit the rupture between philosophy and physics as one of the reasons for technology going out of control, leading to Auschwitz and Hiroshima, and then leaps forward to identify a similar gap opening up between the power of new remote-control technologies and our ability to understand a rapidly changing environment. From this he induces an ethical imperative to rejoin current metaphysical and astrophysical thinking about everything from the beginnings of time to the end of the world as we conventionally know it. Fortunately, he has covered this ground – that is, where the ground in effect gives way to speed – in simpler ways in other works:

> In our situations of televisual experience, we are living in nothing less than the sphere of Einstein's relativity, which wasn't at all the case at the time that he wrote it since that was a world of trolley cars, and at most, the rocket. But today we live in a space of relativity and non-separability. Our image of time is an image of instantaneity and ubiquity. And there's a stunning general lack of understanding of speed, a lack of awareness of the essence of speed. . . . And this passage from an extensive to an intensive time will have considerable impact on all the various aspects of the conditions of our society: it leads to a radical reorganization both of our social mores and of our image of the world. This is the source of the feeling that we're faced with an epoch in many ways comparable to the Renaissance: it's an epoch in which the real world and our image of the world no longer coincide . . . (in Sans, 1991: 139–40)

In *Polar Inertia*, however, the issue entails some heavy wading through, among other difficult works, the writings of Edmund Husserl and Stephen Hawking. The first couple of times I did not get it. Moreover, I thought this was this kind of thing most likely to get the hard-core Protectors of the Virgin Sciences up in arms (*viz.* Alan Sokal of the *Social Text* hoax). After all, Virilio was arguing from the perspective of a post-Einsteinian theory of relativity that not only seemed to play fast and loose with analogical reasoning, but also to violate some of the basic laws of physics, like the impossibility of exceeding the speed of light, or the impossibility of two objects simultaneously occupying the same space. But then, as is often the case with Virilio, the physical world appears to catch up to his metaphysical analysis: news came from Switzerland that objects, albeit sub-nuclear ones, can, *sort of* (to use a technical term) simultaneously communicate at speeds exceeding the speed of light.[4] What Einstein had disparagingly dismissed as 'spooky action at a distance' had been achieved in an experiment in Geneva: 'It was as if some ghostly bridge across the city of Geneva, Switzerland, had permitted two photons of light nearly seven miles apart to respond simultaneously to a stimulus applied to just one of them' (Browne, 1997: C1). As one commentator, George Johnson, later put it, 'two photons ... "correlated" in some funny mathematical way that defies common sense' (1997: E5). Johnson begins and ends his article with the physicists' plaint about the inadequacy of language to describe the results and the field of quantum mechanics in general, confirming, I believe, Virilio's point – and why the reader might have to suffer some conceptual gymnastics to get it:

> Physicists, exasperated at trying to explain to puzzled laymen the meaning of that weird cornerstone of reality called quantum mechanics, complain about what they call 'the word problem.' The counterintuitive manner in which subatomic particles behave couldn't be clearer to those who can sight-read the mathematics, nature's symphonic score. But try translating these truths into language and the trouble begins. . . . But if scientists are surer than ever about the truth of quantum mechanics, they are not any closer to explaining what it means. There is no reason to expect that our linguistic toolkits will contain tweezers fine enough to grasp the slippery concepts that hold in the subatomic realm. (1997: E5)

Yet, for every one of Virilio's oblique concepts or extravagant theoretical claims, there are others which slice right through the sludge that is served up as political analysis.[5] By this quality alone, there is no question that he belongs in the company of Benjamin and Adorno, Debord and Baudrillard, Foucault and Deleuze, Barthes and Derrida, for taking our understanding of the discursive relationship of technology, society and politics to a higher plane of political as well as critical consciousness. He might not always match some of these thinkers in their philosophical consistency, historical knowledge or rhetorical flair. But as the millennium turns, he stands out from the critical crowd, as a conceptual innovator and intellectual provocateur, the one who goes to the edge and sees beyond the traditional maps of modernity. Take, as just one example of many, a 1988 interview, in which he displayed a remarkable prescience about the televisual power of new military technologies and what it would mean for contemporary war and politics:

> When you couple a video camera with a computer on a robot or on a missile like a cruise missile, the gaze, even if for the moment a poor gaze, is a self-sufficient gaze, a blind gaze, the machine looking for itself and no longer for some spectator or telespectator. And I think that this accession of the vision machine demonstrates well to what point meaning, in the rich human, I was even going to say humanist sense, is destined to be superseded. (*Block*, 1988: 4–7)

Virilio's reputation should not stand or fall by the oxyopia of his own gaze. I do believe, however, that his work can judged by the extent to which his conceptual cosomology has infused the debate about late modernity with a critical awareness of dangers extant and future. I can only offer here a rapid-fire proof, that will, I hope, inspire a closer reading of his works.

In his first book (*The Insecurity of Territory* first published in 1976),[6] Virilio introduces the concepts of *deterritorialization, nomadism* and the *suicidal state,* which Deleuze and Guatarri pick up and brilliantly elaborate in their most significant work, *A Thousand Plateaus* (1987: 345, 395-6, 520-1 n.24, 536 n.8, 551 n.56). Virilio draws on Walter Benjamin's fear of an aestheticized politics, but takes it further, showing how politics, no longer willing, no longer able to maintain representational distinctions between the real, the visual and the virtual, *disappears into the aesthetic* (*The Aesthetics of Disappearance,* 1991 [1980]). This disappearance is facilitated by the melding of military, cinematic, and techno-scientific *'logistics of perception'* (*War and Cinema,* 1989 [1984]). All economies of sight and might, remnants of presence like quattrocento linear fields of perception, national-territorial politics, Cartesian subjectivity, Newtonian physics, become coordinated, and eventually subordinated by a relativist, quantum, *transpolitical* war machine (*Negative Horizon,* 1986 [1984]). In political terms, this means that the geopolitics of *extensivity* and *exo-colonization* is displaced by the *chronopolitics* of *intensivity* and *endo-colonization* (*L'Éspace Critique,* 1984). In turn, episodic war gives way, through the infinite requirements and preparations of deterrence and simulations, to a permanent *pure war* (*Pure War,* 1997 [1983]).

Displaying no anxiety of influence, Virilio takes Foucault's panopticon model to an extra-terrestrial level of discipline and control, offering a micro-analysis of how new technologies of oversight and organizations of control, innovated by strategic alliances of the military, industrial and scientific communities, have made the cross-over into civilian and political sectors to create a global *administration of fear* (*Popular Defense and Ecological Struggles,* 1990 [1978]). It is not so much the acuity and reach of Foucault's analysis that is extended by Virilio, as it is the *dimensionality,* showing how the control of space has been force-multiplied if not displaced by the control of pace (*Speed and Politics*, 1986 [1977]). As the individual historically moves from *geocentric* (Copernican) to *egocentric* (Husserlian) to *exocentric* (Einsteinian) perspectival fields, and the species from the sedentariness of the agricultural *biosphere* to the mobility of the industrial *technosphere* to the velocity of the informational *dromosphere*, the once-progressivist identity politics of location loses out to the inertial motility of a real-time *telepresence* (*Polar Inertia*, 1999 [1990]).

And long before Derrida spotted the ghost of globalization haunting post-communist Europe, Virilio was writing that Europe's future would not be decided in the various nations' foreign ministries or on the battlefield, but in the electromagnetic spectrum of informational, *cybernetic wars* of persuasion and dissuasion – that is, deterrence writ temporal and global (*Bunker Archéologie*, 1975). Similarly, he presaged an ever-expanding hierarchy of contemporary virtual realities (*The Vision Machine*, 1994b [1988]), where the pseudo-proximity of live news and *faux* military interventions were displacing the consumptive spectacles of Debord and the seductive simulations of Baudrillard with constant irruptive spasms of '*media-staged strategic events*' ['*stratégico-médiatique*']. This was a diagnosis which Virilio applied early on to a critique of the Gulf War (*L'Écran du désert*, 1991), predicting a *real-time war* of short duration with high if hidden [*furtive*] intensity and costs, in contrast to most liberal intellectuals who were stunned into silence, or even support, by the spectacle of excess as well as seeming success of the war machine. While military strategists and think-tank courtiers were searching for a name for a new kind of warfare without war – was it netwar, cyberwar, infowar? – Virilio had already given notice of the *data coup d'etat* that had shifted the aim of battle from capturing to captivating the enemy through the *media complex* (*The Art of the Motor*, 1995a [1993]). And while environmentalists try to arouse a world consciousness by warning of a possible ecological desertification of the planet, Virilio is one dimension beyond, prophesying the chronological desertification of world time, *global time*, by the negative synergy of the *integral accident* (*Open Sky*, 1997).

What is one to make of this dire scan of the human condition? Probably much less than I have. There is certainly more than a hint of millenarian doom to Virilio's work; but as he has made clear in more than one interview, this is not to encourage quietism but to alert the reader that the time to act is now. 'I don't believe', says Virilio, 'in the end of *the* world – I believe in the end of *a* world' (in Zurbrugg, 1995). More specifically, a technologically induced end – of the body as well as the body politic – is not inevitable but increasingly possible:

> We haven't reached that point yet: what I have described is the end, or a vision of the end. What will prevail is this will to reduce the world to the point where one could possess it. All military technologies reduce the world to nothing. And since military technologies are advanced technologies, what

they actually sketch today is the future of the civil realm. But this, too, is an accident. (Virilio, 1994a)

Other critical thinkers have provided new concepts for investigating the political and social implications of new technologies of reproduction. Yet many of them already seem out of date, stuck in place and, to use a word Virilio favors, *folklorique*, when compared to the restless yet, in all its time*full*ness, strangely rustless conceit of Virilio, that the proliferation of high-speed, real-time, cinematic, global, computer networked – in a word – *virtual* systems of how we see, has forever changed how we know, the other. In an essay which originally appeared in *Le Monde diplomatique*, Virilio maps the social consequences:

> What lies ahead is a disturbance in the perception of what reality is; it is a shock, a mental concussion. And this outcome ought to interest us. Why? Because never has any progress in a technique been achieved without addressing its specific negative aspects. The specific negative aspect of these information superhighways is precisely this loss of orientation regarding alterity (the other), this disturbance in the relationship with the other and with the world. It is obvious that this loss of orientation, this non-situation, is going to usher in a deep crisis which will affect society and hence, democracy. (Virilio, 1995b)

And in an interview he warns, when distance and distinctions between mental and visual images collapse, multiple, intensive, coterminous substitutions of reality begin to *war with another*:

> From now on everything passes through the image. The image has priority over the thing, the object, and sometimes even the physically-present being. Just as real time, instantaneousness, had priority over space. Therefore the image is invasive and ubiquitous. Its role is not to be in the domain of art, the military domain or the technical domain, it is to be everywhere, to be reality.... I believe that there is a war of images.... And I can tell you my feelings in another way: winning today, whether it's a market or a fight, is merely not losing sight of yourself (*Block*,1988: 4–7).

In short, virtuality disappears reality. On its own, perhaps not a great loss; but Virilio has his eye where others do not, on the collateral damage done to the *ethos* of reality, the highly vulnerable public space where individuals responsively interact. For Virilio, the interconnectivity of virtual systems is not ushering in a new day for democracy but a new order of *telepresence*; high-paced interconnectivity is becoming, technically and literally, a substitute for the slower-paced intersubjectivity of traditional political systems. He sees the self as a kind of virtually-targeted ground-zero; once voided, concentric circles of political fall-out spread, leaving in the vitrified rubble all responsibility for the other that forms the prior condition for truly intersubjective, ethical, *human* relationships. This forms the *gravitas* of Virilio's body of work. In practically all of his writings it registers more as a persistent ethical, even spiritual pull than as a moral theory or an explicit religious sentiment (although in interviews Virilio has acknowledged the profound significance of Catholicism in his life).[7] I believe it is also this deep ethical force, more so than his corrosive intellectual critique, which keeps his often elliptical rhetoric and some-times errant concepts in something resembling a coherent orbit.

At the end of a long lunch at *La Coupole* in Paris, Virilio put this all much more succinctly, in the aphoristic style he favors for interviews: 'Interactivity is to real space what radioactivity is to the atmosphere.' Before I could get my head around the thought – I was stuck trying to imagine the virtual equivalent of thyroid cancer – he tempered one hyper-bolic statement by another, declaiming, 'I am in love with technology!' Since I knew from the difficulty in arranging the interview that this was a man without email, fax or even an answering machine, I asked him to explain the apparent contradiction. It's just that he wasn't about to make it easy for the intellectual love of his life. Another aphorism followed: like Jacob, he wrestled with the angel of technology not to prove his disbelief, but to prove his *freedom* to believe. Sound cosmological advice, I believe, for all in search of a livable relationship with the new techno-deities.

Notes

1. 'In Clinton's Words', *New York Times* 18 February 1998: A9.

2. To me, the first sign that the nation had been suborned (in the preferred scandal-ese) by a technologically induced *halluci*nation came when I began to confuse the Bennett brothers, Robert, the President's personal lawyer whose questioning months ago of Tripp's credibility led her to begin secretly taping Monica Lewins-ky's conversations, and William, the ever-virtuous Republican activist who ap-peared on just about every talk show except Jerry Springer, impugning the morals of President Clinton. And things got even stranger. *Time* magazine ran a sidebar (2 March 1998) titled 'Good, Al, but that's with a W'. It reports that Allen Ginsberg wrote a poem in 1949, about a 'Sweet Levinsky', of whom Ginsberg wonders: 'do you giggle out of spite/or are you laughing in delight/Sweet Levinsky, sweet Levinsky'. There's also a line about trembling when the cock crows (it turns out that Levinsky was actually Leon Levinsky, a minor character in Jack Kerouac's first novel, *The Town and the City*). When the Cruise missiles were launched after the embassy bombings in Sudan and Kenya, I imagined the dead poet Allen Ginsberg taking over William Ginsburg's body (there is a resemblance), who would then show up on *Larry King Live* for one last hurrah, chanting Ginsberg's mesmerizing poem, 'Hum Bomb' ('Whom bomb?/We bomb them!/ Whom bomb?/We bomb them!/ Whom bomb?').

3. One waits to see what happens when integral accidents combine with integral crises, as foreshadowed by the testimony of US Federal Reserve Board chairman Alan Greenspan to the US Senate budget committee that the 'Asian Crisis' had entered a 'more virulent phase' (*Globe and Mail* 24 September 1998: B1).

4. See Malcom Browne, 'Far Apart, 2 Particles Respond Faster Than Light' (1997). It would also seem that the *New York Times Sunday Magazine* is catching up with

Virilio. In a special issue on 'What Technology is Doing to Us' (28 September 1997), speed is the ruling concept in just about every essay. See for instance, James Gleick's 'Addicted to Speed' (1997: 54–61), which states on one page that scenes from contemporary television and movies 'speed by so fast they've left the laws of physics behind' (1997: 55); and on the next (after a spread of edited shots from *Men in Black*) quotes an executive from ABC: 'We're all bound by the laws of physics. There are only 24 hours in a day and 60 minutes in an hour and 60 seconds in a minute. Everybody looks at their time with a microscope to get the best utilization they can. It is the only real estate we have.'

5. Since Virilio, in the period of his architectural collaboration with Claude Parent, did make a virtue of the 'oblique function' in urban planning (the theoretical basis for the 1966 parochial center Sainte-Bernadette de Nevers, and the 1969 Thomson-Houston aerospace center in Villacoublay), it might warrant further investigation to see if there is a commensurate conceptual application in his later writings.

6. *Bunker Archéologie* was published a year earlier in 1975, but it was primarily a secondary text to accompany the photography exhibition; and Virilio himself refers to *Insecurity of Territory* as his first book (interview with author, June 1995).

7. This was confirmed during his teleconference at the Ars Electronica Symposium on Infowar in Linz, Austria (8 September 1998).

References

Author – 'In Clinton's Words', *New York Times*, February 18, 1998

Anderson, Ken (1998) 'Entertainer-in-Chief', *New Yorker* 16 February.

Block (1988) 'Paul Virilio', interview in *Block* 14: 4–7.

Browne, Malcolm (1997) 'Far Apart, 2 Particles Respond Faster than Light', *New York Times*, 22 July.

Deleuze, Gilles and Félix Guattari (1987) *A Thousand Plateaus: Capitalism and Schizophrenia*. Minneapolis: University of Minnesota Press.

Dowd, Maureen (1998) 'D.C. Confidential', *New York Times* 25 February.

Friedman, Thomas (1998) 'Iraq of Ages', *New York Times* 28 February.

Gleick, James (1997) 'Addicted to Speed', in *New York Times Sunday Magazine*, Special Issue on 'What Technology is Doing to Us', 28 September.

Greenspan, Alan (1998) *Globe and Mail* 24 September.

Ibrahim, Yousef (1998) 'Despite Threat of Missiles, the Iraqi Capital's People Take a Crisis in Stride', *New York Times* 23 February.

Johnson, George (1997) 'The Unspeakable Things that Particles Do', *New York Times* 27 July.

Patton, Paul (1996) *Deleuze: A Critical Reader*. Oxford: Blackwell.

Sans, Jerôme (1991) 'Paul Virilio', trans. H. Martin, pp. 139—50 in *AA and Philosophy*. Milan: Giancarlo Politi Editore.

Scott, Janny (1998) 'Internet Story Revives Questions on Standards', *New York Times* 6 February.

Virilio, Paul (1975) *Bunker Archéologie*. Paris: Centre Georges. Pompidou, Centre de Creation Industrielle.

Virilio, Paul (1991 [1980]) *The Aesthetics of Disappearance*, trans. P. Beitchman. New York: Semiotext(e).

Virilio, Paul (1984) *L'Espace critique*. Paris: Christian Bourgois.

Virilio, Paul (1990 [1978]) *Negative Horizon*, trans. M. Polizotti. New York: Semiotext(e).

Virilio, Paul (1986 [1977]) *Speed and Politics: An Essay in Dromology*, trans. M. Polizotti. New York: Semiotext(e).

Virilio, Paul (1989 [1984]) *War and Cinema: The Logistics of Perception*, trans. P. Camiller. London and New York: Verso.

Virilio, Paul (1990 [1978]) *Popular Defense and Ecological Struggles*, trans. M. Polizotti. New York: Semiotext(e).

Virilio, Paul (1991) *L'Écran du désert: chroniques de guerre*. Paris: Galilée.

Virilio, Paul (1993) *L'Insécurité du territoire*. Paris: Galilée. (Orig. 1976.)

Virilio, Paul (1994a) 'Cyberwar, God and Television', interview with Louise Wilson, *C-Theory* 21 October.

Virilio, Paul (1994b [1988]) *The Vision Machine*, trans. J. Rose. Bloomington and London: Indiana University Press and British Film Institute.

Virilio, Paul (1995a [1993]) *The Art of the Motor*, trans. Julie Rose. Minneapolis: University of Minnesota Press.

Virilio, Paul (1995b) 'Speed and Information: Cyberspace Alarm!', *Le Monde Diplomatique*, August, translated by Patrice Riemens, and published in *ctheory*, 'Speed and Information: Cyberspace Alarm!', 27 September.

Virilio, Paul (1997) *Open Sky*, trans. J. Rose. London: Verso.

Virilio, Paul (1999 [1990]) *P[olar Inertia*, trans. P. Camiller. London: Sage.

Zurbrugg, N. (1995) 'The Publicity Machine and Critical Theory', interview with N. Zurbrugg, 13 Jan., trans. N. Zurbrugg, *Eyeline* 27: 8–14.

James Der Derrin is Research Professor of International Relations at Brown University and Professor of Political Science at the University of Massachusetts at Amherst. He has written and edited several books, most recently *The Virilio Reader* (Blackwell, 1998). His articles on security, technology and the information revolution have appeared in *Wired*, the Washington Quarterly, *21-C* and *Cultural Values*.

Paul Virilio
A Select Bibliography

Compiled and Introduced by John Armitage

Introduction

This select bibliography of the cultural and theoretical works of Paul Virilio in French and English has been compiled from all the references to Virilio's published works that I have been able to find in books, articles, periodicals, newspapers and Internet sites. However, my efforts have benefited greatly from the research skills and generosity of Virilian scholars and others from around the world.[1] Prior to beginning, some brief notes are in order.

The first section simply lists the main published works of Paul Virilio in French. I have also included in this section one or two second editions of Virilio's main published works where new material (e.g. a new Preface or Afterword) has been added. The second section records all of Virilio's articles, collaborations, working papers, discussions and edited works in French. In some instances, I was unable to verify page numbers and this, rather than inattention to bibliographical detail, explains the occasional absence of page numbers not only in this section but also in all the other sections. Some references in the second section have an asterisk (*) attached. The asterisk simply signals that, in this case, Virilio is not the sole author of the piece but has collaborated in some way, usually through the writing of a working paper or, more generally, through a published round-table discussion or the editorial process. Section 3 catalogues all of Virilio's interviews first published in French. Where I was able to ascertain the name of the interviewer, I have included it. The absence of an interviewer's name indicates only that I was unable to confirm it at the time of writing.

The fourth section lists all of the English translations of Virilio's main published works. Translators are noted where credited or known throughout the English sections. Section 5 is an inventory of all of Virilio's articles that

- *Theory, Culture & Society* 1999 (SAGE, London, Thousand Oaks and New Delhi),
  Vol. 16(5–6): 229–240
  [0263-2764(199910/12)16:5–6;229–240;009968]

have been translated into English. Section 6 itemizes all Virilio's interviews published in English. Interviewers are named where credited or known. I have also noted where an interview published in English is a translation from the French original and where an interview in English has been reprinted elsewhere. Section 7 lists all the studies of Virilio's writings in French and English. I have indicated electronic journals and have included a few details concerning book reviews, chapter sections, a PhD thesis, a conference paper, 'plateaus', Virilio's early writings, and discussions of his work in books that are not, principally, about Virilio. Section 8 is the final section and merely sets down three Internet sites related to the work of Virilio for the reader's viewing pleasure.

My hope is that I have provided the most complete bibliography of Virilio's works available in French and English. No doubt there are a great many Virilian texts contained in obscure journals or still swirling around the Internet that I have not been able to find or access. Indeed, some Virilio publications are so marginal that I often get the impression that once he has finished writing a piece he simply hands it to the first person he meets. Consequently, I would be most interested to receive the details of any omissions from this bibliography at the Division of Government and Politics, University of Northumbria, Newcastle upon Tyne NE1 8ST, UK. Happy reading.

1. Main Published Works of Paul Virilio in French

(1975) *Bunker archéologie*. Paris: Centre Georges Pompidou, Centre de Création Industrielle.

(1976) *L'Insécurité du territoire*. Paris: Stock.

(1977) *Vitesse et politique. Essai de dromologie*. Paris: Galilée.

(1978) *Défense populaire et luttes écologiques*. Paris: Galilée.

(1978) *La Dromoscopie ou la lumière de la vitesse*. Paris: Minuit.

(1980) *Esthétique de la disparition*. Paris: Balland.

(1984) *L'Espace critique*. Paris: Christian Bourgois.

(1984) *Guerre et cinéma 1. Logistique de la perception*. Paris: l'Étoile.

(1984) *L'Horizon négatif: essai de dromoscopie*. Paris: Galilée.

(1988) *La Machine de vision*. Paris: Galilée.

(1989) *Esthétique de la disparition* (2nd edn, contains a new Preface.) Paris: Galilée.

(1990) *L'Inertie polaire*. Paris: Christian Bourgois.

(1991) *L'Écran du désert: chroniques de guerre*. Paris: Galilée.

(1991) *Bunker archéologie* (2nd edn, contains a new Afterword, '1945/1990'.) Paris: Demi-Cercle.

(1991) *Guerre et cinéma 1. Logistique de la perception* (2nd edn, contains a new Preface.) Paris: Galilée.

(1993) *L'Insécurité du territoire* (2nd edn, contains a new Afterword, 'Postface: De l'extrême limite à l'extrême proximité'.) Paris: Galilée.

(1993) *L'Art du moteur*. Paris: Galilée.

(1995) *La Vitesse de libération*. Paris: Galilée.
(1996) *Un paysage d'événements*. Paris: Galilée.
(1998) *La Bombe informatique*. Paris: Galilée.
(1999) *Stratégie de la déception*. Paris: Galilée.

2. Articles, Collaborations, Working Papers, Discussions and Edited Works of Paul Virilio in French

(1967) 'Bunker archéologie', *Architecture Principe* 7 (March.)

(1971) 'Architecture of the Open Systems', *Architecture, Formes & Fonctions*: 155–64.

(1974) 'Le Littoral vertical', *Critique* 30(320): 48–53.

(1975) 'La Guerre pure', *Critique* 31(341): 1090–103.

(1975) 'La délation de masse... ou la contre-subversion', pp. 13–57 in Paul Virilio and Georges Perec (eds) *Le Pourrissement des sociétés*. Paris: Union Générale d'Éditions, collection 10/18.*

(1976) 'Le Soldat inconnu', *Les Temps Modernes* 32(360): 2334–53.

(1977) 'Métempsychose du passager', *Traverses* 8: 11–19.

(1978) *Architecture d'ingénieurs XIXe–XXe siècles*. Paris: Centre de Création Industrielle.*

(1978) 'La Dromoscopies ou la lumière de la vitesse', *Critique* 34(370): 324–37.

(1980) *Le Nouvel Ordre gendarmique*. Paris: Seuil.*

(1980) 'Tabas, la stratégie de l'accident', *Libération* May: 7.

(1981) 'La Ville idéale', *Quinzaine Litteraire* 353: 39.

(1981) 'Les Folles de la Place de Mai', *Traverses* 21–2: 9–18.

(1982) 'Le Compte à rebours a commencé', *Quinzaine Litteraire* 376: 5–6.

(1982) 'Perec, ami paisible', *Quinzaine Litteraire* 368: 4.

(1982) 'L'Accident originel', *Confrontation* 7 spring: 5–10.

(1983) *La Crise des dimensions: la représentation de l'éspace et la notion de dimension*. Paris: 1' UDRA - ESA (Unité de recherche appliqué - Ecole spéciale d'architecture.)*

(1983) *Portes de la ville*. Paris: Centre de Création Industrielle.*

(1984) 'Une ville surexposée', *Change International* 1: 19–22.

(1984) 'Le Cinéma, ce n'est pas je vois, c'est je vole', *Cahiers de Cinéma* 357: 30–3.

(1984) 'L'État nucléaire', *Change International* 2: 9–23.*

(1984) 'Un habitat exorbitant', *Corps Écrit* 9: 25–7.

(1985) 'Guerre des étoiles: la propagande – fiction', *Cahiers du Cinéma* 378: xv.

(1985) 'Le Devoir de dépeupler', *Traverses* 33/4: 154–60.

(1985) 'Un jour, le jour viendra ou le jour ne viendra pas', *Traverses* 35: 5–11.

(1986) *Reinhard Mucha*. Paris: Musée National d'Art Moderne.*

(1986) 'Le Cinéma instrumental', *Cahiers du Cinéma* 385: xiv.

(1986) 'L'Engin exterminateur', *Cahiers du Cinéma* 388: 29–30.

(1986) 'L'Opération de la cataracte', *Cahiers du Cinéma* 386: 35–9.

(1986) (With J.-P. Fargier) 'The Cinema of Speed', *Revue d'Esthétique* 10: 37–43.

(1986) 'Video Technology and the Perception of the Image', *Revue d'Esthétique* 10: 33–5.

(1986) 'Image virtuelle', *Revue d'Esthétique* 10.

(1986) 'Le Cinéma instrumental: "L'imaginaire numerique" à Saint-Etienne', *Cahiers du Cinéma* 385:14.

(1987) *Jean Nouvel*. Paris: Institut Française d'Architecture.*

(1987) 'Permis de détruire', *Cahiers du Cinéma* 401: 29–30.

(1987) 'Le Rest du temps', *Corps Écrit* 24: 11–15.

(1987) 'Un cockpit en ville', *Traverses* 41: 69.

(1988) 'De dromoscopie', *Museum Journaal* 33(5/6): 310–16.

(1988) 'L'Image virtuelle mentale et instrumentale', *Traverses* 44/5: 35–9.

(1988) 'La Lumière indirecte', *Communications* 48: 45–52.

(1989) *De l'instabilité*. Paris: Centre National des Arts Plastiques. Nov.–Dec. Paris: Centre National des Arts Plastiques.*

(1989) 'Le Phénomène Rybczinski', *Cahiers du Cinéma* 415: 64.

(1989) 'Le Mer à vior', *Cahiers du Cinéma* 424: 17.

(1990) 'L'Inertie dromotique', *Techniques et Architecture* 390: 119–21, 181.

(1990) 'La Nouvelle Domesticité', *ARQ: Architecture/Québec* 57: 29–30.

(1990) 'Marcel Odenbach: Die Einen Den Anderen, 1987', in R. Bellour (ed.) *Passages de l'Image*. Paris: Éditions du Centre Pompidou.

(1991) 'L'Insécurité des territoires', in *ART LAB Concept Book*. Tokyo: ART LAB.

(1991) 'Quarante ans d'histoire', *Cahiers du Cinéma* 443/4: 62.

(1991) *L'Odyssée du virtuel*. Paris: Dossiers de l'Audiovisuel. INA Numéro 40, Novembre–Decembre. Sous la direction d'A.-M. Dugent et J.-M. Peyron.

(1991) 'La Guerre des dupes', *L'Événement du Jeudi*: 36–7.

(1991) (With P. Goulet and J. Nouvel) 'Aesthetic des versch windens', *Arch Plus* 108: 32–40.

(1992) 'Une guerre non-conventionnelle', *Transversales* 14: 4–6.

(1994) *Yann Kersalé/L'Instant Lúmiére*. Paris: Hamzan.*

(1994) *Atom Egoyan*. Paris: Distributed Art Publications.*

(1995) 'Alerte dans le cyberspace', *Le Monde Diplomatique* 28 August: 1.

(1995) 'Mémoire de l'ait: une politique du relief', pp. 7–8 in U. Pfammater (ed.) *Cuno Brullman*. Basel: Birkhäuser.

(1996) 'L'Horizon du trait', pp. 74–7 in M. Jacques and A. Lavalou (eds) *Christian de Portzamparc*. Basel: Birkhäuser.

(1996) 'Dangers, périls et menaces', Manière de voir: Internet: L'extase et l'effroi, *Le Monde Diplomatique*: October: 54–6.

(1996) (With C. Parent) *Architecture principe, 1966 et 1996*. Besançon: L'Imprimeur.

(1996) 'Le Musée du soleil', *InterCommunication* 15(Winter): 25–8.

(1997) 'Un monde surexposé', *Le Monde Diplomatique* August: 20.

(1998) 'Le Règne de la délation optique', *Le Monde Diplomatique* August: 20.

3. Interviews with Paul Virilio First Published in French

(1981) 'Vidéo, vitesse, technologie: la troisième fenêtre', *Cahiers de Cinéma* 322: 35–40. (Interview with the editors of *Cahiers de Cinéma*.)

(1984) 'Entretien avec Paul Virilio', *Empreintes* 6: 28–31. (Interview with D. Dobbels and B. Remy.)

(1986) 'Vers l'espace des interfaces: entretien avec Paul Virilio', *Technique et Architecture* 364: 130–3. (Interview with A. Pelissier.)

(1987) 'Paul Virilio', 8 May. (Interview on the French cultural channel, *La Sept.*) (Interviewer unknown.)

(1990) *Architecture Interieure-Crée*, 239: 108–14 (Interviewer unknown.)

(1993) 'La Défaite des faits', *L'Autre Journal* 4: 12–17. (Interview with K. Bros and M. Weitzman.)

(1993) 'Interview avec Paul Virilio', *Archithese* 23(2): 54–6. (Interview with M. Brausch.)

(1994) 'Nous allons vers des Tchernobyls informatiques', *Revue Terminal: Une réflexion sur le concept de technoscience* 62. (Interview with G. Lacroix.)

(1994) 'La Ville, espace mutant: entretien avec Paul Virilio', *Architecture Interieure Crée* 261: 104–7. (Interview with M. Brausch.)

(1995) 'Bientôt, seuls ceux qui seront dans la virtualité s'aimeront', *Supplément multimedia du journal Le Monde.* 30 Septembre. (Interviewer unknown.)

(1995) 'La Guerre de l'information', *Telecom Observer* 11 Octobre. (Interview with F. Burman on Swiss Radio International.)

(1995) 'L'Utopie du cybermonde', *France Culture*. (Radio interview with J. de Rosnay.)

(1995) 'Devant la liquidation du monde', *Black Notes*. (Interview with A. Kyrou and J.Y. Barbichon.)

(1995) 'Vitesse, guerre et vidéo', *Le Magazine Litteraire* 337 (Novembre): 96–103. (Interview with F. Ewald.)

(1996) 'L'Urbanité virtuelle, l'être au monde au temps réel', *Fluctuation fugitive: revue d'architecture*. (Interview with A. Sina.)

(1996) *Cybermonde, la politique du pire*. Paris: Textuel. (Book-length interview with P. Petit.)

(1996) 'Cybermonde, la politique du pire', *Libération* 10 May. (Interviewer unknown.)

(1996) 'Les Formes virtuelles', *Les Sciences de la Forme Aujourd'hui*, Points Sciences (October.) (Interview with É. Noël.)

(1996) 'Caution against the Cyberworld', *Connaissance des Arts* 532(October.) (Interview with P. Jodidio.)

(1996) 'Quand il n'y a plus temps à partager, il n'y a plus de democratie possible', *Les Grands Entretiens du Monde* 3: 37–9. (Interview with J.-M. Frodon.)

(1996) 'Paysage d'événements sur fond de vitesse', *Art Press* 217: 19–26. (Interview with P. Sterckx.)

(1996) 'Virilio, cybéresistant', *Libération* 10 May. (Interviewer unknown.)

(1996) 'Entrer en cyberésistance', *La Rafalé* 19 May. (Interviewer unknown.)

(1996) 'Le Bombardement de Nantes', *Cahiers du Cinéma* 503. (Interviewer unknown.)

(1996) 'Les Grands Entretiens du monde', Chapter 1 in *Dossiers et documents du monde* June: Part 3. (Interviewer unknown.)

(1996) 'Un monde sans espace', *Le Nouvel Observateur* Novembre. (Interview with P. Gari.)

(1997) 'La Révolution de l'information est une révolution de la dénonciation', *L'Événement du Jeudi* 656 (May–June): 60. (Interview with B. Ponlet.)

(1997) *Voyage d'hiver*. Marseille: Parenthèses (Book of interviews with M. Brausch.)

4. English Translations of the Main Published Works of Paul Virilio

(1986) *Speed & Politics: An Essay on Dromology*, trans. M. Polizzotti. New York: Semiotext(e.)

(1986) *Negative Horizon*, trans. M. Polizzotti. New York: Semiotext(e.)

(1989) *War and Cinema: The Logistics of Perception*, trans. P. Camiller. London and New York: Verso.

(1990) *Popular Defense & Ecological Struggles*, trans. M. Polizzotti. New York: Semiotext(e.)

(1991) *The Lost Dimension*, trans. D. Moshenberg. New York: Semiotext(e.)

(1991) *The Aesthetics of Disappearance*, trans. P. Beitchman. New York: Semiotext(e.)

(1994) *Bunker Archeology*, trans. (of 2nd edn) G. Collins. Princeton, NJ: Princeton Architectural Press.

(1994) *The Vision Machine*, trans. J. Rose. Bloomington and London: Indiana University Press and British Film Institute.

(1995) *The Art of the Motor*, trans. J. Rose. Minneapolis: University of Minnesota Press.

(1997) *Open Sky*, trans. J. Rose. London: Verso.

(1999) *Polar Inertia*, trans. P. Camiller. London: Sage Publications.

5. English Translations of Articles by Paul Virilio

(1980) 'Popular Defense and Popular Assault', trans. J. Johnston, pp. 266–72 in S. Lotringer and J. Fleming (eds) *Italy: Autonomia.* New York: Semiotext(e.)

(1981) 'Moving Girl', trans. J. Johnston, pp. 242–8 in P. Lamborn Wilson and J. Fleming (eds) *Semiotext(e) Polysexuality*. New York: Semiotext(e.)

(1984) 'The Overexposed City', trans. A. Hustvedt, pp. 15–31 in M. Feher and S. Kwinter (eds) *Zone 1/2*. New York: Urzone.

(1985) 'Dromoscopy, or Drunk with Magnitude', trans. N. Sanders, *Frogger* 7.

(1986) 'Star Wars', trans. unknown, *Art & Text* 22: 15–18.

(1986) 'The Privatisation of War', trans. M. Imrie, *New Statesman* 112 (10 October):19.

(1987) 'Space, Time, and the City', trans. Unknown, *Lotus International* 51: 25–9.

(1987) 'Nervous Peace', trans. M. Imrie, *New Statesman* 113 (16 January): 36–7.

(1987) 'Negative Horizons', trans. M. Polizzotti, pp. 163–80 in J. Fleming and P.L. Wilson (eds) *Semiotext(e) USA*. New York: Semiotext(e.)

(1989) 'Trans-Appearance', trans. D. Stoll, *Artforum* 27(10): 128–30.

(1989) 'The Last Vehicle', trans. D. Antal, pp. 106–19 in D. Kamper and C. Wulf (eds) *Looking Back on the End of the World*. New York: Semiotext(e.)

(1989) 'The Museum of Accidents', trans. Y. Lawrence, in *The Lunatic of One Idea*, Special Issue of *Public* 2: 81–5.

(1990) 'Cataract Surgery: Cinema in the Year 2000', trans. A. Fatet and A. Kuhn, pp. 169–74 in A. Kuhn (ed.) *Alien Zone: Cultural Theory and Contemporary Science Fiction Cinema*. London and New York: Verso.

(1990) 'The Third Interval', trans. unknown, *Art and Design* 7 (1/2): 78.

(1990) 'The Image to Come', trans. S. Sartarelli, *Art & Text* 36: 90–4.

(1991) 'Head High?', trans. T. Hausman, *Newsline* 3(7): 3.

(1992) 'Gray Ecology', trans. unknown, pp. 186–9 in C.C. Davidson (ed.) *Anywhere*. New York: Rizzoli.

(1992) 'Aliens', trans. B. Massumi, pp. 446–9 in J. Crary and S. Kwinter (eds) *Zone 6: Incorporations*. New York: Urzone.

(1992) 'Big Optics', trans. J. Von Stein, pp. 82–93 in Peter Weibel (ed.) *On Justifying the Hypothetical Nature of Art and the Non-Identicality within the Object World*. Koln: Galerie Tanja Grunert.

(1992) 'The Law of Proximity', trans. W. Nijenhuis, pp. 121–7 in V2 Organization (eds.) *Book for the Unstable Media*. Amsterdam: den Bosch.

(1993) 'The Third Interval: A Critical Transition', trans. T. Conley, pp. 3–12 in V.A. Conley (ed.) *Rethinking Technologies*. Minneapolis: University of Minnesota Press.

(1993) 'Speed and Vision: The Incomparable Eye', trans. unknown. *Diadalos: Berlin Architectural Journal* 47: 96–107.

(1993) 'The Interface', trans. unknown, *Lotus International* 75: 126.

(1993) 'From Superman to Superexcited Man', trans. unknown, *Domus* 755: 17–24.

(1993) 'The Law of Proximity', trans. L.E. Nesbitt, *Columbia Documents of Architecture and Theory* 2: 123–37.

(1993) 'The Primal Accident', trans. B. Massumi, pp. 211–18 in B. Massumi (ed.) *The Politics of Everyday Fear*. Minneapolis: University of Minnesota Press.

(1994) 'The Vision Machine', trans. J. Rose, *Transition* 43: 20–35.

(1995) 'Red Alert in Cyberspace', trans. M. Imrie, *Radical Philiosphy* 74: 2–4.

(1995) 'Speed and Information: Cyberspace Alarm!', trans. P. Riemens, *CTheory* (Ctheory www.com) (Electronic journal.) 27 September.

(1995) 'Critical Reflections', trans. unknown, *Artforum* 34(3): 82–3.

(1995) 'Comforting Light', trans. unknown, *Forum* 38: 17–19.

(1995) 'Politics of Relief', trans. unknown, *Forum* 38: 77.

(1995) 'Memory of Air: A Policy of Relief', trans. I. Taylor, pp. 8–9 in U. Pfammater (ed.) *Cuno Brullmann*. Basel: Birkhäuser.

(1996) 'The Horizon of the Line', trans. S. Pleasance and F. Woods, pp. 74–7 in M. Jacques and A. Lavalou (eds) *Christian de Portzamparc*. Basel: Birkhäuser.

(1997) 'The Overexposed City', trans. A. Hustredt, pp. 381–90 in N. Leach (ed.) *Rethinking Architecture: A Reader in Cultural Theory*. London and New York: Routledge.

(1997) 'Cybernetics and Society', trans. C.T. Wolfe, pp. 1–13, 19–20 in *Any* (editor unknown.) New York: Architecture.

(1997) 'The Museum of the Sun', trans. L. Reijnen, pp. 331–62 in V2 Organization (eds) *Technomorphica*. Rotterdam: V2 Organization.

(1998) 'Foreword', trans. unknown, in J. Rajchman, *Constructions*. Cambridge, MA: MIT Press.

(1998) 'We May Be Entering an Electronic Gothic Era', transcribed and edited by O. Fillion, *Architectural Design* 68(11/12) (November–December): 61.

6. Interviews with Paul Virilio Published in English

(1983) *Pure War*, trans. M. Polizzotti. New York: Semiotext(e.) (Book-length interview with S. Lotringer.)

(1985) 'The Spirit of Defense: An Interview with Paul Virilio', trans. M. Polizzotti, *Impulse* (Death Issue) 11(4): 35–7. (Interview with C. Mellon.)

(1986) 'Speed-Space', trans. D. Miller, *Impulse* 12(4): 35–9. (Interview with C. Dercon.)

(1988) 'Paul Virilio', trans. unknown, *Block* 14: 4–7. (Interviewer unknown.)

(1988) 'Interview with Paul Virilio', trans. H. Martin, *Flash Art*, International Edition 138: 57–61. (Interview with J. Sans.)

(1988) 'The Third Window: An Interview with Paul Virilio', trans. Y. Shafir, with a preface by J. Crary, pp. 185–97 in C. Schneider and B. Wallis (eds) *Global Television*. Cambridge, MA and London: MIT Press and Wedge Press. (Interview with the editors of *Cahiers du Cinéma*. A translation of Virilio's 1981 interview in French with *Cahiers du Cinéma*.)

(1991) 'Paul Virilio', trans. H. Martin, pp. 139–50 in *Art and Philosophy*. Milan: Giancarlo Politi Editure. (Reprint of the interview with Jerôme Sans in *Flash Art*.)

(1991) 'For a Geography of Trajectories', trans. unknown, *Flux* 5: 48–54. (Interview with J.-M. Offner and A. Sander.)

(1992) 'Interview with Paul Virilio', trans. unknown, pp. 74–86 in *100 affiches françaises à Saint-Peterbourg*. Paris: Demi-Cercle. (Interview with D. Joubert.)

(1993) 'Marginal Groups', trans. unknown, *Diadalos: Berlin Architectural Journal* 50(December): 72–81. (Interview with M. Brausch.)

(1994) 'Cyberwar, God and Television: Interview with Paul Virilio', trans. L.K. Wilson, M. Fowler, and R. Stesan, *CTheory* (Electronic journal) 17(3): 1–7. (Interview with L.K. Wilson for *CTheory*.)

(1994) 'Gravitational Space', trans. unknown, pp. 35–60 in L. Louppe (ed.) *Traces of Dance: Drawings and Notations of Choreographers*. Paris: Editions Dis Voir. (Interview with L. Louppe and D. Dobbels.)

(1995) 'Paul Virilio', trans. G. Aylesworth, pp. 97–104 in F. Rötzer (ed.) *Conversations with French Philosophers*. New Jersey: Humanities Press. (Interview with F. Rötzer.)

(1995) 'Cyberrevolution', trans. unknown, *Telecom Observer* 16 October. (Interview with M. Alberganti.)

(1995) 'Critical Mass', trans. unknown, *World Art* 1: 78–82. (Interview with V. Madsen.)

(1995) 'The Publicity Machine and Critical Theory', trans. N. Zurbrugg, *Eyeline* 27(autumn–winter): 8–14. (Interview with N. Zurbrugg.)

(1995) 'Century of Violence', trans. N. Zurbrugg, *Versus* 4: 42–7. (Interview with N. Zurbrugg. Reprint of 'The Publicity Machine' interview in *Eyeline* 27.)

(1995) 'The Silence of the Lambs: Paul Virilio in Conversation', trans. P. Riemens, *CTheory* (Electronic journal) 1(7): 1–3. (Interview with C. Oliveira.)

(1996) 'Speed Pollution', trans. M. Degener, J. Der Derian and L. Osepchuk, *Wired* 4.05: 120–1. (Interview with J. Der Derian.)

(1996) 'The Game of Love and Chance', trans. C. Volke, *Grand Street* 52: 12-17. (Interview with J. Sans.)

(1996) 'The Game of Love and Chance', trans. C. Volke, *Architectural Design* 121: 24–6. (Reprint of the J. Sans interview in *Grand Street* 52.)

(1996) 'Paul Virilio and the Oblique', trans. unknown, pp. 174–84 in S. Allen and K. Park (eds) *Sites and Stations: Provisional Utopias: Architecture and Utopia in the Contemporary City*. New York: Lusitania Press. (Interview with E. Limon.)

(1996) ' "A Century of Hyper-violence": Paul Virilio: An Interview', trans. N. Zurbrugg, *Economy and Society* 25(1): 111–26. (Interview with N. Zurburgg. Reprint of N. Zurbrugg interviews in *Eyeline* 27 and *Versus* 4.)

(1996) 'The Dark Spot of Art', trans. B. Holmes, pp. 47–55 in Herausgeber documenta Gmbtt. (ed.) *documenta documents 1*. Kassel: Cantz Verlag. (Interview with C. David.)

(1996) 'The Dark Spot of Art's Presence', trans. B. Holmes, *Metronome* 0: 7–10. (Reprint, in edited form, of the interview with C. David in *documenta documents 1*.)

(1997) 'Interview with Paul Virilio', trans. J. Der Derian, M. Degener and L. Osepchuk, *Speed* (Electronic journal) 1(4): 1–8. (Interview with J. Der Derian. Reprinted in J. Der Derian [ed.] *The Virilio Reader*, 1998.)

(1997) 'Virilio's Apocalypse', trans. unknown, pp. 70–3 in A. Crawford and R. Edgar (eds) *Transit Lounge*. North Ryde: Craftsman House. (Interview with V. Madsen.)

(1997) *Pure War: Revised Edition*, trans. M. Polizzotti, Postscript translated by B. O'Keeffe. (Contains a new Postscript: '1997: Infowar'.) New York: Semiotext(e.) (Book-length interview with S. Lotringer.)

(1998) 'Surfing the Accident', trans. P. Riemens, pp. 30–44 in V2 Organization (eds) *The Art of the Accident*. Rotterdam: NAI. (Interview with A. Ruby.)

(1999) (With Friedrich Kittler.) 'The Information Bomb: Paul Virilio and Friedrich Kittler in Conversation', edited and introduced by J. Armitage, trans. P. Riemens, in J. Armitage (ed.) *Machinic Modulations: New Cultural Theory and Technopolitics, Special Issue of Angelaki* 4(2.) (First broadcast on the Franco-German television channel ARTE, in November 1995.)

7. Studies of Paul Virilio in French and English

Aidar, M. (1997) 'IDEAL CAR', *Speed* (Electronic journal) 1(4): 1–4.

Armitage, J. (1996) 'The Vision Thing', *Radical Philosophy* 77: 45-6. (Book review of *The Vision Machine*.)

Armitage, J. (1997) 'Accelerated Aesthetics: Paul Virilio's *The Vision Machine*'. in C. Blake and L. Blake (eds) *Intellectuals and Global Culture*, Special Issue of *Angelaki* 2(3): 199–209.

Armitage, J. (1999) 'Paul Virilio', pp. 464–5 in E. Cashmore and C. Rojek (eds) *Dictionary of Cultural Theorists*. London: Arnold.

Armitage, J. (1999) 'Resisting the Neoliberal Discourse of Technology: The Politics of Cyberculture in the Age of the Virtual Class', *CTheory* (Electronic journal) 22(1–2) Article 68: 1–10.

Auber, O. (1997) 'Esquisse d'une position the orique pour un art de la vitesse', *Speed* (Electronic journal) 1(4): 1–10.

Brigham, L. (1992) 'Motion and Destruction', *American Book Review* 14(2): 10. (Book review of *The Aesthetics of Disappearance*.)

Brigham, L. (1997) 'Transpolitical Technocracy and the Hope of Language', *Speed* (Electronic journal) 1(4): 1–6.

Conley, V.A. (1997) *Ecopolitics: The Environment in Poststructuralist Thought*. London: Routledge. (Contains chapter section on Virilio.)

Conrad, P. (1989) 'Screen Spectaculars', *Times Literary Supplement* 1–7 September: 939. (Book review of *War and Cinema*.)

Crawford, T.H. (forthcoming) 'Conducting Technologies: Virilio's and Latour's Philosophies of the Present State', in J. Armitage (ed.) *Machinic Modulations: New Cultural Theory and Technopolitics*, Special Issue of *Angelaki* 4(2.).

Crogan, P. (1996) 'Paul Virilio and the Aporia of Speed'. Unpublished PhD thesis, Sydney, Power Department of Fine Arts.

Crogan, P. (1996) 'Paul Virilio and the Aporia of Speed', Virtual Cultures Conference Paper, Sydney, 13 July: 1–5.

Crogan, P. (1997) 'Metaphoric Vehicles', *Speed* (Electronic journal) 1(4): 1–6.

Crogan, P. (forthcoming) 'Theory of State: Deleuze, Guattari and Virilio on the State, Technology, and Speed', in J. Armitage (ed.) *Machinic Modulations: New Cultural Theory and Technopolitics*, Special Issue of *Angelaki* 4(2.).

Couples, C. (1996) 'Virilio, the Cyborg, and Me'. Archived at: http://ebbs.english.v-t.edu/exper/couples/personal/academia/reviews/art.of.motor.html. (Book review of *The Art of the Motor*.)

Coyle, R. (1992) 'Sound and Speed in Convocation: An Analysis of *The Listening Room* Radio Programs on Paul Virilio', *Continuum* 6(1): 118–38.

Der Derian, J. (1992) *Antidiplomacy: Spies, Terror, Speed, and War*. Oxford: Blackwell. (Contains chapters discussing Virilio's work.)

Der Derian, J. (1998) 'Virtually Wagging the Dog', *Theory & Event* (Electronic journal) 2(1): 1–7. (Book review of *The Art of the Motor*.)

Der Derian, J. (ed.) (1998) *The Virilio Reader*. Oxford: Blackwell. (Contains a reprint of Der Derian's interview with Virilio in *Wired*. Contains 'A Select Bibliography of Works by Paul Virilio'. This bibliography also includes some Spanish, Italian and German Virilio references.)

Deleuze, G. and Guattari, F. (1986) *Nomadology: The War Machine*, trans. B. Massumi. New York: Semiotext(e.) (Contains a critical discussion of Virilio's work. This book is also one of the 'plateaus' in Deleuze and Guattari's *A Thousand Plateaus* immediately below.)

Deleuze, G. and Guattari, F. (1987) 'Nomadology: The War Machine', in their *A Thousand Plateaus: Capitalism and Schizophrenia*, trans. B. Massumi. Minneapolis: University of Minnesota Press.

Drake, M. (1997) 'The Question of Military Technology: Apocalyptics or Politics?', *Speed* (Electronic journal) 1(4): 1–13.

Douglas, I.R. (1997) 'Ecology to the New Pollution', *Theory & Event* (Electronic journal) 2(2): 1–5. (Book review of *Open Sky*.)

Douglas, I.R. (1997) 'The Calm Before the Storm: Virilio's Debt to Foucault, and Some Notes on Contemporary Global Capital', *Speed* (Electronic journal) 1(4): 1–18.

Gilfedder, D. (1994) 'VIRILIO: The Cars that Ate Paris', *Transition* 43: 36–43.

Hake, S. (1989) 'War and Cinema', *Film Criticism* 14(1): 40–2. (Book review of *War and Cinema*.)

Johnson, P. (ed.) (1996) *The Function of the Oblique: The Architecture of Claude Parent and Paul Virilio*, trans. P. Johnson. London: Architectural Association. (Contains Virilio's early architectural writings, drawings, and photographs. Also included is an interview with Parent.)

Kellner, D. (1998) 'Virilio on Vision Machines', *Film-Philosophy* (Electronic journal), Salon review: 1–10. (Book review of *Open Sky*.)

Kerrigan, J. (1997) 'When Eyesight is Fully Industrialised', *London Review of Books* 16 October: 14–15. (Book review of *Open Sky*.)

Koppes, C.R. (1991) 'War and Cinema', *Technology and Culture* 32(2): 447–8. (Book review of *War and Cinema*.)

Kroker, A. (1992) *The Possessed Individual: Technology and Postmodernity*. Basingstoke: Macmillan. (Contains a chapter critically discussing Virilio's works.)

Manovich, L. (1997) 'Film/Telecommunication, Benjamin/Virilio', *Speed* (Electronic journal) 1(4): 1–5.

Messmer, M.W. 'War and Cinema', *The Minnesota Review* 34(3): 175–81. (Book review of *War and Cinema*.)

Oki, K. (1997) 'Decisions at the Speed of Electronic Circuitry', *Speed* (Electronic journal) 1(4): 1–4.

Sokal, A. and Bricmont, J. (1998) *Intellectual Impostures: Postmodern Philosopher's Abuse of Science*. London: Profile Books. (Contains a critique of Virilio.)

Waite, G. (1996) *Nietzsche's Corps/e: Aesthetics, Politics, Prophecy, or, the Spectacular Technoculture of Everyday Life*. Durham, NC and London: Duke University Press. (Contains discussions of Virilio's thought.)

Wark, M. (1988) 'On Technological Time: Virilio's Overexposed City', *Arena* 83: 82–100.

Wark, M. (1990) 'The Logistics of Perception', *Meanjin* 49(1): 95–101. (Review article on *War and Cinema*.)

Weissberg, J.-L. (1996) 'Ralentir la communication', *Terminal* 63: 1–10.

Wilbur, S. (1994/7) 'Paul Virilio: Speed, Cinema, and the End of the Political State', *Speed* (Electronic journal) 1(4): 1–10. (Originally posted on the Net in 1994. Reprinted in *Speed*.)

Zurbrugg, N. (1995) '"Apocalyptic!" "Negative!" "Pessimistic!": Baudrillard, Virilio, and Techno-culture', pp. 72–90 in S. Koop (ed.) *Post: Photography: Post Photography*. Fitzroy: Centre for Contemporary Photography.

8. Internet Sites Related to the Work of Paul Virilio

Paul Virilio (Off) line
http://web5.netculture.net/~ovk/virilio/index.html.
Enterprise: Theoretical: Virilio
http://www.uradio.ku.dk/~enterprz/virilio.html
Speed
http://proxy.arts.uci.edu/~nideffer_SPEED_/

Note

1. In this regard, and apart from a large thank you to Virilio himself, I must thank James Der Derian, Patrick Crogan, Wim Nijenhuis, Mark Little, Andreas Broeckmann, Kevin Robins, Nicholas Zurbrugg, Gerard Greenway, Patrice Riemens and Andreas Ruby. Lastly, I would like to thank Joanne Parkes, Assistant Divisional Administrator in the Division of Government and Politics, University of Northumbria, UK. Suffice it to say that Joanne's magical skills with a Word for Windows character map are a wonder to behold.

Index

Theory, Culture & Society

Theory, Culture & Society caters for the resurgence of interest in culture within contemporary social sciences and the humanities. Building on the heritage of classical social theory, the book series examines ways in which this tradition has been reshaped by a new generation of theorists. It also published theoretically informed analyses of everyday life, popular culture, and new intellectual movements.
EDITOR: Mike Featherstone, *Nottingham Trent University*

SERIES EDITORIAL BOARD
Roy Boyne, *University of Durham*
Mike Hepworth, *University of Aberdeen*
Scott Lash, *Goldsmiths College, University of London*
Roland Robertson, *University of Pittsburg*
Bryan S. Turner, *University of Cambridge*

THE TCS CENTRE
The Theory, Culture & Society book series, the journals *Theory, Culture & Society* and *Body & Society*, and related conference, seminar and postgraduate programmes operate from the TCS Centre at Nottingham Trent University. For further details of the TCS Centre's activities please contact:

Centre Administrator
The TCS Centre, Room 175
Faculty of Humanities
Nottingham Trent University
Clifton Lane, Nottingham, NG11 8NS, UK
e-mail: tcs@ntu.ac.uk
web: http://tcs@ntu.ac.uk

Recent volumes include:

Love and Eroticism
edited by Mike Featherstone

Polar Inertia
Paul Virilio

Peformativity and Belonging
edited by Vikki Bell

Feminist Imagination
Genealogies in Feminist Theory
Vikki Bell

Michel de Certeau
Cultural Theorist
Ian Buchanan

The Cultural Economy of Citites
Allen J. Scott